THE RILKE ALPHABET

The
Rilke Alphabet

ULRICH BAER

Translated by Andrew Hamilton

FORDHAM UNIVERSITY PRESS
New York   2014

Library of Congress Control Number: 2013957597

Printed in the United States of America
16 15 14   5 4 3 2 1
First edition

CONTENTS

List of Abbreviations   vii

Preface: "The Whole Dictation of Existence"   ix

Acknowledgments   xv

a   for Ashanti   1

b   for Buddha   10

c   for Circle   27

d   for Destiny Disrupted   36

e   for Entrails   45

f   for Frogs   53

g   for God   61

h   for Hair   71

i   for Inca   76

j   for Jew Boy   87

k   for Kafka and King Lear   104

l   for Larean   111

m for Mussolini   116

n   for Nature   125

o   for O   132

p   for Proletarian   133

q   for *Quatsch*   139

r   for Rose   146

s   for Stampa   149

t   for Tower   162

u   for Un-   171

v   for Vagabond, or Being Outside   178

w for Worm   192

x   for Xaver   200

y   for Y   203

z   for Zero   204

Notes   215

Works Cited   233

Index   241

ABBREVIATIONS

All works are by Rainer Maria Rilke unless otherwise noted.

AAP   *Ahead of All Parting: The Selected Poetry and Prose of Rainer Maria Rilke*

ALT   *Briefe* (1980)

ANI   Rilke and Anita Forrer, *Briefwechsel*

BOI   *The Book of Images*

BSF   *Briefe an die Schweizer Freunde*

BZP   *Briefe zur Politik*

GB   *Gesammelte Briefe*

HAT   Rilke and Magda von Hattingberg, *Briefwechsel mit Magda von Hattingberg*

NAL   *Briefe* (1991)

JBL   *Selected Works, Volume 2: Poetry*

KA   *Werke*

LOL   *Letters on Life*

LOU   Rilke and Lou Andreas-Salomé, *Briefwechsel*

LYP   *Letters to a Young Poet*

MLB   *The Notebooks of Malte Laurids Brigge*

NP   *New Poems*

POR   *The Poetry of Rilke*

SID   *Briefe an Sidonie Nádherný von Borutin*

SIZ   *Briefe an Gräfin Sizzo*

SW   *Sämtliche Werke*

TAX   Rilke and Marie von Thurn und Taxis, *Briefwechsel*
UP   *Uncollected Poems*
WUN *Briefe an Nanny Wunderly-Volkart*

PREFACE: "THE WHOLE DICTATION OF EXISTENCE"

"Diktat des Daseins"

> The longer I live, the more urgent it seems to me to endure and transcribe the whole dictation of existence [*das ganze Diktat des Daseins*] up to its end, for it might just be the case that only the very last sentence contains that small and possibly inconspicuous word which transforms into magnificent sense everything we had struggled to learn and everything we had failed to understand.[1]

Rilke wrote these words to Ilse Erdmann on December 21, 1913, close to the end of a year during which he had met Sigmund Freud in person, spent more time with Lou Andreas-Salomé, and drafted a poem that he would not complete for another decade as the first of the Duino elegies. By writing down "the whole dictation of existence," Rilke hopes to register those experiences that we normally go through without noticing. Do not overlook anything, pay attention to everything, spell it all out up to the most minuscule and negligible word and letter: That is Rilke's aesthetic motto and his guide for life. In order not to miss anything or get distracted in the task of living mindfully and honestly, the poet must not decide in advance between important and unimportant things. He has to write in the conviction that each experience and every word possesses a value all its own.

Rilke's ambition to copy down the entire "dictation of existence" rests in an animistic thought, as if the greater universe finds in us humans its diligent secretaries, whose lowly service can find the key to the universe's hidden meaning as long as we don't miss a word. Poetry becomes the record of the universe, and one of the countless words in this great and faithful transcription might reveal the universe's hidden meaning to us. The language of poetry does not turn away from the world toward a greater, transcendent Meaning but opens up the world, and opens us *to* the immanence of the world, in which we live. This is Rilke's ambition: to write attentively about the world in the hope that our lives, as we are already living them, might be transformed "into magnificent sense."

This book honors Rilke's call to copy down the dictation of existence. *The Rilke Alphabet* presents twenty-six words that cast new light on Rilke's oeuvre (including his poetry, prose, and letters) from unexpected angles. Some of the chapters examine what scholars and critics have "struggled to learn," to adapt Rilke's term for our often reflexive tendency to resolve any challenge by relying on secondhand opinions and common-places, while other chapters open our eyes and ears to what many readers have "failed to understand."[2] Many readers have not yet grasped Rilke's poetry because they have elevated his poetry above life and search for "a magnificent sense" and inspiration in books of Rilke's verses instead of grasping that Rilke's poetry, even when addressing flamingos, angels, and hydrangeas, presses us *more deeply into life.* Rilke copies down the dictation of existence as "the secretary of the invisible" (in his own memo-rable phrase), yet each one of the words examined here shows that this secretary knows us humans to be physical, mortal beings at once blessed and trapped in our human bodies with desires, longings, and fears.

This work takes its origin in many years of study and in a deeply *sensory* experience of reading Rilke. It shows but two things. First, it shows that Rilke, the poet who among modern poets most insistently and convinc-ingly promises salvation and even redemption *within* our disenchanted, secular modernity (and not in another religion or ideology, not even that of "art"), had a body. Second, it also demonstrates that when it comes to poetry and life, a single word may change everything. One word may upend your sense of yourself and end your world in its entirety. One single word. That is poetry's insistence, and it is the reason why we tend to turn to poetry, Rilke's in many cases, at moments of transition, or when due to a calamity or loss it seems that one way of being in the world has ended for us. But a single word may also console and provide salvation, and turn everything "we had struggled to learn and everything we had failed to understand" into "magnificent sense."

The twenty-six words that were taken from Rilke's writings open up the veins of Rilke's work, from which existence pours out, fierce and fervid, red and pulsing. They challenge the prevalent picture of Rilke as a poet of transcendence (also often called, simplistically, "love," "romanticism," "mysticism," "belief," or "art," or what some critics define as poetic language referring to itself). Not all of these twenty-six words are commonly discussed in critical works on Rilke. (Some have been repressed by scholars and critics for years; others have been sanitized or willfully misunderstood.) Some of them may make us cringe. Cringe we must—Rilke used these words to "transcribe the whole dictation" for *all* of existence and to mine each word's potential to transform into sense those parts of our lives we tend to overlook by relying on social conventions that define how we love and live, or on systems of belief that promise to bestow transcendent meaning (a greater cause; an ideal) on our actions. These twenty-six words attest to Rilke's bold balancing of our euphoria for the radical openness and immanence of life (as we may experience it, if we are blessed, in love, which for Rilke always includes physical love) with our despair in the face of the equally radical openness that defines our relationship to death. Each of these words reminds us that we are suspended in life between two radically open moments: for Rilke the experience of being reborn in love and the capacity to know death as part of life.

The following chapters trace and explain the strange logic by which poetry wrests from ordinary language, from the words we all use all the time, extraordinary meaning. That meaning is shaped in its relation to other words found in Rilke's work, including his prose and letters, which I consider here as much an essential part of his oeuvre as his poetry, following Rilke's own instructions in his last will and testament. Like small coves or tiny shells sheltering another sense amid the vast sea that is Rilke's language, these words deepen the meaning of Rilke's oeuvre for us today. They have resisted Rilke's drive toward sublimation (an ultimately failed attempt to turn desire into art, as outlined in several of the chapters here). They mark the places where his work bears witness to those haunting and hallucinatory, sublime and devastating experiences and sensations in life for which there are no words. They are motes of reality embedded in a lyrical work that throw into relief nothing less than the possibility of living fully under modern conditions with all of our world's often very entertaining distractions and temptations to be inauthentic. Even when we think we know so much about it, life constantly surprises us with the richness of its highs and the devastation of its losses. The words examined here remind us that life cannot be grasped or fully understood but that life can be experienced only as the interruption of what we, with the aid of science, religion, reason, faith, and politics, call "life." Paradoxically, life seems impossible to grasp at these moments of its interruptions even though we also feel *most* alive during those apparently timeless, ex-static, and abyssal moments of bliss and loss. The twenty-six words examined here stand in relation to Rilke's oeuvre in the same way as such experiences stand in relation to our daily lives. They interrupt Rilke's work with the force that is the unique capacity of poetry to turn words against themselves and make them speak for more than what they refer to. Misfits, truants, outliers: That is what those words are. They are the stuff of poetry.

Some of the words selected here seem to disturb the Rilkean "completeness" and "perfection," which Robert Musil identified as a rare, distinguishing trait of Rilke's work in his eulogy in January 1927, a few short weeks after Rilke's exceedingly painful death from complications from too-late-diagnosed leukemia on December 29, 1926.[3] The later critic Paul de Man, as editor of Rilke's poetry in French translation, considered Rilke's capacity for turning words against their literal meaning without letting them slip fully into metaphor the great, if paradoxical, "promise" of Rilke's poetry.[4] In his assertion of Rilke's perfection, Musil also recognized to what a remarkable degree Rilke devoted himself to the irritating factors in our existence: "And there is one great poem that cannot forget the unrest, inconsistency, and fragmentary nature of life [. . .] That is Rilke's poem."[5] The words examined here disrupt the surface perfection of Rilke's poetry. They promise not transcendence but immanence unrivaled in modern poetry, real toads, à la Marianne Moore, notwithstanding. A few of the words examined here offer new insight into Rilke's (sometimes short-lived) political commitments and personal predilections. True to Rilke's imperative not to divide life a priori, before living, into what's important and what's insignificant, these words chronicle the eruption of the contingencies of life into his work. Some of these words simply document what scholars pointedly and fastidiously overlooked for decades, and what even many fans of Rilke's poetry occasionally forget: that Rilke had a body. They attest to Rilke's commitment to endure in the face of life, in order to copy it all down.

I encountered these twenty-six words during a period of two years spent reading all of Rilke's works—all of his poems, all of his prose, and as many as possible of his boundless correspondence totaling more than fourteen thousand letters.[6] These words struck me, during a difficult personal time triggered by a loss I couldn't put into words, as keys to Rilke's insistence that we can be *pressed into* life more deeply, and that poetry, far from being an esoteric commentary *on* life, is one of the paths *into* a life that we often forget in the business of living. These words are placed into the largest possible context that I explored with students in teaching Rilke for many years at New York University, following the methods of philology. I examine these words in the belief that each entry elucidates a distinct and valuable direction in Rilke's thought, a particular structure of his poetic method, a different way of dealing with a motif, or a controversy sparked by Rilke's work. The chapters function as free-standing essays. They revise commonly held notions about Rilke by explaining that he is a poet of immanence—a poet of life as it is lived, not as it is reflected philosophically or as art.

By "immanence" in this context I mean Rilke's insistence that we do not accept or reject existence, we *live* it. To put it differently: Life lives us, and whatever we think of it comes only later and at an inevitable remove. In Rilke's only novel, *The Notebooks of Malte Laurids Brigge*, the narrator confesses that he places life above knowledge, experience above reading, even when our hard-gained knowledge would shelter us from suffering: "I am sometimes surprised at how readily I give up everything that was expected in favor of the real, even when it is terrible."[7] *The Rilke Alphabet* follows the sequence of the European alphabet, where no single letter is more important than any other. It makes the claim of elucidating, adumbrating, deepening Rilke's writing in twenty-six words by cataloging those splinters of language that refract our existence like prisms through which we can for a moment grasp "the real," which we are after all.

ACKNOWLEDGMENTS

The translation of this work was funded by Geisteswissenschaften International—Translation Funding for Humanities and Social Sciences from Germany, a joint initiative of the Fritz Thyssen Foundation, the German Federal Foreign Office, the collecting society VG WORT, and the Börsenverein des Deutschen Buchhandels (German Publishers and Booksellers Association).

Additional funding was provided by the Humanities Initiative at New York University.

Thank you for advice and conversations about Rilke and his ever-widening circles over a period of many years to:

Tina Bennett, Harold Bloom, Fritz Breithaupt, Peter Burgard, Michel Chaouli, Robert Cohen, Andrea Dortmann, Amir Eshel, Paul Fleming, Eckart Goebel, Eva Geulen, Patrick Greaney, Cyrus Hamlin, Karen Hanson, Lyle Ashton Harris, Geoffrey Hartman, Winfried Hörning, Amy Hosig, Huang Jiankun, Carol Jacobs, Daniel Kehlmann, Li Shuangzhi, Karen Leeder, Catriona MacLeod, Herb Marks, Sandra Nadaff, Jiří Pehe, Eyal Peretz, Judith Ryan, William Waters, Jane Tylus, Shelley Rice, Simon Richter, Avital Ronell, Richard Sieburth, Elke Siegel, Thomas Sparr, Emily Sun, Helen Tartar, Johannes Türk, James Wagner, Glenn Wallis, Will Murphy, Friedrich Ulfers, Liliane Weissberg, Lawrence Weschler, Ellen Weschler, my family, my students at New York University, and Sifu Shi Yan Ming of the USA Shaolin Temple.

a

for Ashanti

How do Africans feature and fare in Rilke's work? A group of men, women, and children from West Africa (most likely today's Ghana) were put on display like animals in the Jardin d'Acclimatation in Paris, where Rilke saw (or, as it turns out, didn't see) them in the spring of 1902. Before that there had been similar shows of individuals and groups of people from the African continent in 1896 in Vienna and shortly afterward in Budapest: A village full of Africans from the Gold Coast (today's Ghana) alongside antelopes, parrots, and flamingos, put on show for predominantly white Europeans. These wildly popular human exhibitions, which toured Europe from around 1875 until the third decade of the twentieth century (and also occurred in the United States, including at the Bronx Zoo), were also a fashionable topic in literary circles. Prior to Rilke, another Austrian writer named Peter Altenberg—whom Rilke praised as "the first herald of modern Vienna"[1] in 1898—published a book of prose poems dedicated to the "African men of paradise" titled *Ashantee*.[2] With abyssal irony Altenberg, whose love affair with an African woman had been thoroughly caricatured and ridiculed, with racist overtones, in the Viennese press, exposed his own weaknesses as well as the racism and bigotry of his milieu.

Rilke's "The Ashanti" is more subdued than Altenberg's charged prose. But this poem is as problematic (and "disconcertingly obtuse"[3]) as it is important in his oeuvre. The fact that it is so rarely discussed in the boundless secondary literature leads one to suspect that most critics would prefer to disavow this racist moment in Rilke altogether. But ignoring "The Ashanti" will not solve the problem. "The Ashanti" represents an important point in Rilke's body of work because it deals with the poet's—and thus our—ability and willingness to perceive another person on his or her own terms. It is also a link between the sentimental poems in *The Book of Images,* where it first appeared in 1902, and the "objective" thing poems in *New Poems* of 1907 and 1908 for which Rilke is so rightly renowned. I consider "The Ashanti" here in light of Rilke's wish to approach the world as a poet, honestly and without judgment.

In a letter dated October 19, 1907, Rilke explains that to pick and choose from what is given (that is, in this case, to excuse "The Ashanti" as an embarrassing and youthful faux pas, since this poem doesn't fit with our image of Rilke) would constitute a sin for any artist:

> First, artistic contemplation must have so thoroughly conditioned itself to see what is there, even in the ugly and the seemingly repulsive, which, like everything that exists, counts. It is not permitted for the artist to pick and choose, nor to turn away from any part of existence: a single rejection at any time expels him from the condition of grace, makes him a sinner, through and through. [. . .] To turn yourself towards the leper and share the warmth of your body with him, down to the warmth of the heart in a night of love: this must be a part of the artist's existence, as the striving for a new blessedness.[4]

Blessed is the artist who refuses to turn away from "existence." Yet this is just what Rilke does in "The Ashanti" (and what the critics have done in turn): He turns away, he fails to look, he privileges the animals and hardly leaves room in his text for the humans right in front of him. The poem piles up seven consecutive negations, whose objects are born of Europe's racist images that attribute to the Africans a lascivious sexuality, a raw violence, an authentic nature.

> No vision of far-off countries,
> no feeling of brown women who
> dance out of their falling garments.

No wild unheard-of melodies.
No songs which issued from the blood,
and no blood which screamed out from the depths.

No brown girls who stretched out
velvety in tropical exhaustion;
no eyes which blazed like weapons,

and the mouth broad with laughter.
And a bizarre agreement
with the light-skinned humans' vanity.[5]

Keine Vision von fremden Ländern,
kein Gefühl von braunen Frauen, die
tanzen aus den fallenden Gewändern.

Keine wilde fremde Melodie.
Keine Lieder, die vom Blute stammten,
und kein Blut, das aus den Tiefen schrie.

Keine braunen Mädchen, die sich samten
breiteten in Tropenmüdigkeit;
keine Augen, die wie Waffen flammten,

und die Munde zum Gelächter breit.
Und ein wunderliches Sich-verstehen
mit der hellen Menschen Eitelkeit.[6]

With the blood that screams out "from the depths," Rilke evokes both
the Europeans' image of Africa and the violence done to Africans by
European weapons, past and future. Likewise, Rilke's figure of the "brown
women" operates on two levels: By dancing "out of their falling garments"
they act out the erotic, orientalist fantasies of Europeans, to fantasies with
deep roots in the German tradition. As early as Friedrich Hölderlin's
poem "Remembrance" of 1803 (where Hölderlin refers to the Mediterranean people) there appear in the gaze of the German poet "brown
women . . . on silken surfaces." Hölderlin's poem, according to a
commentary by Martin Heidegger, is about "becoming familiar with one's
own" through contact with the foreign.[7] Rilke's poem is about the same
experience. Yet Rilke's projections onto the Africans fall apart at the

moment when the Africans laugh in the Europeans' face. Instead of being able to distinguish himself dialectically in the encounter with the other, and thus define himself, Rilke encounters the Africans' willingness and desire to interact with the "light people." The Europeans' "vanity," enshrined in a Hegelian notion of the dialectic of self and other shared by poets from Hölderlin to Rilke, consists of Europeans looking at Africans only for the purpose of defining themselves, of perceiving the Africans not on their own terms but as other.

At the same time that Rilke, in the letter quoted above, forbids the artist to "turn away from any part of existence," he wanted to turn away in his poem: "It made me shudder seeing that."[8] At the center of the poem is Rilke's fear of being seen. And in this poem to be seen means to be defined. It is not the Africans who are exposed in this poem but the poet himself, who cannot abide by the tenets of his own aesthetics.

In *The Book of Images* Rilke explains his fear of seeing the Ashanti. This fear comes from the recognition that the Ashanti are active in being seen and themselves want to see. The Ashanti disappoint Rilke and partly defeat his project of finding oneself through close and patient observation of the world. Strangely enough, however, his aesthetic triumphs in this disappointment. The way Rilke sees the Africans is determined by the Africans themselves. Since they cannot be seen by the poet in the way he wants to, the Ashanti become just what Rilke, as he writes in his letters, wishes to see in all of existence—that which is seen unfiltered, without "selection," "turning away," and "rejection."[9]

The artist must "overcome" himself in order to see the Ashanti. He must rein in his "vanity"; he must not judge everything from a distance, but rather should see the various parts of the world from their own perspective and on their own terms (and so for a short time exchange his own perspective for another's experience of the world). The Ashanti enter Rilke's vision as beings with their own wishes, desires, vanity, and projections who do not distinguish between themselves and the "light people": In the words of the letter cited at this chapter's beginning, they "count." These qualities attest to their humanity: the expectation that they will be seen by others, and that they see.

Allowing Africans displayed in the zoo "to count" means, for Rilke, not to show them in his poem. And by disappearing from his poem, they escape, at least in part, from Europe's racist imagination. Their absence in the poem attests to their inaccessibility as a theme for the poem, and this absence, paradoxically, attests to their humanity.

The verses quoted above are followed by a freestanding line:

> And it made me shudder seeing that.[10]
> Und mir war so bange hinzusehen.[11]

In the poem's concluding stanza, Rilke confesses his fondness for animals: "O how much truer are the animals" ("*O wie sind die Tiere so viel treuer*").[12]

In the book titled *Ashantee*, Altenberg's narrator urges one of the two children he has taken to the Prater (Vienna's amusement park and zoo) to also look at the animals: "There is no shame in dreaming from the point of view of an animal."[13] Rilke first dreamed from an animal's point of view in *New Poems*: His efforts to inhabit the perspective of flamingos, parrots, gazelles, cats, and panthers made Rilke a completely "modern poet." In "The Ashanti" Rilke dreams of animals that offer the poet a sealed inner life:

> O how much truer are the animals
> that pace up and down in steel grids,
> unrelated to the antics of the new
> alien things which they don't understand.
> And they burn like a silent fire
> softly out and subside into themselves,
> indifferent to the new adventure
> and with their fierce instinct all alone.[14]

The animals are true only to themselves. They do not depend on us; rather, they are—as the end of the poem puts it—"with their fierce instinct all alone." The instinct of the Africans—in the rhetorical figure of negation and the image of their "blood"—cries out against that. The brutal and inhumane exhibition of the Ashanti in a zoo sets free their humanity. Rilke recognizes that man uses his consciousness to set himself apart from his animal nature and seeks a relation to the world and himself that was there all along but still must be discovered. He prefers animals, because they do not incorporate the poet into their world, and thus can be viewed as objects. The Ashanti, on the other hand, form a connection with the poet by sharing their wish to be recognized and defined by their observer.

This insight hardly exculpates Rilke for the racism he shared with most Europeans of his time. He wants to keep his aesthetic project in a space that remains outside of politics and ethics, since in those fields it is necessary to make judgments or "pick and choose" from what there is. This idealized space, where no picking and choosing is permitted but into which everything enters unfiltered, is disturbed by the insistent presence of the Ashanti—in Rilke's poem the image of their mouths wide open with laughter. Yet this is precisely the meaning of that pre-ethical, transcendent space: that all that exists is permitted there. The poem about the Africans exhibited in a zoolike setting enacts Rilke's poetic principles, although it describes the poet at a moment where this all-encompassing vision fails.

Without mentioning "The Ashanti," the critic Paul de Man once described Rilke's method as follows: It is "the reversal of the traditional priority, which located the depth of meaning in a referent conceived as an object or a consciousness of which the language is a more or less faithful reflection."[15] In "The Ashanti," Rilke carries out this reversal of referent and meaning by not letting the Ashanti themselves appear and presenting only their inaccessibility—and therefore also their resistance to any rhetorical or imaginative appropriation. The Ashanti are figures in Rilke's language and not actual, embodied referents. De Man characterizes Rilke's devaluing of meaning (that is, of reference) as a form of "liberation": "On the level of poetic language, this renunciation corresponds to the loss of a primacy of meaning located within the referent and it allows for the new rhetoric of Rilke's 'figure.'"[16] De Man says nothing about the ethical and political meaning of this "loss . . . of meaning located within the referent." As soon as Rilke has freed himself from the convention that ties meaning to an actual object (de Man's "referent"), he can present the Ashanti without portraying them as "genuine" Africans. If he had stuck with a conception of meaning as equivalent to reference, it would have been impossible for the Ashanti to be represented on their own terms, apart from the semantics of a racist Europe.

Rilke's decision not to describe the Ashanti, and instead to show how they share (and therefore disappoint or block) the poet's expectations, projections, and "vanity," corresponds to the liberation of "meaning located within the referent." Does that mean that Rilke denies the

Ashanti their actual existence and turns them into the mere product of discourse, into mere figments of his imagination? Of course. But even so, in this dialectical poem the Africans escape the racist European imagination that had landed them in the zoo in actuality. In Rilke's poem, they win the autonomy of vanity, which they do not have in the Jardin d'Acclimatation, where (as Rilke's ironic subtitle also states) they are supposed to fit in and "acclimate" to the climate of Europe. Their mouths are prepared not only for laughter, but also for speech.

Rilke's poem is not postcolonial, nor is it a protest poem. Such interpretations would keep the Ashanti prisoners in the European imagination, as if their humanity and freedom depended on the judgment, politics, perception, and goodwill of Europeans and of a European poet. Africans had already featured as performers in a mass spectacle in Rilke's early and all-but-forgotten "Visions of Christ" from 1896, in which he dryly describes an African entertainer who forgets his part because of a primitive homesickness:

> And yonder, as if rooted to the spot
> A black man stood who should have bellowed, but
> Became enraptured of a coconut.[17]

How is it possible to free such a figure from the pernicious web of European racist projections?

De Man emphasizes that the "urgency" of Rilke's promise of a transcendent level of meaning (above the political reality in which these humans are prisoners in a zoo) cannot be separated from the "equally urgent, and equally poetic, need of retracting it at the very instant [Rilke] seems to be on the point of offering it to us."[18] Rilke's fear of looking directly at the Ashanti constitutes this simultaneous promise and retraction. At the linguistic level, Rilke's fear at being looked at by the Ashanti is the fear of losing his protective layer of poetic self-consciousness. Its second, literal meaning is the frisson experienced by a light-skinned European on a Sunday afternoon at the zoo before the cheap replica of an African village with a few Africans dressed to look exotic, other, strange. Rilke's fear is that the Ashanti will recognize his gaze in a way different from how animals behave. Rilke can promise transcendence and retract it at the same time, because his fear is simultaneously the metaphorical fear of the poet and the literal fear of the visitor to the zoo. By speaking to both the figurative and literal levels at once, this poem can simultaneously show (and thus make a spectacle out of) and not show (and thus grant meaning to) the Ashanti.

On March 8, 1907, Rilke explains in a letter how the patient observation of the outside world allows an artist's internal vision to develop independently. The potential of "The Ashanti" may be found in this directive on how to unleash one's creativity:

> To look at something is such a wonderful thing of which we still know so little. When we look at something, we are turned completely toward the outside by this activity. But just when we are most turned toward the outside like that, things seem to take place within us that have longed for an unobserved moment, and while they unfold within us, whole and strangely anonymous, *without us*, their significance begins to take shape in the external object in the form of a strong, convincing, indeed their only possible name. And by means of this name we contentedly and respectfully recognize what is happening inside us without ourselves touching upon it. We understand it only quietly, entirely from a distance, under the sign of a thing that had just been alien and in the next instant is alienated from us again.[19]

When we observe something very patiently and closely, "strangely anonymous" things take place inside us. A new knowledge forms in us and overtakes us, since we can name this new awareness only with a "possible name" from "without." What does that mean? That something is changed by Rilke's "The Ashanti," something "inside us" but without our conscious control: a new (in)sight, which cannot fix or recognize, approve or condemn, the meaning of what is seen before it is seen—in this case Rilke's meaningful poem about Africans in the zoo. Here emerges a new concept of the everyday, which Rilke thinks of as "part of everything else," but which could, at any moment, become no longer "everyday," no longer a "part of everything else." This notion of the everyday and what is right in front of us as the potential for completely new meaning exists in every single one of Rilke's poems. In "The Ashanti" this potential is the possibility of seeing the Africans as humans, which means not regarding them as "other" but rather, based on our understanding that they are "alienated from us again," seeing them, like all humans, as unique and yet part of the everyday at once.

The Ashanti block or interrupt Rilke's artistic project of "blessed contemplation." They mark the limit of the European imagination, which retreats from the task of recognizing other humans as such. Rilke addresses this limit in a later poem:

> For there is a boundary to looking
> [. . .]
> Work of the eyes is done, now
> Go and do heart-work.[20]

In the Jardin d'Acclimatation such "heart-work" would be the beginning of empathy and recognition, which would compel one to turn away. And that would be the beginning of the end of such inhumane exhibitions of people like animals. Rilke turns away, but the political intervention does not follow.

Rilke's project of artistic self-overcoming and of finding the right way of seeing, of a practice of *seeing* as a step past the "boundary to looking" from the "work of the eyes" to "heart-work," encounters the Ashanti. This encounter challenges the racist European view of the world, which locks people in actual and metaphoric cages and recognizes the meaning of these people *only*, blindly, in relation to Europe. The Ashanti throw Rilke's poem and project off course. They shamefully interrupt the stanzas and cause his rhythm to falter: In the original Greek meaning of the word, the Ashanti are Rilke's stumbling block, his *skandalon*, his scandal.

b

for Buddha

Can Rilke's writings, from the perennially popular and often-cited *Letters to a Young Poet* to the hard-won consolations of *Duino Elegies*, offer a guide to life?

In 1907 the Viennese bookseller Hugo Heller began a survey, the results of which were published by Hermann Bahr in a paperback volume entitled *Books for Real Life* (*Die Bücher zum wirklichen Leben*) that in a very short time sold forty thousand copies, an appreciable figure. In addition to bankers, philosophers, and politicians, famous authors listed the books that might be "indispensable [. . .] necessities for existence" for young people.[1] In his foreword, Hermann Bahr said of Heller's survey: "The question asked here is not about books, but rather about the future. What we think of it, what we want it to look like, what kind of belief we have in it."[2] Although it was only 1907, two participants in the survey cited Rilke's poetry, even if it did "not find a large audience" in the present, as a "major work of the future."[3] In his contribution to the book, Rilke wrote: "My relationship to books is not without an aspect of imprisonment, and it can happen that in a large library I find myself as if I had fallen into the hands of a powerful enemy force, against which any resistance by an individual would be useless."[4]

This is certainly an understandable response. The sheer mass of books to grapple with can cause even motivated and fast readers to break into a sweat. This response seems so much more honest than the famous passage from Rilke's novel, *The Notebooks of Malte Laurids Brigge*, so beloved by young poets and haughtily titled "Bibliothèque Nationale," in which the narrator writes with childlike (feigned) pride: "I am sitting here and have a poet. What a fate. [. . .] But just imagine my fate: I, perhaps the shabbiest of all these readers, and a foreigner: I have a poet. Even though I am poor."[5] In the novel, the euphoria doesn't last long. The library's august reading room can only briefly support the illusion of equality among its visitors. The passage ends with the narrator trying without success to lose himself in the fantasy of his future life as a poet, in which he has an old country house to call home, looks out onto a gentle green garden, and apart from a comfortable armchair owns nothing but flowers, a loyal dog, "and a strong walking-stick for the stony paths. And nothing else."[6] It is a fantasy of the writer as a perfectly self-sufficient creature that offsets the poet's "poverty" for a few minutes. The destitute Malte cannot find a home in the Bibliothèque Nationale and must be content with much less than a country house: "But life has turned out differently, God knows why. My old furniture is rotting in the barn where I left it, and I myself, yes, my God, I have no roof over me, and it is raining into my eyes."[7] Eventually the Paris rain rinses the nostalgia for such rural kitsch, to which Malte clings for a while, out of Rilke's narrator's eyes and mind. Rilke's language grows harsher over the course of the novel, and the thought first formed in the formidable library that one could feel truly at home in the work of another poet, or "have" another poet as a metaphoric soul mate, muse, guardian angel, or mentor, collapses. The disillusioned Malte learns that one cannot be truly at home in a country house, least of all by oneself.

Rilke's admission of the overwhelming power of books anticipates what he writes in *The Notebooks of Malte Laurids Brigge* after the detour into "a quiet house in the mountains" with its solid middle-class and respectable "mahogany desk" and its "potbellied dresser at the back of his bedroom."[8] That is, Rilke admits that dealing with books can sometimes be torture. That the sheer mass of books already written can demoralize the budding poet, rather than offer him a comfortable home in the grand library. That one often has no chance against so many books. That one must find that stony path alone. Yet this admission of anxiety also reveals the great influence books can have: If books can be so threatening, they must also have the potential to help in real life. In his response to the bestselling survey *Books for Real Life*, Rilke suggests that the path to real life is the path away from books. He puts the text behind him and deliberately misunderstands the title of Heller's survey. For Rilke, "books for real life" does not mean books that give advice *about* life, but rather books that lead *into* life. The Danish author Jens Peter Jacobsen, who features prominently in Rilke's famous *Letters to a Young Poet*, "opened" such a "path" for Rilke: "To the same degree that books have made an impression on me, they also point me beyond them into nature" and "support me in my inner certainty that even the quietest and most inaccessible parts of us have a sensual counterpoint in nature. The only task is to find it."[9] The way to himself, and to what seems "most inaccessible" in his own nature, is opened to Rilke as soon as he puts away books written by others. On August 2, 1904, he writes in a letter: "In the end there are only two or three things I would trust myself to write about, and there are probably no books that make the list."[10] Another passage in *The Notebooks of Malte Laurids Brigge* reads: "thus it became clear to me that I was never a real reader."[11]

Between the short-lived magic of the library scene in his only novel and his recommendation in the response to *Books for Real Life*, Rilke seeks to learn his way *in* life from books, without turning away from life. How does one achieve a balance between the stultifying anxiety of "falling into the hands of a powerful enemy force" in the library—that is, of surrendering to another's ideas—and the illusory belief that one can "own" and assimilate another poet to improve oneself? Where is the path between letting go and holding on; how does one free oneself from the influence of others without becoming spiritually adrift and without any guiding stars, or, in Rilke's terms, "poor"?

Rilke charted a path for even the most critical of his readers. In the midst of a devastating, war-hungry age, the conservative German poet Gottfried Benn, in notebooks written between 1936 and 1940, cited the final line of Rilke's poem "Requiem for Wolf Graf von Kalckreuth," written for a young man who took his life at age nineteen, as a tough motto for a generation headed into disaster: "Who talks of victory? To endure is all."[12]

But it was not only fellow poets to whom Rilke showed the right path. Even during his lifetime he did not resist the "temptation" to give comfort to less prominent, directionless souls. In 1920 he wrote: "Oh love, there are so many people who expect something of me, I no longer know what—help, advice (from me, who finds himself so helpless in the face of everything important in life!) and even though I can see that they are lost, that they are deceiving themselves,—I am tempted to share a few of my experiences with them, and offer them a few fruits of my solitude."[13]

Rilke's ambition to share his works as "fruits of [his] solitude" landed his work in the self-help section of today's booksellers. In many difficult situations, a Rilke quote offers support and guidance. (I have relied on Rilke's words when I've found myself speechless in the face of loss.) Rilke is often thought to have done more than other poets did for other generations, which had been largely to sweeten their well-earned leisure time with pleasant rhymes. But in spite of the uses of Rilke's words on calendars, on coffee mugs, in poetry blogs, and in Hollywood movies, it does not matter if people read the right books for the wrong reasons or listen to the right poets for the wrong reasons, as long as they read the right books and listen to the right poets. But how well does Rilke truly fit alongside Deepak Chopra and Rumi in the New Age section? Is the poet whom W. H. Auden famously called the "Santa Claus of loneliness" a fitting prophet for our age?

Times change. Gottfried Benn's war-torn generation had picked Rilke's steely "Who talks of victory? To endure is all" as a motto and sidelined Rilke's other works, the allegedly effete stuff with unicorns, fragrant hydrangeas, and especially the angels. In the 1960s, other poets protested against this partial appropriation of some of Rilke's lines by hard-boiled types like Benn. Paul Celan, who had grown up reading Rilke in his hometown of Czernowitz before his world was engulfed and destroyed by the Second World War and then the Holocaust, during which his parents were murdered by Germans, found the lines chosen by Benn less than inspiring.[14] Celan implicitly accused Benn of having used these lines of Rilke's to bury the debate about who in Germany had been raving about "victory" and who was really entitled to speak of "enduring." "Enduring" and "surviving" were no longer "all" for Celan and many of his readers. For Celan, what mattered was the responsibility to remember what the cost of survival had been. And Rilke's "to endure" included for Celan also the endurance of those persecuted by the Germans in an unspeakable fashion, and not only the endurance of the Germans as Benn had understood the term. In the 1970s, as a younger generation of German readers tried to escape from the regulated lifestyles of their respective countries, East and West Germany, and come to terms with the legacy of vast crimes committed by their family members, Rilke experienced a second renaissance in the English-speaking world alongside Hermann Hesse and Carl Jung. During this period another line of Rilke's became the motto of a generation. It was the famous final line of his enigmatic poem about a fragment of a Greek statue, "Archaic Torso of Apollo": "You have to change your life."[15]

I believe that today, when some of the liberationist impulses of the 1960s have settled into institutions and a new generation seeks meaning in ways not even conceivable only decades ago, there is another line that takes on relevance and meaning. This line hovers between resignation and control, melancholy and sovereignty, and captures the zeitgeist: "All of life is lived" (*"Alles Leben wird gelebt"*).[16]

"All of life is lived." This line from *The Book of Hours* may speak the most directly to the mood of our times, because it makes a place for life as something yet to be imagined, instead of giving the subject complete decision-making power and control over his own being. To put it differently: Precisely the thing that we do not understand, that we cannot grasp intellectually, that we do not want to face and suppress from our lives, ultimately forces its way back and, even if in a different form, is lived. This line essentially comes down to: Live every moment in full consciousness that you are alive.

The apparent tautology "All of life is lived" connects seamlessly to such Buddhist teachings as the *Dhammapada* of Buddha, which says more or less that "the *dhamma* is the *dhamma* because of the *dhamma*." Glenn Wallis explains that this "means something like: 'The teaching is the proper way of living because of the way things are.' And, unlike in theistic traditions, 'the way things are' is, in the Buddhist view, readily observable, here and now, to anyone who would develop precisely the skill to discern it. The *dhamma*, as teaching, is precisely the means to this skill."[17]

Compare this to Rilke's thinking, in a letter:

> Most people have no idea how beautiful the world is, or how much majesty there is in even the smallest things, in a random flower, a pebble, a piece of tree bark, or a birch leaf. Grown-up people, who are busy with various things and worries and who torment themselves with trivial concerns, completely lose sight of this abundance [. . .] And yet the greatest beauty of all would be if all people [. . .] would not lose the ability to take the same intense delight in a birch

leaf, the feather of a peacock, or the hopping of a crow as in a majestic mountain range or a glorious palace. What is small is just as inherently not small as what is great is in itself great. The world is shot through with a great and eternal beauty, which touches equally all that is great as what is small; for in the most important and essential matters there is no injustice on earth.[18]

One should not be distracted by Rilke's use of the term "beauty." In a typically subtle transformation of a concept into its opposite, Rilke would consider it "the greatest beauty of all" if people did not take *beauty* as the only valid way of perceiving the world. But it's not simply that the world *would be* beautiful if people stopped prejudging what is beautiful and what is not. The world *is* beautiful in this way. It's only that people do not see that, and thus prevent this beauty. Like his predecessors Baudelaire and Rimbaud, Rilke challenges a prevailing tenet in the European aesthetic tradition, which takes the world and divides it into the beautiful, ugly, sublime, important, and meaningless. He wants to reach a kind of thinking or, more precisely, a sensory experience, that—like Buddhist teaching—allows for everything on equal terms. "Who still believes," Rilke writes, "that art can portray the beautiful which has an opposite (this little term 'beautiful' belongs to a concept of taste). Art is the passion for the whole. Its result: equanimity and the equal participation of everything."[19]

Does this mean that Rilke's writings are correctly placed in the self-help section, next to Khalil Gibran's *The Prophet*, paperback editions of *The Teachings of the Buddha*, meditation manuals, and celebrities reading sections of the *Dhammapada*? It may seem that the booksellers are correct and that the way to Rilke passes through Eastern thought. But in fact Rilke's path no more leads to Buddhism (which, like all teachings, he rejected) than Buddhism leads to Buddhism, as long as we understand "Rilke" and "Buddhism" as teachings instead of results, as knowledge and not as everyday practice. The path, that is, the teaching, does not lead away from life, nor run through it, but *is* life: "All of life is lived." In light of the striking similarity between the central teaching of Buddhism, that the way things are can be experienced directly, and Rilke's "passion for the whole," the connection between Rilke and the Buddha is well worth exploring.

A year after Rilke's response to the survey for *Books for Real Life*, Clara
Rilke sent her husband a copy of a new and widely celebrated German
edition of *The Teachings of Gotama Buddha*. Does the Buddha put Rilke
on the right path? Karl Eugen Neumann's 1902 German translation, the
first full edition of the Buddha's teachings in any European language, had
quickly become a bestseller.[20] Many important authors who had first
encountered Indian philosophy in the works of philosopher Arthur Scho-
penhauer found this edition indispensable. Thomas Mann "carried with
him the *Teachings of Gotama Buddha* in the translation by Karl Eugen
Neuman [. . .] safely through all the stations of [his] wanderings,"
including his move to the United States, and counted this work "among
the great translations of world literature."[21] Hermann Hesse mentioned
Neumann's translation in his essay in *Books for Real Life* as an important
contribution, since "recent research has not yet produced any [other] truly
classical work." George Bernard Shaw likened the translation to Luther's
translation of Scripture: "I can say that in placing a complete translation
of the Buddhist canonical scriptures within the reach of the German
people you are rendering as great a public service as that of the first
publishers of Luther's translation of the Bible, and I hope your enterprise
will be adequately rewarded." Hugo von Hofmannsthal attributed great
importance to the book, which appeared "at the moment of a world-
historical crisis—which was not a spiritual crisis, unless it were also a crisis
of language"; once Edmund Husserl began reading Neumann's translation, he "could not, in spite of other more important work, tear
[himself] away." For the founder of phenomenology, in "this time of the
collapse of our culture which is being degenerated by superficiality [. . .]
this coming-to-see the Indian way of transcending the world" constituted
"an important experience."[22] Rilke, in contrast to these effusive apprecia-
tions of the Buddha's writings, thanks his wife for giving him the
Buddha's writings in a letter and immediately explains why he, unlike his
contemporaries Mann, Hesse, Hofmannsthal, Shaw, and Husserl, who
took the book enthusiastically as a spiritual and cultural "great experience," will not read the teachings of the Buddha:

> I opened the book, and already several of the first words I glimpsed
> made me shudder [. . .] Why do I experience this new gesture of
> hesitation, which puts you off so much?—It may be that I do it for

the sake of Malte Laurids, whom I have been neglecting for too
long.[23]

After this initial shudder over "several of the first words [he] glimpsed,"
Rilke closed his edition of *The Teachings of Gotama Buddha* and,
presumably, forgot it. Rilke then explains how he must defend his projects
against any rivals for his attention, including any powerful author, any
teacher, and his wife. When he writes that leafing through the Buddha's
texts makes him shudder, this gesture is the uncanny shudder of *recognition*. Rilke feels that he has been called upon to write his own Buddha
book. Of course, Rilke rejects other influences at this moment in his life:
for example *Goethe's Correspondence with a Child*, "this strong, imploring
testimony against" Goethe, or ultimately Auguste Rodin as an overbearing and unfair teacher. But while Rilke at least briefly engages with
Goethe's text to deflect the precursor's influence, he pushes Buddha out
of his mind without opening the book again. He reads Goethe, "while
Buddha is made to wait. Please don't judge me. Please, let me be and
have faith. Don't ask anything else of me, not even in spirit."[24] He engages
with everything, especially Goethe, just long enough to move it out of the
way. Only Buddha is not given a chance.

But it is hard to be more Buddhist than this, for we do not learn the
way from the teachers who point it out to us, but rather by walking it
ourselves—in Rilke's case, by writing himself.[25] "Don't judge me," writes
Rilke, and implores his former spouse, "let me be": I can rely on nothing
but myself.

"Let me be," in the letter to Clara, also means: Let me go. Let me be
on my way. Rilke was well on the way to becoming a master, even while
he was still working as a secretary for the great sculptor Rodin. He then
had a falling-out with Rodin—on a petty pretext, but also because on the
way to Rodin he had "mistakenly" glimpsed his own path as going beyond
all masters, gurus, and analysts to himself as a poet who, full of "passion
for the whole," made no more distinction between life and teachings.
Rilke doesn't need to read *The Teachings of Gotama Buddha*: Wherever it
might take him, Rilke—and we can't ask any more of him than this, "not
even in spirit"—has been there all along.

"It is best to simply take notice of some things that will no longer
change, without either lamenting these facts or even judging them."[26]
This plea not to judge underlies Rilke's confession in *The Notebooks of*

Malte Laurids Brigge that he was "never a real reader." It also constitutes the first step toward contemplation as a Buddhist practice.

Three years before Clara had sent her husband the Buddha book, the young and still unknown Rilke lived for a short spell in Meudon, near Paris, in a tiny cottage on the estate of Rodin, from whom Rilke hoped to learn how to live an artist's life. The grounds were filled with Rodin's works, which Rilke watched being created in the large workshop every day. From his window he looked upon a massive sculpture, *Buddha at Rest*, in Rodin's garden.

> After dinner I soon take leave, and am in my little cottage at 8:30 at the latest. In front of me I see the wide sky blooming with stars, and down below the window the gravel path rises up a small hill to where a statue of Buddha rests in fanatic reticence and expends the unspeakable completeness of his gesture under the skies of day and night in quiet withdrawal. C'est le centre du monde, I said to Rodin. And then he looks at one so kindly, so much like a true friend. That is very beautiful, and a great deal.[27]

Rilke is unusually stable during his brief sojourn as Rodin's secretary. He recognized himself in the Buddha statue. But whenever Rilke uses "so" as an adverb ("so kindly"), he is usually not being quite honest. And to be sure, instead of remaining in "fanatic reticence" as Rodin's student, he draws on his own "quiet withdrawal" and the distance from the Buddha (and of course from Rodin) to find the strength to express the "unspeakable completeness" of life and death, heaven and earth, inner and outer worlds. (Ultimately Rodin fired Rilke for contacting one of his wealthy clients under his own, rather than Rodin's, name.) Rilke, living in a little cottage in the shadow of the master and across from his Buddha statue, explains to the great and famous man, the unexcelled creator, Rodin: Every evening, after I have left you, when I am alone with myself, I behold the center of the world.

Rilke tries to communicate from within the center of his existence, without either betraying it or wrapping it in silence. In his poetry Rilke strives for the balance between the interiority of an object and the consciousness of the poet and reader, which necessarily remains external to the object. On the linguistic level this effort often takes the form of a series of rhetorical inversions, which flood the poem's point of departure (the original referent, or the poem's apparent "theme" and central figure) with a series of new figures and thereby, like countless layers of thick glaze, eventually make it unrecognizable. The resulting poems begin with images and often expansive metaphors, which are then superseded to make these metaphors disappear in the texture of more metaphors, meta-metaphors, if you will, and a newly formed language.

In Rilke's *New Poems* there are three such poems about the Buddha. They focus on physical objects to examine whether these objects exist independently of our looking at them. They treat this basic inaction and indifference of things as their immanence—which is no different than the immanence of Rilke's poetry, which occasionally treats words for their sound, for instance, instead of their signification within a language. Each of the three Buddha poems is a self-portrait. As the Buddha eventually disappears into the descriptive metaphors, so does Rilke's self disappear in his writing. The larger context, which Rilke calls the "passion for the whole," is evoked in all three poems, as Rilke places the pure materiality of the statue above the spiritual significance of Buddha, so that ultimately the material itself is recognizable as a higher order.

This is one of Rilke's most characteristic poetic methods: In poems about the inner essence of a given thing, he takes what seem to be its secondary qualities and ancillary objects (such as the material of which a relic is made, the color of a flower, the shape of an object, or, also in *New Poems*, the "vinegar-soaked sponge" and "hard brush" used for washing a corpse[28]) and emphasizes these properties in such a way that the thing in question is pried from its familiar context, emptied of its allegorical meaning, and glimpsed as if for the first time. The idea in the Buddha poems is to layer the metaphors of transcendence (star, distance, sublimity, majesty, gold, eternity, center) in such a way that they eventually give up all meaning in the face of the unmoving presence of the Buddha. Rilke takes the metaphors literally, develops more images from them, and thus leads them *ad absurdum*. The metaphors are stripped of their value; the poem, however—as one of the Buddha poems says— "endures." The first Buddha poem, which is titled "Buddha," likens the Buddha to a star:

> As if he listened. Stillness: something distant . . .
> We check ourselves—and do not hear it.
> And he is Star. And throngs of giant stars
> which we do not see stand around him.[29]

Als ob er horchte. Stille: eine Ferne . . .
Wir halten ein und hören sie nicht mehr.
Und er ist Stern. Und andre große Sterne,
die wir nicht sehen, stehen um ihn her.[30]

Rilke is looking at himself. He writes to Clara: "Don't be dismayed—but I am so overly sensitive, and when anyone's gaze rests on me, I grow weak in that spot. I would like to know from now on that only the stars linger on me, they see everything at once from their distance, the whole, and so do not tie anything down, but rather release everything in everything . . ."[31]

He wants to "release everything in everything": The wish for complete consciousness, the underlying gesture of meditation, the complete disinhibition and relinquishing of the self for the sake of the self, is always in conflict with the knowledge and awareness that in consciousness and meditation the desire (as well as knowledge and even awareness) and the self are supposed to disappear. Rilke's "Stillness" in the first line of "Buddha" describes not only the state in which Rilke discovers a statue of Buddha or imagines the Buddha to be. "Stillness" ("*Stille*") is also an imperative, a call, and a command, "Hush!"—to abide, to yield, to behold the Buddha, to sink into yourself, to read this poem. But as soon as we fall quiet with no purpose in mind, according to Rilke, we no longer examine that which so suddenly made us still. In the letter to Clara, Rilke expresses the monomaniacal wish to know that all "the stars linger on [him]." This wish corresponds to his longing for freedom from everything, a freedom that makes him the center of the world. It is Rilke's wish for complete stillness, for "releas[ing] everything in everything," which is tantamount to wishlessness, the end of desire, ignorance, repose in a stillness that can no longer be grasped.

Oh, he is everything. Really: do we stand here
until he sees us? What would he want?
And if instead we threw ourselves before him,
He'd remain deep and idle as a cat.[32]

O er ist Alles. Wirklich, warten wir,
daß er uns sähe? Sollte er bedürfen?
Und wenn wir hier uns vor ihm niederwürfen,
er bliebe tief und träge wie ein Tier.[33]

The Buddha is no golden calf, but rather an unmoving and unmoved, indifferent animal. It has no relation to us, since the Buddha meets our wishes with less than his own being. There is nothing but the inertness that underlies consciousness. And it is just this that we want to learn from the Buddha: to be—without the discontinuousness of the self that makes us aware of our being. "Let me be and have faith. Don't ask anything else of me. Not even in spirit," Rilke writes to his wife after she sends him the Buddha book. The final strophe of the Buddha poem should also simply exist, merely *be*. So it is structured around the words "tugs," "circled," "forgets," "denied" (in German: *"reißt," "kreist," "vergißt," "verweist"*), all of which literally contain the hidden promise of pure being—the German *ist*, for "is"—without appearing, without being redeemed.

> For what tugs us roughly to his feet
> has circled in him for a million years.
> He, who forgets what our life teaches
> and abides in the wisdom we're denied.[34]

> Denn das, was uns zu seinen Füßen reißt,
> das kreist in ihm seit Millionen Jahren.
> Er, der vergißt was wir erfahren
> und der erfährt was uns verweist.[35]

The Buddha's being is not a fulfillment, nor a revelation. We cannot experience it as long as we think of that experience as a step on the way to knowledge. For the Buddha "abides in" what we are "denied," that which leads us away from experience to reflection, awareness, thinking, understanding, memory, and knowledge.

The second Buddha poem in the same part of *New Poems* is also called "Buddha." It deals with the base materiality of a Buddha, whose inscrutability confuses the pilgrim. The Buddha does not rise out of "kingdoms full of penitence," as the icons in a church do, whose art- and craftworks are meant to be signs of the coming majesty that compensates for the rejection of this world. The power of the Buddha arises rather from its seeming lack of connection with the world of the pilgrims. This distinguishes it from Christian icons, which draw their strength from the believers' material and spiritual sacrifices.

Already from afar the wary foreign
pilgrim feels how it drips from him goldenly:
as if whole kingdoms full of penitence
had heaped up all the secrecies.

but drawing nearer he grows confused
before the loftiness of these eyebrows:
for this is not their drinking cups
and the earrings of their women.[36]

Schon von ferne fühlt der fremde scheue
Pilger, wie es golden von ihm träuft;
so als hätten Reiche voller Reue
ihre Heimlichkeiten aufgehäuft.

Aber näher kommend wird er irre
vor der Hoheit dieser Augenbraun:
denn das sind nicht ihre Trinkgeschirre
und die Ohrgehänge ihrer Fraun.[37]

The Buddha does not care about his pilgrims; he makes them grow
confused and lose their way, instead of offering himself as the destination
and purpose of their pilgrimage. The pilgrims see that the gleam of his
gold cannot be compared with anything from the world they live in. The
"loftiness of these eyebrows" comes from indifference to the objects and
values of this world. Yet the pilgrim is amazed and confused that the
material of the Buddha remains so present. With the emphasis on the
material, which even the Buddha cannot overcome by virtue of a transcen-
dental meaning, Rilke proposes something like a koan, an impossible
riddle in the Buddhist tradition. It goes like this: If the only goal in
Buddhism is being, then a bejeweled statue dripping with gold, just like
Gotama Buddha, does nothing more or less than—be. The body, the
statue, the gold, the material cannot be separated from the spirit. In a
letter Rilke describes this philosophy, which is in fact not a philosophy
but merely life: "You know that I am not one of those who neglect their
body to offer it up as a sacrifice to the soul. Mine [i.e., my soul] does not
at all care to receive such an offering, since the entire motion of my spirit
begins in my blood."[38]

The unknowability of the materiality of the Buddha, which—like Rilke's body and its rushing blood—cannot be forgotten just because of its spiritual meaning, creates a broader connection:

> Is there someone then who could say
> what things were melted down to erect
> this image on this flower chalice:
>
> more hushed, more peacefully yellow
> than a golden one and all around
> touching space the way it does itself.[39]

> Wüßte einer denn zu sagen, welche
> Dinge eingeschmolzen wurden, um
> dieses Bild auf diesem Blumenkelche
>
> aufzurichten: stummer, ruhiggelber
> als ein goldenes und rundherum
> auch den Raum berührend wie sich selber.[40]

What "touches space the way it does itself" is neither self-involved nor lost to itself. Here is the key to Rilke's belief, his faith, his system of thought (really it should be called his poetics, since it is too materialistic for a credo): that the things of this world constitute the entire context that can be given to us. Hence Rilke's conviction that a simple life would prepare him for his work, which led him to becoming a vegetarian, and forgoing (unlike his French precursor poets) alcohol, tobacco, and drugs. To make up for this sobriety he took "air baths" in the nude, had a passion for walking barefoot, and relished erotic communion with many of the women in his life. His poetry exists not in opposition to his body, because he finds the reason for his poetry in the rushes of the body. Instead of seeking a supernatural moment of transcendence, Rilke stands by the unmoving material composition of the world.

The result: The pilgrims in the Buddha poem "grow confused," because they want to experience the meaning of the Buddha as something extramaterial—something spiritual as opposed to material. But the meaning of the Buddha is nothing but his physical presence, his goldenness. To express the fact that the Buddha overcomes himself simply by being what he is, through his own physical presence as a statue, Rilke never once makes a distinction in either of the two poems called "Buddha," nor in the third Buddha poem in *New Poems*, called "Buddha in Glory," between God and idol, saint and statue, idea and icon, spirit and matter, language and referent. We don't know if he means the Buddha himself or an image like the large statue in Rodin's garden. For it is just this distinction, so fundamental for Western thought, between essence and substance, spirit and body, language and meaning, appearance and reality, imagination, will, and world, that Rilke makes unrecognizable. Nothing remains but a poem in which these distinctions are invalidated and in which the subject, in the sound of the rhymes (in German, the final six lines rhyme in a pattern of A-B-A-C-B-C: "*sagen, welche*"/"*Blumenkelche*"; "*wurden, um*"/"*und rundherum*"; "*ruhiggelber*"/ "*wie sich selber*"), touches the empty space of the page "the way it does itself." The enormous spiritual meaning of the Buddha is not distinguishable from his being absolutely material.

But Rilke would not be Rilke if he left the blatantly phallic "Buddha in Glory," in which the "thick fluids rise and flow," in its position as the center of the universe. In an opening stanza that takes off with a prayer's intensity and the urgent energy of one of Rilke's erotic poems to Lou Andreas-Salomé, he focuses the quasiatomic centrality of the Buddha, who shines like the sun at the center of the solar system:

> Center of all centers, core of cores,
> almond self-enclosed, and growing sweet—
> all this universe, to the furthest stars
> all beyond them, is your flesh, your fruit.[41]

> Mitte aller Mitten, Kern der Kerne,
> Mandel, die sich einschließt und versüßt,—
> dieses Alles bis an alle Sterne
> ist dein Fruchtfleisch: Sei gegrüßt.[42]

That poem embeds the traditional lyric image of a fruit in its rind in the very modern conception of the universe, of which Rilke was an adherent (he followed with enthusiasm newspaper accounts of the "great success" won by Albert Einstein against the opinion of conservative scholars at a conference).[43] Ultimately "Buddha in Glory" looks beyond itself:

A billion stars go spinning through the night,
blazing high above your head.
But in you is the presence that
will be, when all the stars are dead.[44]

denn ganz oben werden deine Sonnen
voll und glühend umgedreht.
Doch in dir ist schon begonnen,
was die Sonnen übersteht.[45]

The Buddha as embodiment of the "unspeakable closeness" that for Rilke represents the apotheosis of the work of art contains a force that overcomes this unity. What outlives the sun and billions of stars? Rilke's poetry, naturally—at least that is what the poet means to say in the final poem of *New Poems*. It remains the center, the core, and the flesh of the Buddha, and thus that material of the divinity, as in the second Buddha poem, where unknown materials were melted down to "erect this image on this flower chalice." What outlives the sun and stars is all that endures beyond our expectations and hopes as mere materiality. And this is what Rilke wants to achieve in his poems: that his words carry on, simultaneous with and independent of the meaning we find in them. This is impossible, utopian. And yet Rilke comes close to this by letting the white metaphors of truth—the suns and stars in his poetry—burn themselves out. What endures is nothing but the poem, which in its final lines leaves its metaphorical matrix behind. *New Poems*'s final poem also leaves behind the two earlier Buddha poems, whose metaphors all orbited the unnamed, white metaphor of the sun, as our guiding star, as truth. Thus, in the first Buddha poem:

And he is Star. And throngs of giant stars
which we do not see stand around him.[46]

Und er ist Stern. Und andre große Sterne,
die wir nicht sehen, stehen um ihn her.[47]

And the final stanza of the second Buddha poem:

more hushed, more peacefully yellow
than a golden one and all around
touching space the way it does itself.[48]

stummer, ruhiggelber
als ein goldenes und rundherum
auch den Raum berührend wie sich selber.[49]

In the final poem, "Buddha in Glory," these golden metaphors have been melted down. The self-sufficient sun is called autopoetic and onanistic, after having centered the poem around itself as "center of all centers, core of cores [. . .] all this universe to the furthest stars." But something "will be" after the sun has blazed out. And what "will be" is no deeper insight, no wisdom, no improvement of thought. It is the poem that lets its metaphors flare out in its midst.

C

for Circle

In late fall of 1926, Rilke was on his deathbed. He was suffering terribly from leukemia, which had been diagnosed too late, and entrusted himself to the Swiss doctor Dr. Haemmerli despite his lifelong fear of having his body interpreted by another person. "It's bad enough that the needs of my body have forced me to hand myself over to an intermediary and negotiator, that is, to a doctor."[1]

In his despair, Rilke had, a year before his death, called on another person as "intermediary and negotiator": the friend of his youth and his erstwhile lover Lou Andreas-Salomé, who as early as 1913 had been trained under Freud's supervision as one of the first female psychoanalysts. In 1912 Rilke had turned down a chance to be psychoanalyzed, saying, "If one were to exorcise my demons [. . .], this would also be a small, indeed very small scare, to put it thus, for my angels."[2] He considered Freud, whom he had personally met in 1913, "important and memorable" after that first meeting, even if his writings struck him initially as "unsympathetic" (he later revised his judgment and had new publications by Freud sent to him as soon as they appeared); ultimately he viewed Freud to be a representative of "that human science which does not yet, in fact, exist."[3] As a poet, he feared this "straightening up" of the thus "disinfected soul" not because he considered analysis useless, but rather because he viewed it as too effective, too powerful; Rilke's rejection of psychoanalysis was based on his great confidence in its healing power to cure his neuroses, on which his productivity depended.[4]

Faced with a serious illness that the doctor could do nothing to relieve, Rilke writes to Andreas-Salomé to ask for help. In the letter he identifies a presumed bodily cause of his suffering: masturbation.

> Dear Lou,
>
> [. . .] for two years now I have been living more and more in the grip of something horrible, the most immediate cause of which (a stimulation I carry out on myself) I keep aggravating with a devilish obsession, even when I think that I have overcome this temptation. It is a horrid circle [*ein entsetzlicher Cirkel*] of black magic that encloses me like a Bruegel-style picture of hell. Now, for the last month, I've had visions that preserve that particular phobia in me [. . .] It has been two years since I first concocted a scheme to outwit that repugnant desire to carry out that stimulation [. . .] I traveled to Paris [. . .] in order that such a complete change of environment and every influence would, at one go, tear me out of the rhythm of senseless temptation [. . .] But victory did not come [. . .] Just imagine: this compulsion to do the same old damage to myself, with all its after-effects and threats, was stronger, more powerful [. . .] and if I [. . .] stayed in Paris, it was only because I was ashamed to go back to my tower still entangled in the same snares, where I was afraid that in my isolation these pesky devils would really start to overdo their game with me.[5]

And so on.

Rilke suffers terribly from these "defeats," whose absurdity he fully comprehends. For in the same year that his compulsive behavior torments him as "the most immediate cause" of his suffering, he without a doubt read André Gide's novel *The Counterfeiters*, in which the French author seeks to strip onanism, among other things, of its social taboo.[6] But Andreas-Salomé does not liberate Rilke from his compulsions when she links his masturbatory urges to his work. In Rilke's work, as we shall see, there is already an empty space prepared for masturbation, which cannot be filled with analytical or other explanations.

Rilke's letter to Andreas-Salomé is a final call for help, a desperate plea, a last reproach to his first serious lover and great maternal figure—you are not there for me! In her answer, Andreas-Salomé tries to dissuade Rilke from locating the root of his illness in onanism. The doctor had informed Andreas-Salomé about Rilke's acute leukemia. He considered sharing this knowledge with Rilke too risky for the patient, who had requested that his diagnosis be shared exclusively with Andreas-Salomé and his close friend and patron Nanny Wunderly-Volkart, but not with Rilke, the patient, himself. But with her psychoanalytic explanations, Andreas-Salomé makes Rilke responsible, if indirectly, for his suffering. Because he is still caught up in old-fashioned guilt complexes, as Andreas-Salomé analyzes his call for help, his onanism is unconsciously manifesting itself as a pathological symptom in other organs. Onanism is not a mistake, as Andreas-Salomé says, but Rilke's feelings of guilt are.

"Rainer, this is what it comes down to: it is not a devilish obsession at all! *Because* it gives you all these feelings of guilt, and has ever since childhood, *that's why* it has such ill effects."[7] Andreas-Salomé attributes Rilke's bodily pain to an indirect overstimulation of various body parts, which are now working "as something very like [. . .] erotic sensations on the penis," displaced onto that organ.[8] The final letters between the two are deeply disquieting. Rilke's despair in the face of his deadly illness is not assuaged and despite Andreas-Salomé's best intentions, her psycho-analytic interpretation—that feelings of guilt and fear and the erotic excitement of onanism have been displaced onto other organs—only strengthens Rilke's mistaken belief that onanism is the cause of his sickness.

Although Rilke did not want to write to Andreas-Salomé anymore after this exchange, in his last days, spent in great physical pain, he believed—as Wunderly-Volkart reports in a letter written shortly after Rilke's death—"that Lou [would have been] the only one to understand." Andreas-Salomé had made Rilke into a poet, taken him under her wing as an experienced woman, given him his identity as a writer, driven the sentimentality out of him. But she could not take away his adolescent urges for "this compulsion to do the same old damage" to himself, nor his despair in the face of a sickness that he wanted to experience in full but that he saw from the wrong perspective of a "horrid circle" in which his shameful "obsession" trapped him.

The remote stone cottage in Muzot, which a well-meaning Swiss patron had provided for Rilke as a residence, had given him the necessary peace to complete his masterpieces *Duino Elegies* and *The Sonnets to*

Orpheus. In this old building, where Rilke asked for "great solitude" from his housekeeper, because "when occupied with literary work, he did not wished to be disturbed," he becomes a plaything of the autoerotic "pesky devils."[9] Although Andreas-Salomé's suggestions trail off helplessly, they could have hit upon the right way out of this terrible "circle." For Andreas-Salomé's final piece of advice to Rilke was that he, in a kind of self-therapy, read his own works, take up "R. M. Rilke's elegies (as some of my sickest patients do)."[10] Rilke's "lapse into frustration, into despair, betrayed by [his] own body," was for the artist not only a discharge "after tense work [but also] something belonging to it, the reverse side of the matter, as the devil is only a *deus inversus*."[11] The work is supposed to heal the poet. This attempt to interpret masturbation as the necessary inverse of Rilke's creations, however, does not succeed. Masturbation remains Rilke's unsolvable problem since the "circle" of pure, unproductive waste in which Rilke is caught cannot be broken open nor brought into a productive context, since it doesn't result in any growth.[12] Andreas-Salomé's suggestion places onanism alongside his work and thus keeps it in the "circle" of Rilke's self-doubt, instead of recognizing that it is in fact, as Rilke wrote in his letter, "senseless." By applying Rilke's work as the cure for her own patients (including the author), Andreas-Salomé instrumentalizes the work in the same way that she ascribes Rilke's masturbation a function as the "inverse of creation."

As pure *"dépense"* (expenditure), to rely on a later definition by philosopher Georges Bataille, Rilke's masturbation in his tower at Muzot is functionless and therefore neither a distraction from his work (what Andreas-Salomé calls the inverse of creation) nor its condition.[13] To call Rilke's regular self-pleasuring a part of his work, as Andreas-Salomé suggests, means to explain a bodily, wasteful *"dépense"* either as a condition for or as an obstacle to writing poetry, and thus ascribe a (positive or negative) value to it. Rilke avoids this kind of attribution and evaluation of everything in *Duino Elegies*. The work that Andreas-Salomé regarded as a counterweight to masturbation and prescribed to her patients is precisely the attempt to simply let some things be, without assigning them a value.

When Andreas-Salomé urges *Elegies* upon Rilke, she recommends to Rilke his own work as a self-imposed therapeutic control of the compulsion to pleasure himself. But in *Elegies* Rilke actually wants limitation *and* freedom, constraint *and* moderation, desire *and* sublimation, both faraway locations *and* a home. He himself thought that the elegies "reach out endlessly beyond themselves."[14] He suffers from onanism because he continues to understand his compulsive behavior as the edge of "a horrid circle of black magic" and not as a self-imposed limitation, beyond all "circles," on something that reaches "beyond itself." When the well-intentioned Andreas-Salomé assigns to Rilke's onanism the function of an "inverse God," she proceeds precisely with the thought of a closed system of energy, which is as inappropriate for masturbation as a worldly context (such as assigning his poems a healing, therapeutic function) is for Rilke's works. Rilke's *Elegies* cannot heal. Many of his texts are unapologetically phallic. They deal with the sexuality that ministers to a man "even before [the girl] could soothe him, and as though she didn't exist," and into which a man throws himself while "sleeping,/yes but dreaming, but flushed with what fevers."[15] Eros is for Rilke a curse and a blessing at once; ultimately eros, the bittersweet, and sexuality unleash powers that surpass us. When Rilke, in his letter, describes masturbation as "the grip of something horrible" and a "horrid circle," he is using the same words he uses in "The Third Elegy" to reduce a young man's experience of love to something "fearful," "horrid," and "repulsive."[16] While the lover thinks she is holding him secure in his sleep, the youth falls in love "*inside*" himself—Rilke's emphasis—"not one who would someday/ appear, but/seething multitudes [. . .] all this, my dear, preceded you."[17] The experience of love is a primal, elementary experience of unrestrained power in Rilke's imagination—even if it takes place in the embrace of two people. In "The Third Elegy" the softness of the girl in love is neither reassuring nor provides relief for the youth, whom the "lord of desire [. . .] often, up from the depths of his solitude, even before she could soothe him, and as though she didn't exist, held up his head [. . .]/erect, and summoned the night to an endless uproar."[18] Eros is an autonomous power that seizes a man—here Rilke is uncharacteristically bound to conservative gender roles—against his will, and that even in sexual activity is not necessarily sated. For Rilke this illustrates the powers inside us that are greater than us.

Andreas-Salomé's attempt to ascribe a healing power to *Elegies* or to think of Rilke's onanism as the inverse of creation betrays a logic that no longer applies in *Elegies*, but with which Rilke himself, in his letter, condemns his masturbation as "devilish obsession." In *Elegies*, a man's "entanglement" (Rilke uses the same word as in his letter about masturbation; the word later appears as a euphemism—unexplained, although the letter to Andreas-Salomé is quoted—in certain biographies) in his original sexuality remains unresolved.[19] Every attempt, including Rilke's own, to see onanism as an antibourgeois provocation, as the introduction of the unreal into the work, or as the inverse of creation only encourages this "entanglement" in this "circle."

In 1915 Rilke wrote seven erotic poems. The poems link sexuality and creative achievement in surprisingly direct images of male potency. The reanimation of poetry for Rilke bursts out of the "full bud of his vitality" in the hand of the "rose-gatherer."[20] Yet Rilke's descriptions cannot be neatly accounted for as metaphors for poetic production. The sexual images are both erotic and, as some critics maintain, obscene. The parts of them that cannot be understood as allegory are no longer purely lyrical or aesthetic. But precisely because Rilke crosses the boundaries of good taste, these poems offer a key to his creative process. Without these concrete images of an *unrestrained*—that is, occasionally indecent— excess, the refined passages from *Elegies* ("our own heart always exceeds us"[21]) remain incomprehensible. The sexual dimension cannot be removed from Rilke's work, but it cannot be completely integrated into the work, as Rilke did not experience sexuality reliably as something that always exceeded him. His phallic poems, of which there are quite a few, have a different function than analogous poems by other poets. In Rilke, these erotic poems contain an additional meaning, which neither destroys nor fundamentally determines the sense of the poems. The erotic poems can no more easily be incorporated into a full understanding of Rilke's poetry and his existence than can his masturbation. They remain excessive and superfluous.

Such a devaluation of onanism as pointless waste was possible in Rilke's time. In Sigmund Freud's circle, for instance, masturbation was defended only by such figures as Wilhelm Stekel, who was soon excluded from the weekly analysts' meetings. Andreas-Salomé's explanations remain derivative of Freud's heavily debated and conservative opinions on onanism, and Freud, on account of his own clinical observations, argued to "not eliminate the rubric: damaging effects of onanism."[22]

Here stands the great poet, who makes a tremendous contribution to world literature from his Swiss hideaway, pleasuring himself the whole time. A century after the first major psychoanalytic discussions about onanism in Vienna, our understanding of Rilke's "devilish obsession" remains caught up in unproductive reflections on productivity. Andreas-Salomé plays Rilke's work against the "unproductive" onanism, furthering his obsession with a closed system of angels and devils, creation and destruction. To her credit, one can say that Rilke always liked his devils. She had no other choice but to argue from inside this economy and to address the situation directly. Rilke wanted to ignite himself with guilt.

In much of the secondary literature, Rilke's sexuality is not mentioned at all. In Andreas-Salomé's memoirs of Rilke, written a year after his death, she quotes the passage from the letter with the "horrid circle" and the "Bruegel-style picture of hell," the "rhythm of senseless temptation" and the "compulsion to do the same old damage to myself," without once mentioning the actual reason for Rilke's horror, which she had referred to in her private letter unabashedly as "erotic sensations on the penis."[23] Andreas-Salomé comments on the masturbation letter, without naming onanism, and interprets for Rilke's later readers the poet's terror as fear of the superior power of the beauty he has created, in the presence of which everything "material"—and that included Rilke's body—was hit "with a terrible stamp of non-admission to the kingdom of angels."[24]

The portrait of Rilke as a sublimated genius who suffers at having a body at all perseveres as myth. Until 1952, a solid quarter of a century after Rilke's death, Rilke's stepson and daughter avoided the publication of his letters to Lou Andreas-Salomé, because they revealed "too many symptoms of psychogenic suffering."[25] Only in 1975 did the publication of these letters finally seem justified, because, as the editor put it then, "their contents have become history."[26] The story of these letters is in fact dodgy, since Andreas-Salomé's explicit reply was "not found in the Rilke archive" at the time of the first publication of the correspondence, but had been copied and cataloged by a researcher in an archive years before.[27] The belated publication of this letter, once suppressed, and then known only in a copy, has not productively revised our understanding of Rilke. In more recent biographies Rilke continues to be portrayed as a sublime, angelic being of pure inspiration, who either has no body or—what amounts to the same thing—suffers terribly from having one. Donald Prater paraphrases Rilke's letter to Andreas-Salomé in his biography, without explaining that Rilke's "stimulations applied to himself" are compulsive masturbation.[28] Ralph Freedman's extensive biography corrects this mis-estimation in a few lines, but without adding any real insight into the role of this behavior for our understanding of his work.[29] And a five-hundred-page cultural history of masturbation, *Solitary Sex*, mentions Schiele, Wittgenstein, Stekel, and Freud, but does not catch Rilke in the act.[30]

Andreas-Salomé could have known better. And that even without knowing about *Viennese Psychoanalytic Discussions* (1913), a publication in which several analysts in Freud's circle question the discussion of onanism in terms of "usefulness." Already in *The Book of Hours*, the volume of poems that Rilke had dedicated to his lover Andreas-Salomé in 1899, Rilke describes a young man's difficulties in keeping his hands still and not too much to himself. In a poem from *The Book of Hours*, "To the Young Brother: You, a Boy Just Yesterday, Taken Over by Confusion," this inner struggle leads to an empty line in a poem:

> And suddenly you are left all alone
> with your hands that hate you so—
> and if your will does not produce a miracle:
>
> ————————

> Und plötzlich bist du ganz allein gelassen
> mit deinen Händen, die dich hassen –
> und wenn dein Wille nicht ein Wunder tut:
> ————————[31]

"Self-love" is abruptly turned around here. The hands, with which the "younger brother" could autoerotically divert and satisfy his growing love for God, are near to taking hold of him and, by succumbing to this vice, "hating" him. But Rilke does not trust the miracle of will; the poet's hand lets go of the pen for one line. Does the young brother . . . ? Or doesn't he . . . ? The poem does not provide an answer. The empty line shows only that either way, it does not lead to anything. The sublimated drive conceives either an empty space, which pours itself out as a wondrous interruption in the poem, or a silent pause, during which the brother-poet, "left all alone," cannot refrain from himself. This distinction cannot be made for good and doesn't matter at this moment, since in both cases nothing is achieved, said, or conceived. No "circle" is closed, and no "reverse side of the matter" reveals itself. There is a straight line but no circle. It is pure waste.

Andreas-Salomé could have recognized this. The fact is that as early as 1899, at the age of twenty-four, Rilke was fighting with his hands, which hated him (or did he hate them?), because he couldn't keep them off himself. The fact is that at age fifty he was still fighting. He had been with many women but still couldn't stop himself. And the fact is that the "miracle" that Rilke—who was able to work with such discipline— demanded from his will was precisely that he spent and surpassed himself. He could not separate this "miracle" of self-surpassing from his obsessive autoerotic activities. The fact that Lou did not recognize this fact that was staring her in the face is all the more astonishing given that Rilke's *Book of Hours* bears the dedication "Placed in Lou's Hands." Why placed in her hands? Perhaps because Rilke's hands were all too busy ————.

d

for Destiny Disrupted

In the charming Hollywood romantic comedy *Only You* (1994), Peter
Wright (played by Robert Downey Jr.) tries to convince the beautiful
Faith (Marisa Tomei) that he is the right man for her as they take an
evening stroll through Rome. As her name suggests, Faith is a firm
believer in prophecy and fate. When she was eleven she learned the name
of her true love, Damon Bradley, from a Ouija board and now travels
through Italy in pursuit of the thus-named prince. By happenstance Peter
knows about Faith's idée fixe and acts as though he is the Bradley in
question. In order to fool Faith, he recites, in a halfhearted Italian accent,
the lines of a great German poet:

> Peter: There's this poem by . . . Goethe . . . yeah, Goethe, and it's
>   about two people who come from different places, but they hear
>   the same bird singing.
> Faith: "Perhaps the same bird echoed through both of us yesterday,
>   separate, in the evening."
> Peter: That's it. Exactly.
> Faith: Wow . . . yeah, it was Rilke.
> Peter: Rilke? Oh . . . same country. How'd you know that?
> Faith: Oh, I could tell you some things.

Oh, you have a lot to learn from me, Faith explains to the besotted man. What can Peter learn from Faith? What can we learn here? The Hollywood genre of the romantic comedy does not leave any doubt that the two main characters (easy to recognize, since they are the stars) will find themselves, after many obstacles, together at the end. What is there to learn when everything is already known?

The lines Peter quotes are from Rilke's poem "You Who Never Arrived," which Rilke wrote in Paris during the winter of 1913–14 but did not publish. The melancholy poem attests to a love—à la Baudelaire's "To a Passerby"—that befalls us just after a missed chance or opportunity. "I have given up trying/to recognize you in the surging wave of the next/ moment," sighs the poet self-pityingly, and in the second stanza gives up the naïve belief in the promise of love: "You, Beloved, who are all/the gardens I have ever gazed at,/longing." But the final lines, cited by the Hollywood screenwriters, promise fulfillment once again and attest to belief in true love:

> [. . .]—Who knows? Perhaps the same
> bird echoed through both of us
> yesterday, separate, in the evening.[1]

> [. . .]—Wer weiß, ob derselbe
> Vogel nicht hinklang durch uns
> gestern, einzeln, im Abend?[2]

The three final lines give the melancholy poem a hopeful ending, since the birdcall links the unknown beloved who had been assumed "lost/from the start," without her knowledge, to the poet, "yesterday [. . .] in the evening." The poem considers whether this unknown connection had always been there: The unheard birdcall, audible to only two people, becomes the promise of a connection, which existed even *before* the shared call. With this notion Rilke opens the poem to a future predestined on the previous evening by a birdcall the two lovers didn't know they shared. The melancholy "from the start" in the poem's opening line, according to which all love is lost to melancholy a priori, is undercut by the fact that the unknowable and yet insistent "yesterday [. . .] in the evening" has initiated another sense of time, another logic of belonging that skirts the loss of the beloved. The poem, so to speak, is suspended between two states of the anterior future: of something (love as experience) lost "from the start" and something (love as destiny) predetermined "from the start."

For the birdcall is the poet's deceptive and mystifying mating call, is Peter Wright's arrow in his seducer's quiver, is the line of the poem that claims (without quite saying it) that when in love, we are destined for one another "from the start." The birdcall can open a future that interrupts the pattern of disappointment and frustration prevailing until now, because this future had already been lived.

In *Only You* we learn that there is something like destiny, a greater order, predestination, that constitutes the film's plot; but there is also disruption, an unexpected and even uncanny correspondence between people and things that cannot be known, an event, a birdcall. There is something that one can learn (as the steadfast Faith learned, early in life, the name of her future beloved) and something that one cannot learn (how to fall in love). This is the reason why Peter, acting on his belief that love cannot be learned, learns nothing on the plot level and symptomatically attributes to the wrong author (Goethe) the poem he quotes to show off to Faith. He still has a lot to learn from the woman his heart is set on, or at least he hopes so.

This notion of an overarching structure, including that of destiny and predetermination, that is disrupted by an imminent event is found throughout all of Rilke's works. Much in Rilke's works seems to be predetermined, including the return to the great themes of love and death and human possibility in *Duino Elegies* and *The Sonnets to Orpheus*, finished not until 1922, themes that also occur as early as Rilke's poems from his adolescence and student years prior to 1900. Following this logic of an interruption to a pattern that can be recognized only in retrospect, the birdcall, which stands for the disruption of anything that is predetermined, resounds at odds with destiny and intersects with the illusion of having life under control. This poem, written in 1913, used in the Hollywood movie, is not the first time Rilke sounds a birdcall.

A birdcall resounds already in Rilke's work in the poem "Apprehension" in *The Book of Images*, written in Berlin in December 1900.

> In the faded forest is a birdcall
> that seems meaningless in this faded forest.
> And yet the rounded birdcall rests
> in this interim that shaped it,

wide as a sky upon the faded forest.
Everything pliantly makes room in the cry:
the whole landscape seems to lie there soundlessly [. . .][3]

Im welken Walde ist ein Vogelruf,
der sinnlos scheint in diesem welken Walde.
Und dennoch ruht der runde Vogelruf
in dieser Weile, die ihn schuf,
breit wie ein Himmel auf dem welken Walde.
Geräumig räumt sich alles in den Schrei:
Das ganze Land scheint lautlos drin zu liegen [. . .][4]

This birdcall, which no longer celebrates nature or attests to its beauty, has become senseless. It is no longer a traditional metaphor (as the flight of the lark) for the transcendence of poetry, but rather a metaphor for that which creates and expends itself, holds and is held, in the same gesture. This type of inversion (of figure and referent) is typical for Rilke's work: the "senseless"-seeming birdcall in "the faded forest" ultimately holds "the whole landscape" in its sound, instead of just trailing off, small and mournful. For many interpreters such a reversal of actual relations is mere poetic window dressing and mystification, with which Rilke pulls the rug from under our feet but puts it back in the same image to create the impression that the poem has written itself, or at least that what he says there is inevitable and destined to be so. But Rilke does not invert the relation between structure and event, ground and figure, the rhetorical devices of poetic speech and the experience of reading simply to create a literary effect. He does so in order to reflect in our experience of reading the poem the inversion of the relation between life and experience, between destiny and its accidental, miraculous disruption.

Here the event is nothing other than the opening of time onto the "interim," which the poem now takes on and without which this poem simply couldn't exist. For an interim needs to be created: in nature there is no interim because there time is empty. The theoretical demystification, by various critics, of Rilke's rhetorical inversions is as clever as it is endless and ultimately frustrating; such deconstructions show again and again that Rilke's poems "are the outcome of poetic skills directed towards the rhetorical potentialities of the signifier."[5] And thus Rilke's deconstructive critics demonstrate that the experience of poetry is not something you prove, but something that happens. This, indeed, is correct. But the "rhetorical possibilities" of a signifier like "birdcall"—as for instance Paul de Man, one of the most important interpreters of Rilke, never tires of emphasizing—cannot be delineated by the poet himself. With "birdcall," Rilke sets free precisely the possibility that a word says more than its meaning, that something happens that cannot be predicted, proven, or explained.

Just as the birdcall in "You Who Never Arrived" disrupts the structure of a predetermined destiny, it also disrupts the composition of Rilke's entire oeuvre, in that this metaphor, despite being a figure for unremembered experience, resounds repeatedly as something new and unique. In a short essay on *Letters of a Portuguese Nun* by Marianna Alcoforado, which Rilke translated in 1907, he writes: "Just as the nightingale breaks out not only in song, but also in a silence that encloses the unfathomable night, so is the entirety of feeling to be found in the words of this nun, the speakable and the ineffable. And her voice is just as devoid of destiny [*schicksalslos*] as the voice of the bird."[6] In his introduction to the poems of Anna de Noailles, which Rilke also wrote in 1907, the birdcall is a very similar metaphor of lamentation: "And when her heart suffers, the same sorrow breaks out like a plague over all the land, and in the now-desolate evenings her lament lingers like a birdcall."[7] Here, just as in the essay about the Portuguese nun and in the early poem "Apprehension," the birdcall at once creates space in the landscape and also expresses the "unexpected and undeserved poems" of Noailles, which then divide this space and give voice to a unique love. It is the "ever-recurring lament, the single eternal sorrow; the lament of a love that is too great, that has grown beyond every beloved."[8]

The same metaphor of the birdcall resounds throughout Rilke's texts, again and again, as an index of the unique. In *The Notebooks of Malte Laurids Brigge* it is the metaphor for the lament of the unhappy lover: "No other lament has ever come from a woman [. . .] it is recognized again, like a bird call."[9]

In 1908 an infamous birdcall sounds at the end of a long poem in *New Poems* as a sign of decline, the rise and fall of which Rilke develops as an allegory of human life.

> As on stairs, with every lightest gale
> clammy leaves descend from every side there,

every bird-cry seems as though decried there,
poisoned every nightingale.[10]

Immer geht ein feuchter Blätterfall
durch die Luft hinunter wie auf Stufen,
jeder Vogelruf ist wie verrufen,
wie vergiftet jede Nachtigall.[11]

In 1911 Rilke wrote "Judith's Return," in which the resonant lament of a
woman turns into a birdcall:

Heart, famed heart, beat on the countering wind:
how I stride, stride
and swifter the voice in me, mine that will call, bird-call,
before the locked-in city of fear.[12]

Herz, mein berühmtes Herz, schlag an den Gegenwind:
wie ich geh, wie ich geh—
und schneller die Stimme in mir: meine, die rufen wird, Vogelruf,
vor der Not-Stadt.[13]

In 1913 the birdcall resounds several times. In the prose piece "Experience," in which the poet describes the mystical experience of the unity
between consciousness and world, the birdcall is the prelude to a mystical
moment of unmediated consciousness: "He recalled the hour in that other
Southern garden (Capri) when a birdcall outside was in harmony with
what was inside him, because it was (so to speak) unbroken by the surface
of his body, treating its inside and outside together as an uninterrupted
space in which, secretly protected, there remained only one unified region
of the deepest and most pure consciousness."[14]

And in the "Improvisations from the Capri Winter," written at the
same time, the birdcall motif appears in a variant form as a world-
constituting "bird sound": "Because what good to me/are the innumerable
words that come and go,/when the cry of a bird/uttered again and again,/
makes a tiny heart so vast and one/with the heart of the air, the heart of
the grove."[15] If you look through Rilke's work for all the birdcalls, you
start hearing them all over. In the dedication to Merline Klossowska that

Rilke added to his translations of the sonnets of Elizabeth Barrett Browning, he describes his own creations as a "birdcall."[16]

A further birdcall occurs as the germ of all his later texts in a letter to Lou Andreas-Salomé from 1912: "I am going on long, long walks out here [. . .] when I hear a small birdcall singing out to me."[17] In another letter written two years later Rilke adumbrates this metaphor: "The reason why we so easily allow a birdcall to penetrate our inner being is because it seems as if we could translate it without remainder into our emotion. Indeed, for a moment a birdcall can turn the entire world into our inner space since we feel that the bird makes no distinction between its heart and that of the world."[18]

The birdcall recurs even more frequently as a leitmotif in Rilke's work (which begins to resemble an aviary once you start to listen). From a psychological perspective Rilke suffered from an idée fixe. But both the philological tracking of this motif and the notion of an idée fixe depend on the same conception of an all-encompassing structure, which the appearance of a birdcall confirms as overarching, by interrupting it. For every birdcall in Rilke's work constitutes an event that disrupts the normal course of things and thereby confirms the presence of a different and yet immanent level, on which things assume an additional meaning. In each passage the birdcall marks the point where it no longer serves as a metaphor, but rather depicts the disruption and interruption of such rhetorical conventions and the logic of the poem.

Each of the passages quoted above shows in a new way how the birdcall breaks through the invisible structure (of our consciousness and thus by extension of the text, the work, of language as a whole) that makes the relationship between world and body possible in the first place, since it "was to some degree unbroken by the surface of his body, taking its inside and outside together as an uninterrupted space." It is precisely a birdcall in the middle of human words: sonorous, auspicious, beautiful, ephemeral, unintelligible, foreign.

It is remarkable, therefore, that Rilke seems to have envisioned this penetrating, singular, unplannable "experience" of an unbroken consciousness, in which body and spirit are one, and deliberately prepared the unplannable through the repeated use of this metaphor of the birdcall. Already in 1900 Rilke wrote in "Apprehension": "everything pliantly accommodates to the call." What is sworn, envisioned, anticipated, and proposed poetically for the massive, all-encompassing work, and hoped for, reappears frequently in later poems—in "Judith's Return," in the letters to Lou, in "You the loved one lost / in advance," in the prose texts—and always as a "birdcall" that disrupts all plans, intentions, contexts, expectations, destiny, and finally even the work itself. "Birdcall" stands for Rilke's attempt to experience the interruption, the unhoped-for, the unexpected, again and again. It is destiny disrupted.

The screenwriters for *Only You* get it just right. With uncanny intuition they took not just any line from Rilke's poetry to stand in for the quintessence of poetry. The birdcall stands for the experience of love, which is not part of life for Rilke, and which breaks free of all plans and anticipations. In *The Notebooks of Malte Laurids Brigge*, Rilke writes: "The loving woman always exceeds the loving man because life is greater than fate."[19] When in *Only You* Faith explains to Peter that the poem is in fact by Rilke and not Goethe, and that he still has a lot to learn, we can learn three things.

First, Faith lets us know that both she and her suitor are familiar with the same love poem (even if he does not know its correct author), just as if the same birdcall had struck them independently and without their knowledge. She thereby confirms Wright's claim—even though she is correcting him—that there is such a thing as true love. Second, she is unimpressed by Wright's efforts at seducing her, unmasks his mistake, and shows that love is never free of errors and never goes according to a plan. Third, Peter still has a lot to learn: He has to learn that love cannot be planned or drawn up in advance.

Rilke's birdcall stands for an event that not only penetrates everything but is complete in itself. Everything "accommodates to the call": The birdcall *is* everything. (For readers bothered by the mystifying rhetoric of the previous sentence, here is a more technical explanation: As a rhetorical figure, the metaphor of the birdcall serves as both container and content.)

The action of *Only You* revolves around a woman who believes in destiny, prophecy, and structure. Faith's happiness, she believes, is predetermined and only has to fulfill itself. On the other hand, Peter knows about chance and the contingencies of events, of encounters, of happiness. The charm of the film is that because of the external circumstances Peter Wright must enact a love as if it has happened at first sight (he must seduce Faith), while Faith, in spite of her belief, falls in love with the "wrong man" (who, in keeping with the rules of Hollywood, turns out to have been the [W]right man all along).

The "rounded birdcall," which simultaneously penetrates the hearts of two people destined for each other, is both an all-encompassing structure, destiny, life as lived, and a disruption, the intrusion of the unforeseen, an interruption of the predetermined life plan. The medium of film, writes the philosopher Stanley Cavell, is "as if meant for philosophy—meant to reorient everything philosophy has said about reality and its representation, about art and imitation, about greatness and conventionality, about judgment and pleasure, about skepticism and transcendence, about language and expression."[20]

The experience of happiness in love, the momentary, ephemeral meeting of the rhythms of two souls, finds expression in *Only You* when Faith recognizes the Rilke quote about the harmony of souls and is thus able to contradict and correct Peter. Immediately the roles of seducer and seduced, man and woman, are reversed, and with them the standard received romance narrative, which the birdcall is intended to disrupt; and so, as happens several times in every Hollywood romantic comedy worthy of philosophical consideration, what it means to know and what it means to learn are reversed. Love is poetically rewritten as a birdcall, as an all-encompassing, ever-present harmony of the world. The birdcall is Rilke's metaphor for the attempt and at the same time for the experience, for structure and play, for matrix and contingency, for an undivided thinking of language and event.

Peter says to the woman he loves that there is such a thing as destiny only if you also believe in its disruption, that only disruptions can be destined. And that love is the divided experience of a unity. That after all the showing off and playacting, seduction, deception, flirtation, manipulation—there comes a disruptive event, an accident beyond this structure. (In case you have been wondering about what Martin Heidegger means by an "experience of language" in this context, it is what happens between the Hollywood creations Faith and Peter as a shared Rilkean birdcall.)

In a letter to a confused reader, Rilke wrote that this reader should not try to decipher, investigate, or understand an unfamiliar name in one of Rilke's poems, but rather listen to it like the sound of an unknown bird in the forest: sonorous, seductive, mysterious, incomprehensible. It should sound like the "I love you" in a conversation: "completely forsaken by the surrounding languages: ignored, disparaged, or derided by them, severed not only from authority but also from the mechanisms of authority (sciences, techniques, arts)."[21] *I love you, only you*: this unknown birdcall. You can't learn that.

e

for Entrails

What, exactly, is "world's inner space (*Weltinnenraum*)"? Hardly any other word of Rilke's has provoked so much skepticism from critics and so much mystical approval from admirers. "Through all beings reaches the *one* space: world's inner space." Says Rilke.

With "world's inner space," a neologism that fuses three words, *Welt* (world) + *innen* (inside) + *raum* (space), Rilke describes an experience that accords as much significance to the imagination as to reality. He calls this the "deep dimension" of consciousness, which "does not even need the dimensions of space in order to be nearly immeasurable in itself."[1] In a posthumously published poem written in the late summer of 1914, the notion of *Weltinnenraum* captures a sense of nondivision between emotion and experience.

> Through all beings extends one space:
> World's inner space. Silently the birds fly
> through us. Oh I who want to grow,
> I look outside, and in *me* grows the tree.

> Durch alle Wesen reicht der *eine* Raum:
> Weltinnenraum. Die Vögel fliegen still

durch uns hindurch. O, der ich wachsen will,
ich seh hinaus, und in mir wächst der Baum.[2]

For the existentialists, the matter is clear: "The poem creates a space in
which everything returns into its deep being [. . .], where we find unham-
pered access to a place where nothing holds us anymore."[3] But this
interpretation of "world's inner space" as granting access to an atemporal,
groundless "being" gives so much weight to "space" that Rilke's "inner" is
at risk of getting lost. For historically oriented readers, on the other hand,
Rilke's inner space is not worldly, not sufficiently grounded in his
historical context. The existentialists want to derealize this "world's inner
space" in which much of Rilke's poetry originates, which they understand
as an ontological category, while socially and critically oriented critics try
to re-create the historical context that presumably gets lost in such
mystical musings. How to understand Rilke's "world's inner space"
depends on the definitions of two ideas. Human existence is either
contingent being-in-the-world or an abstract value. Depending on which
option you subscribe to, reality is either an observable reality or something
only created by consciousness. But neither the existentialist readers of
Rilke nor the historicists locate Rilke's inner space quite correctly. The
"world's inner space" does not lie somewhere halfway *between* the experience of being (as fulfillment or as loss) and the "occurrences [. . .] which
shook up the course of history"[4] somewhere within language itself, as
some critics have argued. It lies inside Rilke himself.

It was Rilke's stated purpose and artistic credo not to exclude any
dimension of our experience from consideration. In this regard, a central
problem for him was our presumably modern, Western understanding of
death as the opposite of life. When we admit death only as an abstraction
and the outer boundary of our experience, according to Rilke, we limit
our range of possible experiences. Only death (and—for women—the
birth of a child, and ultimately, in Rilke's understanding of the world, the
experience of sexuality) opens our consciousness to the mysteries of life in
our modern, disenchanted, and godless Enlightenment world. Instead of
suppressing this experience or being overwhelmed by the thought of it,
and thus having a major part of our experience happen against our will,
Rilke tries to get closer to death.

Only in the confrontation with death do we recognize the full scale of
our existence: "Through such a great, such an immeasurable loss, we are

finally introduced to the whole. Death is only the inexorable means of making us familiar with and accustoming us to the side of our existence that is turned away from us."[5]

Rilke does not deny the horror of death. On the contrary, he seeks, patiently, poetically, to acknowledge this horror as part of our existence. In his "Requiem," written for the painter Paula Modersohn-Becker, who died at the young age of thirty-one, Rilke tries neither to suppress the death of a person whom he had loved nor to be overwhelmed by grief. The result is a long, strange poem, in which Rilke describes how he tries to "learn" death. He wants to take away from death the strangeness that cultural practices and modern forms of thought attribute to it. The goal of this work of "integration" is not, however, to completely take away death's "full and unmasked cruelty" or its disturbing strangeness.[6] Instead, the "inexorable" strangeness that exists independent of conventions should be recognized. Rilke seeks an adequate relationship to death that neither covers up its harshness nor recoils from this harshness and thus removes it from our consciousness.

In a condolence letter written in 1919 Rilke blames religion for this suppression of death:

> My reproach to all modern religions is that they provide their
> believers with consolations and embellishments of death instead of
> offering them the means to get along and come to terms with it.
> With death, with its complete, unmasked cruelty: this cruelty is so
> immense that it ends up completing the circle: its cruelty reaches
> the extremity of a gentleness that is so great, so pure, and so utterly
> *transparent* (all consolation is murky!) in ways we never imagined
> mildness possible, even on the sweetest spring day![7]

The suppression of death leads to the false assumption that we can "recover" from suffering a loss due to death. Rilke writes in the same letter: "Even time does not 'console,' as people say superficially; at best it puts things in their place and into a certain order."[8] In "Requiem" Rilke describes a similar kind of placing things into a certain order. But it is clear in that poem *where* death is to be "placed": not in the abstract ideas of philosophy and religion, but rather deep within ourselves, inside the lungs, in the "last chamber" of the heart, and finally in "our entrails

[*Eingeweide*]." There, inside our internal organs, our intestines, "world's inner space" rules.

Rilke had first met the painter Paula Becker around 1900 in Worpswede. He had fallen in love with her and her close friend, his future wife Clara Westhoff, at the same time. The young artists embodied for Rilke that ideal mixture of (as he saw it, anyway) childish naïveté and feminine vision that appears as a muse in his early poems. Rainer, Paula, and Clara were a clover leaf, as they liked to say at the time (they composed and signed together a three-part poem for the painter Heinrich Vogeler, which Rilke transcribed into a gift book half-filled with aphorisms and poems).[9]

Paula married the painter Otto Modersohn in 1901, and shortly thereafter Rilke was engaged to Clara, who seven months later gave birth to their daughter, Ruth. By the fall of 1907, when for several years Rilke had been living separated from his wife in Paris, Paula Modersohn-Becker died while giving birth to her daughter. The poem, inscribed "to a friend," is one of several requiems Rilke composed. This poem, beginning with the lines "I have my dead and I have let them go/and was amazed to see them so contented,"[10] takes psychologically astute measure of the steps of mourning as a bodily pain that cannot be avoided: the letting go, the initial disbelief, the anger, the guilt and helplessness of the grieving person left behind. But the long poem, which Rilke composed over the course of three days, is not a para-Freudian or pre–Kübler-Rossian essay, and also not a requiem in the classic sense. It is a ghost story. The poet is haunted by the dead woman so that he will "mourn her." Instead of describing the shock of an early death for those left behind, Rilke projects his surprise onto the deceased herself, who haunts the poem.

As an artist Modersohn-Becker had, according to Rilke, grasped existence in its full scope: "for you understood that: the ripe fruits."[11] One would have suspected that Modersohn-Becker, as a fulfilled artist who had taken stock of existence in its entirety, would have found a measure of peace in death.

> But that you yourself were still afraid,
> Where fear no longer holds[12]

> Doch daß du selbst erschrakst und auch noch jetzt
> den Schrecken hast, wo Schrecken nicht mehr gilt.[13]

Modersohn-Becker could not understand her own death, the poet surmises. He tears himself away from the mourning fantasy into which the poem was beginning to lull the reader ("requiem" means "peaceful rest") at the moment when he starts to adjust to his loss: "O do not take from me what I am slowly picking up." His sense of mastery over the loss, what we would consider coming to terms with it, is interrupted: "it wakes me, often, in the night, like a thief breaking in."[14] He turns Paula's restless ghost into a representation of his own grief. This ghost now tears Rilke out of the numbness brought on by grief and pain. Since Paula has a voice only through the poem, Rilke tears himself out of, but also awakens himself to, his pain.

> I have my dead and I have let them go
> [. . .]
> Only you, you come
> back to me; you brush up against me, you haunt me, you want
> to knock against something, so that it makes a sound,
> and gives you away.[15]

> Ich habe Tote, und ich ließ sie hin
> [. . .]
> Nur du, du kehrst
> zurück; du streifst mich, du gehst um, du willst
> an etwas stoßen, daß es klingt von dir
> und dich verrät.[16]

These lines should be read in full knowledge that Rilke participated in many séances during his lifetime, where the movement of chairs and tabletops hinted at the presence of ghosts amid the living. Since in Rilke's age professional mourners were no longer employed at European funerals, it falls upon the poet to "make up for lost mourning" for the dead. But since Rilke is writing a poem, "Requiem" is from the outset in its form and convention a spiritualized and sublimated form of grief, which as a work of art can never adequately convey the concretely felt, draining inter-actions with the errancy, the frights, pleas, ranting and raving, and lamentations, of the dying and dead. Paula accuses the bereaved of some-thing that cannot be reconciled with the harmonious sounds of poetry and therefore emerges as creaturely, discordant pain: "but no, you want something. It penetrates me/to the bone, grumbles [*querrt*] through me like a saw."[17]

In "Requiem" the dead's accusation against the still living finally takes on its own voice.

> The accusation you might make, you ghost,
> against me, when at night I retreat
> into my lungs, into my entrails
> into the last and poorest chamber of my heart,—[18]

> Ein Vorwurf, den du trügest als Gespenst,
> nachträgest mir, wenn ich mich nachts zurückzieh
> in meine Lunge, in die Eingeweide,
> in meines Herzens letzte ärmste Kammer,—[19]

Lungs, entrails, and heart are the only organs that make a sound (which is why an examining doctor listens to them). By detecting the breath, heartbeat, and sounds of digestion, you can tell whether a human being is alive or dead. In "Requiem" the poet retreats from the haunting visit of the ghost of his dead friend into these inner organs. But his dead friend follows him there, too. She contaminates the metaphors of poetry: "lung" and "heart" are age-old poetic images for human identity and emotion, and also representations of Rilke's "world's inner space." The entrails do not work this way. Unlike the lungs and heart, the entrails cannot be used as any expansive metaphors like the ones Rilke often uses as images for human existence: breath and blood. After the entrails there is nothing more; after that comes waste, excrement, *merde.*

The path from the metaphorical image of the "heart" to the concrete image of the "entrails," which are no longer a rhetorical expression of bodily grief, is part of Rilke's project, to cross from linguistic representation to the bare body, in which one finds a truth (often in the form of pain) that coincides with an experience.[20] The body becomes a sounding board, on which the dead sound out their requests directly, that is, not through linguistic representation, but as sounds, as "grumbling." Not until then and from this spot—from the depths not of Being but of our entrails—does the dead person's lament become audible. Only then is the death of Paula Modersohn-Becker, who blocks herself from Rilke's understanding, no longer the opposite of life—and the living body—but literally a part of it.

The unusual terms Rilke uses in "Requiem" for "bones" ("*Gebein*") and "entrails" ("*Eingeweide*") are expressions of the unspeakability of grief, which is audible in the body itself. Only in the entrails can the sounds of grief be heard, can death reverberate. Rilke writes to Sidonie Nádherný von Borutin: "Do not believe that anything which is part of our pure realities could ever really cease to exist, or come to an end [. . .]. All of our true relations, all of our enduring experiences reach through *Everything*, Sidie, through life and death, *we have to live in both and make our home in both*."[21] Rilke is well aware of the difficulty of this task. But this "living in both" does not mean residing in the abstraction of "Being." It means living in the body. It means not explaining away death but recognizing pain as something that cannot always be sublimated. On the contrary: "This cruelty [of death] is so immense that it ends up completing the circle [. . .] I do not mean to suggest that one should *love* death. But one should love life so unreservedly and without calculation or deliberation that death (the half of life that is turned away from it) is at all times unwittingly included in and loved along with life [. . .]"[22] In the straightforward language of "Requiem," this means: Listen to your stomach, pay attention to its processes and grumblings during joy and pain. The accusation of Paula's ghost becomes a lamentation at the moment when she gets into the poet's entrails, grows loud, and "grumbles" ("*querrt*").

The onomatopoetic word "borborygmus" refers to the sounds made by gas in the intestines; in French the word has come to mean "unintelligible and meaningless remark." Rilke's "grumbling" ("*querren*" is an age-old, now-obsolete German word that also echoes the German "*quer*," for "askance" or "angled") is such an onomatopoetic word: It imitates the sound of a rumbling stomach and is thus not a representation of it, but in fact the sound itself. Something "grumbles" in Rilke's guts. Only when it is no longer possible to evade death by retreating into your own entrails, or rather when the pain of mourning has followed you deep into those depths, can death come to the senses as something no longer abstract, but as physical pain. What you hear then does not belong to knowledge or understanding—it is simply experienced. Only then is it possible, as Rilke puts it, to be "finally introduced to the whole." The "reverse side of our existence," of which Rilke writes, does not transform our life into an experience of Being in its totality, nor does it consist of the overarching reality of our historical living conditions. It is the grumbling inside us, the borborygmus, which cannot be translated into sense but is nevertheless something real. Entrails. *Querren*. Borborygmus.

Only in certain cases is it possible to transform the grumbling of the body into poetry. In a short text about Rilke, Samuel Beckett characterizes with typical dryness and acidic accuracy Rilke as an exceptional case, since Rilke successfully translated the fidgeting of his body into great poetry. "He has the fidgets, a disorder which may very well give rise, as it did with Rilke on occasion, to poetry of a high order." But for Beckett there are limits to sublimation: "But why call the fidgets God, Ego, Orpheus and the rest? This is a childishness to which German writers seem specially prone."[23] The grumbling of the entrails in "Requiem" constitutes an exception, for here there is no name foisted upon the body's movements and sounds.

Rilke wrote "Requiem" between October 31 and November 2, 1908. Already, four years earlier, literature had tried to get into our entrails. In James Joyce's *Ulysses*, whose action famously takes place on June 16, 1904, the fourth chapter is dedicated to the guts: "Kalypso," where the narrative action is designed to mirror peristalsis, the incremental movement of matter through the intestines. The bowels, our digestion, peristalsis, defecation: For Joyce, this, and not the entirety of Being à la *Weltinnenraum*, is our unavoidable reality. Without this reality literature gets lost in flights of fancy and undermines the part of our existence that grounds us on earth—Joyce's *Ulysses* would then be little but myth, Rilke's "Requiem" little more than a fantastical ghost story.

"World's inner space"? It is that inside us which reverberates independently of language and philosophy—it grumbles. It is that which creates distortions across the metaphysical divisions between subject and object, spirit and body, Rilke's lofty "angels" and earthly "puppets." We are the sounding board and echo chambers of reality, the "heart" and "lung," when we make poems out of blood and breath, but also entrails when we—no, when *something in us* grumbles and growls. Borborygmus. Listen! "World's inner space" is what's going on in your guts.

for Frogs

In her memoirs, Rilke's close friend and confidante Princess Marie von Thurn und Taxis-Hohenlohe explains that she and Rilke's other wealthy patrons "received so much more" from the poet than they could ever give him. Rilke regularly received money from various supporters. He was invited by different patrons to stay at their vacation homes off season, or was allowed to live rent free for months at a time on their estates, among them the Duino castle of the Thurn und Taxis family near Trieste and their property in Lautschin in Bohemia, while the owners were traveling. The contributions that Rilke occasionally received seem high, considering what a poet could earn with publications and readings at the time. It wasn't enough for a comfortable life. But the work, which Marie von Thurn und Taxis held so dear, demanded a higher price.

When you add it all up, the money Rilke received in his lifetime was just sufficient to accrue as dividends the jealousy and mean-spirited barbs of fellow poets. Gottfried Benn concluded, with a mix of the artist's resentment of inherited wealth and envy: "Even these hundreds of counts and countesses from their fifty castles—, it's hard not to find it funny [. . .]. Finally it all comes together nicely, and another aristocrat's castle opens up, where you can write poems about the poor."[1] Thomas Mann, no stranger to wealthy patrons himself, added: "Those Rilke-hags surely must have been awful, and I'm not making an exception for the princesses and countesses with whom the Austrian snob maintained a correspondence."[2]

How to counter these jealous accusations that Rilke allowed society ladies to play sugar mama while he wrote poems about the poor, the beggars, and the wretched of the earth? After his time in Paris, from 1902 to the beginning of the First World War in 1914, when Rilke was primarily working on his novel *The Notebooks of Malte Laurids Brigge* and *New Poems*, he glimpsed those social outcasts mostly from protected interiors well insulated from the outside world by cast-iron gates, silken wallpapers, and lace curtains. Is Rilke's reliance on the rich remedied by his lifelong financial support of wife and daughter, or by the fact that he used his influence to help others and to arrange for the education of his lover Baladine Klossowska's sons (who grew up to become the painter Balthus and the writer Pierre Klossowski)? In the reckoning of Rilke's life that continues to this day, with critics faulting him for relying on the rich while writing about the poor, we can draw up such a tally. Up to the present we witness the occasional cri de coeur of disappointed readers who discover that their favorite poet had many lovers, chose not to stay married, did not actively raise his daughter (who grew up with her grand-parents), and was generally a selfish narcissist who failed in his parental duties. It should be mentioned that Rilke reproached himself throughout his whole life. "We live our lives so poorly because we arrive in the present always unprepared, incapable, and too distracted for everything. I cannot recall a time in my life without this reproach or even worse misgivings. Only for the ten days directly following [my daughter] Ruth's birth, I think, did I live fully and without any loss; only during those days I found reality to be as indescribable, down to the smallest detail, as it is probably all the time."[3]

But the accounts hardly square in Rilke's favor. Even the memory of the short spell of happiness after his daughter's birth is put to the service of his work, which is why this moment "without waste" also passes quickly. For while Rilke was openly asking his wealthy friends to pay for fancy soaps and shirts, to buy him stationery, custom-made standing desks, beige underwear from "Système Dr Lahmann," and bed socks, and cover his bills for month-long stays in elegant hotels, he left his wife, Clara; daughter, Ruth; and various girlfriends mostly in the lurch. Rilke was in fact a moocher and a spoiled dandy who let himself be taken care of by flattered baronesses, unattached princesses, and prestige-hungry industrialists, and while doing so failed to do right by his child. Even the kindly Princess Marie von Thurn und Taxis-Hohenlohe, to whom Rilke dedicated *Duino Elegies*, did not suspect in what currency Rilke was repaying his debts to his patrons.

In a direct response to the accusation that he was an irresponsible father, Rilke recommended that Ruth's fiancé, Carl Sieber, assess the totality of his failures and mistakes—including his dependence on rich patrons—against his work. On the occasion of Ruth's wedding, which Rilke chose not to attend, he wrote to his future son-in-law: "I can be accused of the fact that my strength and my constitution are not adequate for *both* (the realization of my *inner* life [and . . .] the work required to achieve an *external* life); I have nothing to counter such criticism, except to point quietly to those areas to which I have devoted all of my abilities, and to wait and see whether I am acquitted or condemned in the end."[4] It is not a pleasant thought that Ruth Rilke had had to do without her father from infancy so that today we can enjoy the poems and letters to which Rilke "devoted all of [his] abilities." Rilke's calculation does not exculpate him: A parent cannot, as most would agree, be replaced by anything, not even Rilke's letters and writings, which Ruth and Carl spent their adult lives editing and publishing. But the fact is this: Poetry does not necessarily originate from pleasant thoughts, and certainly not always from good conduct. Rilke makes his art without Ruth—ruthlessly, so to speak—instead of caring for his daughter, and thus brings her suffering, grief, and injustice. Thus critic Marjorie Perloff rightly faults Rilke for "raiding his daughter's trust fund" to pay for expensive hotels. (Ultimately Ruth lived off her father's works, which she edited and published during her adult life.) But when Rilke uses his patron's funds, is it a different matter? To be sure, Rilke's work is worth more, especially from today's perspective, than such assessments, and also more than the fur coats, grand dinners, and hunting trips that his rich patrons would otherwise have spent their money on and that have long been forgotten. But this surplus value is the result of another system that has its share of inequities and lies at the origin of the wealth of the bankers, industrialists, factory owners, and aristocratic heirs who were Rilke's patrons. By sponsoring artists, many of these wealthy patrons hoped to legitimate their wealth. Rilke sets aside moral considerations in taking this money. The wealthy "princesses and countesses" do indeed receive much more than they ever gave Rilke. For Rilke pays back their magnanimity by softening the appearance of their specious morality with his art, for which he leaves his own child and instead of saving, squanders the money.

Let's wipe the slate clean of these calculations, which only tell us something that Rilke first learned upon reading Charles Baudelaire, whose collection of provocative prose poems inaugurated our modernity in 1860: that for him there exists no difference between writing poetry and committing a horrible crime. Rilke had already taken this maxim on as his own in 1901, the year his daughter, Ruth, was born, in an open letter published in *Die Zukunft* (The Future). The context was a long commentary on the trial of a Viennese man who carried out an emergency operation on his son without the help of a doctor. When the son died, he cut the body into pieces and burned them in an oven. Rilke saw in this horrible case no possibility to "create and arrange categories of crime": "That, on the contrary, the unavoidable presence of such categories is dangerous, since every crime, *like every work of art*, is a unique case, with its own roots, its own development, under its own sky, which rains and shines down on the strange sprouts of unfathomable acts."[5]

Rilke views art and horror as individual cases (he makes a similar point in one of the letters in *Letters to a Young Poet*) that cannot be offset by or compared to anything else. The work of art and a criminal act, according to Rilke, both stand in equal measure for the complete absence of morality.

Let's try a more modest calculation. And since this is a calculation about a seriously impractical poet who couldn't do the "work required to achieve an *external* life," let's simply replace one metaphor with another. Rilke, after all, attained supreme mastery at the ingenious substitution and multiplication of words with the help of metaphors, metonyms, and synecdoches that we call poetry.

In the summer of 1914, Rilke received (along with Georg Trakl, Oskar Kokoschka, Adolf Loos, and Else Lasker-Schüler) an anonymous contribution of twenty thousand Austrian crowns from the heir and (yet-to-become) philosopher Ludwig Wittgenstein. That is a lot of money. To put it crudely (and why not be crude when it comes to money): That's a lot of toads, according to a quick and conservative calculation, more than US $440,000 in 2013. (Rilke was living on about four thousand crowns a year at this point.) Since Rilke never found out who made this donation, it remained a genuine gift, even though Wittgenstein, without knowing it, would later profit from Rilke's help. (In 1919 Wittgenstein was looking for a publisher for his *Tractatus Logico-Philosophicus*, and Rilke offered a mutual friend, though unbeknownst to Wittgenstein, to use his [Rilke's] influence to help get it published.[6]) Nanny Wunderly-Volkart and her cousin Werner Reinhart gave Rilke an even larger sum of money, on which he lived in Switzerland from 1919 to 1926. He considered Nanny Wunderly-Volkart a dear friend (and solver of all sorts of household problems). Rilke made it quite clear to all of his patrons that his work would not free them from their vague feeling of guilt at being wealthy capitalists. In fact, Rilke occasionally found ways to rub in the fact that these patrons hoped to sponsor an artist, but that he would not be owned by them. Thus Rilke spent a pile of money, with which he could have financed his simple life for quite some time, during a long stay in a Berlin luxury hotel, and then asked for more financial support and defended himself vehemently against the objection of his sponsors that such a life-style was not appropriate for poets.[7] These criticisms by his rich patrons, who hoped to wipe their conscience clean but also put Rilke in his place, as if poets were less entitled to live in certain ways, thus overlap with the mean-spirited remarks of jealous fellow writers Benn and Mann, and later critics venting their frustration after gleaning a few gossipy details about Rilke's life off the Web. From the perspective of bourgeois morality, Rilke should have cared for his child instead of traveling the world on someone else's bill.

After all the calculations, and after all has been said about the selfish poet, Rilke is still in debt. Wittgenstein's financial contribution does not simply reappear, without remainder and fully transubstantiated from Austro-Hungarian currency into metaphor, in the form of Rilke's angels, his version of Orpheus, swans, nuns, priests, and panthers. In all of his work Rilke relies on such metaphors not in order to surrender entirely to a specific trait or feeling (such as courage, fear, astonishment, piety, hope) or to create a poetic atmosphere, but rather to use the poetic figure to examine such feelings dispassionately. Let's be humble, then, and exchange the twenty thousand Austro-Hungarian crowns, the metaphorical toads, for a few simple frogs. And then I will leave it to you, dear reader, to decide whether Rilke gave back "so much more" than he received from his patrons, or whether he was just a spoiled and selfish shmuck.

Rilke wrote the following letter in April 1921 to Nanny Wunderly-Volkart. It's not a poem, not a crafted story, only one of 470 letters to one of his most generous supporters. Yet it is also the self-portrait of a poet trying to get the creative juices flowing with the description of a reedy pond (Rilke thought of his letters as an "ascent into consciousness"[8]). In this letter Rilke takes his writer's block, from which he had been suffering intermittently between 1914 and 1921, and turns it into a poem. Rilke writes about the difficulty of writing poetry during the war years, his military service, and his loss of citizenship. As a non–French citizen, he had been expelled from Paris, which he left with little but a suitcase, overnight in 1914; at the end of the First World War his homeland, the Austro-Hungarian Empire, had disappeared as a political entity and suddenly, after having no passport and no claim to Austrian citizenship, he had become a Czech in a newly formed state. During this decade-long time of uprootedness, Rilke wrote countless letters and several hundred uncollected poems (many of which were only published posthumously), but he recovered his true lyric voice only when he was able to move to Switzerland after the end of the war. The small, cast-off letter, written in a temporary Swiss residence with park views to "little Nike," as he called the well-heeled Wunderly-Volkart, dwells on some of Rilke's major themes: the expansiveness of our heart; the glorification of love; the poet as visionary; the beloved as muse; the notion that art is unanswerable to other values; the sobering insight that even beauty and love pass away.

> I am worried about the frogs. They had already achieved their ideal mating temperature and were behaving quite June-nightishly in the pond. They have such a heart to which their whole rubbery body yields, and with this heart they were singing. Elastically.—But during the night before the weather changed, one of them suddenly stopped, right in the middle of loudly poeticizing, and ceased singing along with the others. They all paused; a momentary break; you could hear the fountain. He pulled himself together, began again, entered on the wrong beat, corrected himself, recited half a stanza, got stuck,—said something unintelligible, fell silent. They were silent along with him, disconcerted. Suddenly, into this next pause, one of them shouted at him from the pond's opposite edge: ".......," (an untranslatable swear word in froggish) "Out with your love!" He apologized in a hoarse voice,—apparently another lead singer was chosen, a small group joined him,—a few measures, forced, without passion,—it didn't work, he too broke off and was

silent. Now the first one, the spoilsport, this visionary, who had the whole thing on his conscience, once more did all he could to save the general mood. He put hand on heart, lifted his head up into the peculiarly indifferent April night, and said: I'll try again.—Oh no, how phony that sounded, dry, dismal.—Jointly they discouraged him, enough, enough . . . Then, finally, silence. But his beloved whispered to him: "My God, you're not getting sick?!"—I am afraid that indeed he's fallen sick, out of rebuffed love and poetry, and she has probably also caught a cold and has the sniffles; not a flattering look. He, feverish and lethargic, stares at her, who three days ago had been so dear to him, and thinks: her mouth is actually quite ordinary, vulgar—, to even marvel at her eyes has become an effort for him, and takes serious concentration, her golden eyes, out of which stares the flu.[9]

One hesitates to translate this passage. Parts of the letter are in froggish, and in froggish it is perfectly clear. It is Rilke during the war years and afterward, in Switzerland, ill from "rebuffed poetry," and it is coming out of him only slowly. They are screaming at him, across the borders, from all of the spots where poetry is read: *Keep writing!* Rilke puts hand on heart, wrestles with himself, but it sounds forced. Like a frog, which only wakes from hibernation bit by bit, when there is a steady increase in temperature, Rilke has not "overcome the lingering torpor in [him] from the war years—a few Summer months [. . .] would be a good start."[10] Someone offers him a free stay in a small, old, and drafty château with a pond and fountains near the Swiss town Berg am Irchel, where he stays from November 1920 to May 1921; an infinitely patient publisher does not push him, but keeps sending him a monthly allowance; others manage to get him a highly coveted residence permit for Switzerland, vouch for him with affidavits, take care of his financial needs; a new lover not only prepares the new residence but even refurbishes it, washes his socks, paints, weeds and plants, blocks up rodent holes, makes coffee, breakfast, lunch, and dinner; loves him. But all too soon even this lover, the painter Baladine (Merline) Klossowska, begins to look a bit ordinary, her problems begin to seem a bit too worldly, her money and marriage problems with a Russian man in Paris and their two young sons become almost—vulgar.

And nevertheless the frog story sounds lighthearted, lively, effortless; we join the chorus of his fans who call out to Rilke: More, more, keep writing! The "rebuffed love and poetry" result in a letter more precious than reams of short stories by other authors. Although the inhibited poet can hardly lift his head up above his windowsill, he weaves from a bit of quiet, some scraps of time, and a premature concert on the pond that went bust a finely spun bit of froggery, in which his whole weepy suffering and his self-pity are released in froggish.

Who's still counting the dividends of Wittgenstein's twenty thousand toads? Who can give a proper account of the pathos of the suddenly rebuffed beloved, "the one who three days ago had been so dear," with her froggy "golden eyes," and measure this pathos of a suddenly cooled love against the gift of a few crowns, francs, marks, lire, which Rilke wasted on expensive soap and sleep in luxury hotels, only to beg for more? Who can provide a ledger that tallies the poet's behavior in life against his work, when it's really all about expansive hearts in slimy rubber bodies, and the nearly inhuman effort of wresting songs from the mundane experiences of the flu?

Whoever makes such calculations has obviously come down with a very bad cold.

for God

Is Brecht correct? He writes, "[T]he way Rilke expresses himself when he writes about God is totally gay. No one who has ever noticed this can ever read a single line of these poems without a disfiguring grin on his face."[1]

"Totally gay" (*absolut schwul*). This is typical early Brecht, in the twenties, when the words "gay" and "queer" were still decades away from being rehabilitated by activists. When Brecht spoke about God, he adapted the Marxist bon mot about "the opium of the masses"—he called religion the circus of the masses. Rilke, on the other hand, used the word "God" often and without the supercilious sneer of bona fide atheists, and without being ashamed of it. Did his face at those moments contort into the grimace of the "inverted," as some of Rilke's contemporaries thought of themselves at the time? Does the perversion flash from his eyes like a lilac handkerchief from his breast pocket? Does reading Rilke's verses give every reader an involuntary "disfiguring grin," as Brecht claims? Is Brecht correct?

What did Brecht mean to say with this remark? As with some other mean-spirited remarks by important writers about fellow authors, he hit the mark. If we turn Brecht's statement around, voilà: A new criterion for understanding Rilke is introduced. We know that over the course of his life Rilke was involved with a good number of women. Brecht knew this too. We should not read Brecht's statement as a snide, sharp-tongued provocation from the macho, Marxist playwright from Augsburg (or rather, read it not *only* as such), but rather as real food for thought. Let us consider the charge of queerness from a different direction, for example on the basis of Rilke's love poems to God and a series of surprisingly visionary letters about sexuality Rilke sent to a young woman named Anita Forrer. If we hastily dismiss Brecht's remark as a politically incorrect insult (even if back then "gay" could have been a progressive term), we are doing both Rilke and Brecht a disservice.

Brecht is not alone in making this association. Other artists also did not approve of Rilke's refusal to take on gender-specific roles. For them, to simply write in this way, neither as a man nor as a woman, was a scandal. Karl Kraus, who was terribly jealous of Rilke's relationship with his friend Sidonie Nádherný von Borutin, an Austro-Hungarian heiress who maintained an important salon for artists and intellectuals, chided Rilke's progressive attitude toward women as "feminine-aesthetic" and in his letters called Rilke—whom he knew to spend time alone with his friend Sidonie—always, pointedly, "Maria" (and never "Rainer").[2] Rilke's good friend Rudolf Kassner found *The Book of Hours*, of 1899 (published in 1905), in which Rilke turns with great intensity and intimacy to our "neighbor God," "embarrassing."[3] Franz Blei calls Rilke a "poet for women. Which in no way means a feminine poet."[4] Rilke's adamant challenge: "Learn, inner man, to look on your inner woman," from a later poem, dedicated to Rudolf Kassner, remains a provocation.[5] One year after Franz Blei's remark, Thomas Mann declared: "Rilke or [Stefan] George—[. . .] they were indeed both aesthetes: the one [Rilke] in feminine form, the other in manly, masculine, sadistic, dictatorial form."[6] A later critic cautiously quotes (in inverted commas) " 'lap' and 'member,' " before turning away from Rilke's "embarrassingly bombastic sexual metaphors."[7] There are a few defenders: Hans Carossa mocked the "people who always reproach the nightingale for not being an eagle, [. . .] and keep putting Rilke down by denying the elemental masculinity in his poetry."[8] What is the truth of the matter?

"Lord: it is time. The huge summer has gone by."[9] One of Rilke's most famous poems, "Autumn Day," is a single unreasonable demand of God, who has almost slept through the beginning of autumn. Hello? Is anybody listening? Are you sleeping on your pillow of clouds? It's high time to please get autumn started, since we've had enough of summer. Rilke addresses God informally: "and you, you've fallen from the nest/you're a young bird with yellow claws/and big eyes and you pierce my heart/(my hand must seem gigantic to you)."[10] He feels sorry for him (Rilke only sometimes capitalizes "him" when writing about God, and does not capitalize "you" when addressing God directly), demands an answer, makes him small and helpless, provokes, insists on his own opinion, appeals, is condescending, almost fights. Rilke is bothersome. Has little respect and much to say. At another point, in another famous poem—"I live in ever-widening circles"—God is an "old tower," which the poet circles in ever-widening gyres as either a majestic falcon, violent storm, or great song. It gets more disrespectful. In a great inversion, Rilke turns the fear of one abandoned by God into God's concern. "What will you do, God, when I die?/I am your jug (and I will shatter)/I am your drink (and I'll go bad)."[11] The thought that God is dependent on us is arrogance, presumption, blasphemy. Is that what sounded "gay" to Brecht's sensitive ears?

Most critics consider the early poems of Rilke's *The Book of Hours*, modeled on a medieval prayer book marking the times of day when specific prayers were to be said, too ornate, and overly laden with rhymes. They consider these poems unsalvageable. But that is a rush to judgment. In a further blasphemous inversion, Rilke makes "God" into something he must himself create, instead of understanding God as a superior instance of his own being. As a result everything is turned around: Thus "God" presents the temptation to create him. For Rilke, religion was the challenge of inventing faith anew: "I cannot understand religious-minded natures who accept and devote themselves to God as a given, without striving to create something anew through his presence."[12]

In *The Book of Hours*, Rilke strives creatively toward God. He writes, while identifying himself with the monks ("I've many brethren in my life of prayer/in southern cloisters where the laurel grows"[13]), letters to "God" as the great beloved:

> If sometimes, neighbor God, my knocking on
> your wall at night disturbs you out of season,
> that I've scarce heard you breathing is the reason,
> and know you're in your room alone.[14]

> Du, Nachbar Gott, wenn ich dich manchesmal
> in langer Nacht mit hartem Klopfen störe,—

so ists, weil ich dich selten atmen höre
und weiß: Du bist allein im Saal.[15]

Why did Brecht find this "gay"? Because Rilke takes away the hierarchy
of the relationship between God and man, without robbing it of the
tremendous power that resides in it as a relationship of love. Because for
Rilke the relationship to God is not the recognition of "given" hierarchies,
but rather the overcoming of them, which leads to a possible loss of
identity. Because Rilke makes the erotic connection with God, which
marks the writings of all female mystics from Hildegard von Bingen to
Teresa of Ávila, into an open question for all men of faith. In the poems
of *The Book of Hours*, which Brecht found "gay," Rilke poses an old
problem: What are men to do with their love for God, when its intensity
spills over into an erotic connection (if devoted women already, as Rilke
says, misuse Christ as a "bedfellow" and "a sweet substitute for a man, the
most tender lover that can be found")?[16] The possibility of having an
unspeakably intense relationship without an innate hierarchy between the
two lovers is recognized by Brecht and marked with the word "gay."
"Gay" signifies here an emotional and erotic love affair that cannot be
classified in advance by socially accepted (in the jargon of academia,
"heteronormative") roles of power and submission, active and passive,
masculine and feminine, a man who loves a woman, a woman who loves
a man—all of what Rilke means by "given." "Gay" means a form of life
that must be invented, which from Rilke's point of view applies to every
kind of genuine faith.

Rilke refrains from the reverent attitude of the devout believer, who
turns to the church to make his God into the instance of the law: "And
I—I should call you father?/That would mean to separate myself from
you a thousand times."[17] The father must be overcome before he can truly
be loved. Without probably intending to do so, in his toxic remark Brecht
recognized this radical relationship with God to be a relationship without
hard and fast roles. "You are my son," Rilke writes, and then: "And my
soul is a woman before you."[18] Rilke's love poems to God make ever-new
combinations. In ever-different arrangements they demand nothing less
than the fungibility of the believer and the believed-in.

"Gay," therefore, has nothing to do with any actual lived relationship
between men or between women. The word classifies the utopian possibility of a relationship whose roles and structure are not yet determined.

For Brecht it marks the difference between Rilke's understanding of God and the church's codified relationship to God as a normative hierarchy (which Brecht ably deconstructed, like all social institutions, including heterosexual love, in his work). To this extent Brecht's remark may harbor a veiled plea for Rilke.

In "gay" love, which is here not meant empirically, but rather as a potential, two people may recognize themselves in roles other than the socially sanctioned roles of lover and beloved, submissive and dominant. Once gender equality has been achieved, Rilke writes in *Letters to a Young Poet*, "[t]his kind of progress will transform and fundamentally change (very much against the will of men who have been surpassed) our experience of love, which currently brims with confusion. Love will no longer be a transaction between man and woman, but the relationship of one human being to another. Much closer to our humanity, this love will be infinitely considerate and quiet, and good and clear both in how it begins and how it ends. It will resemble the love which we prepare through our arduous struggles: the love of two solitudes that protect, delimit, honor and recognize each other."[19] And if people are still forced into socially defined roles, the relationship is possibly less fixed than heterosexual relationships, in which people can continue in the social roles of man and woman. For Rilke, these roles are analogous to the Christian convention of the relationship between God and the believer. "Gay" in this sense means: pure potential.

Since for Rilke the function of God must be forged anew every time, and is potentially "on equal terms," he can describe his faith as an ocean current:

> With this rushing and flowing and running
> with widening banks into the open sea's door,
> as during ever repeating rendezvous,
> I want to profess and proclaim to you
> as no one before.[20]

> Mit diesem Hinfluten, mit diesem Münden
> in breiten Armen ins offene Meer,
> mit dieser wachsenden Wiederkehr
> will ich dich bekennen, will ich dich verkünden
> wie keiner vorher.[21]

Brecht dismissed this as gay. In his own *Buckow Elegies* Brecht writes such tender verses as: "It is evening. Two simple boats/glide by, in them/ two naked young men: rowing side-by-side/they speak. Speaking/they row side-by-side."[22] Rudolf Kassner called Rilke's verses the "sex drive of Narcissus."[23] Rilke was well aware of these critical reactions to his provocation: "is that presumptuous?" he asks in *The Book of Hours*, and "if that is arrogance, then let me be arrogant."[24] He is not interested in masculine or feminine, but rather in the contingencies of a religious relationship, for which he (like the rabbinical tradition long before him) uses the metaphor of erotic love. Although Rilke's faith is not completely new, it seeks to be inspired and creative. "I believe in all that has not yet been said"—in Rilke's faith, God is created in each prayer for the first time.

Rilke was raised by a pious Catholic mother. Because his feminine side was not as much of a problem for him as it was for many of his male contemporaries, the drive toward God turns into blasphemy. He pushes through faith, beyond its received forms, to find again a sensual, intense, and deeply personal love for God. In doing so, he leaves behind many conventions—of faith as well as of society. And in this internal and unconventional intimacy and closeness to God, he becomes, as Brecht puts it, "gay." Without a doubt, Brecht is thinking of other lines by Rilke: "I want my conscience to be/true before you; want to describe myself [. . .] /like my mother's face."[25] For this line is no compliment to God. In a poem written in 1915, which was not published during Rilke's lifetime, he writes:

> Alas, my mother is breaking me down.
> I have laid stone after stone upon myself,
> [. . .]
> Now my mother is coming to break me down.
> [. . .]
> From her to me, no warm wind ever blew.
> She does not live out there in the fresh air.
> She stays inside a barricade of the heart
> And Christ comes every day and washes her.[26]

> Ach wehe, meine Mutter reißt mich ein.
> Da hab ich Stein auf Stein zu mir gelegt,
> [. . .]

Nun kommt die Mutter, kommt und reißt mich ein.
[. . .]
Von ihr zu mir war nie ein warmer Wind.
Sie lebt nicht dorten, wo die Lüfte sind.
Sie liegt in einem hohen Herz-Verschlag
und Christus kommt und wäscht sie jeden Tag.[27]

And finally Rilke stands there before God in his glory: "Don't you see my soul, how it/stands before you in a cloak of silence?"[28] And this in the heat and dampness of all the young brothers crowded together in the tight space of the cloister: "I find you in all these things/to which I'm close, to whom I'm brother; as you/take glory in all that is small/and among the great you offer your greatness to others."[29] For the writer Klabund, Rilke was "a monk who wore a crimson cowl instead of a gray one, who loves the blessedness of heaven, but does not scorn worldly pleasures."[30] The emphasis here on the erotic and bodily "worldly pleasures" lifts these religious poems out of the tradition of bodiless mysticism, which is often ascribed to Rilke. This romanticization of Rilke is seen in such claims as Rudolf Kassner's remark that *The Book of Hours* is "embarrassing."[31] Kassner misses the important connection between *The Book of Hours* and the tradition of medieval books of hours or *horaria*, to which Rilke is consciously alluding. These often artfully illustrated prayer books contain pictures and phrases that may seem obscene to modern eyes and ears but would still have been viewed without offense by medieval readers, in whose eyes Rilke believed there was "still a look which thought this was possible."[32] Brecht, who said meaner things as a person than he wrote as a poet, is wrong on this count. But he is on the right track. His remark about Rilke's being gay does speak to Rilke's understanding of God, as long as we understand "gay" as the pure potential for a not-yet-defined love relationship that separates itself from the conventions of church and society.

But now let us consider Rilke's attitude toward God, and Brecht's charge of Rilke's "gayness," from the other side. Rilke's "gay" relationship with God can be read from the perspective of his pursuit of freedom in a love beyond gender-specific norms. Evidence of this attitude can be found in *Letters to a Young Poet* and, more pointedly, in the politically progressive prose of a letter written on February 2, 1920, to a young Swiss woman, Anita Forrer, who was seeking Rilke's advice. Rilke called Forrer, who had written out of desperation, "an ardent adolescent male, trapped inside a mild-mannered girl"[33]—and he became a kind of mentor for her, and, as Forrer recalled when she had grown into a well-respected woman, gave her the courage and the "impetus of a certain liberation and transformation."[34] Anita Forrer said, describing a close friendship with a woman her own age, whom she considered an "ideal (without blemish), the omniscient (who could teach me)," "something came to pass, which I must now think of as very wrong.—But then, we were children."[35] In his response to the confessions of a young woman whose attraction to another woman gave her such a feeling of guilt that she suffered "torturous agony," and who had been sent to a psychiatrist by her parents, Rilke wrote:

> [. . .] what two people could give and grant each other in their intimacy remains for all time a secret of their always indescribable mutual confidence. If they thought at a particular moment that they could give each other pleasure even more tenderly, this might have been a small error since they did not serve their happiness but their longing in this way and thus cast disturbances into their blood that could prove distressing after the fact—but who is to judge that? Perhaps they were justified after all in thus surrendering, which is so indescribably innocent, like everything in love that is born of simple having-to-do and not-knowing-any-differently—nobody may dare to judge from the outside what took place there. Such rapture and such joy, no matter how far they go, may yield a moment of transformation that concerns nothing but *the soul*.[36]

Rilke's defense of a socially condemned kind of tender, erotic happiness between two people, in this case two women, which exonerates Anita Forrer from all "guilt and ugliness" in her love affair with another woman, segues into his political appeal for free sexuality—including homosexuality—in society: "Sensible people have long struggled to relieve love relations within the same gender of the ugly suspicions placed there by convention—but even this effort and viewpoint does not seem the right one. It isolates a process that ought to be considered always only within the full range of its contexts, and it turns an inexpressibly unique occurrence into something general and even ordinary only because it could happen to anyone. And ultimately this approach retains only the physical manifestation of such an event and forgets in what inaccessible and exuberant relations this one thing (which only appears capable of being described) is placed."[37]

In the modern political understanding of equal rights for minorities, Rilke would stand apart from "identity politics," according to which gays and lesbians demand their human right to recognition and full equality. His passionate defense of homosexual love affairs, whose "center," according to Rilke, "may be found in the final and sweetest physical intimacy (also between women),"[38] insists on the distinctiveness of homosexuality and not on its equality with other types of relationships. These thoughts reinforce the poems in *The Book of Hours* and Rilke's declaration of a faith that he thinks must be a productive engagement with a God with whom one must "challenge" oneself, and who, according to Rilke, can never be taken as a given. Rilke's letters enable the grateful Anita Forrer to see "the spiritual element of a human relationship, regardless of gender." In his defense of homosexual love Rilke does not suppress the sensual element at all; his letters are political precisely because he does not call for any sublimation of bodily desire. Rilke's political demands for equal rights in the form of granting value to difference give rise to a definition of same-sex love that renders Brecht's remark about Rilke's being "gay" in one sense appropriate, but on the other hand misses the fact that for Rilke love can never fit into preexisting patterns.

Rilke insists that a true erotic love be able to live on in all possible ways, even those that are unknown or unsanctioned by society. In a relationship this means that "no tenderness must impose itself with the force of mindless repetition."[39] This means that *every* conceivable and reachable tenderness is allowed, so long as it is not simply regurgitated. This attitude applies equally to serving and praying to God. Every relationship that deserves the name of love must be invented anew by the lovers.

Rilke's poems about God can be read, in light of his letters to Anita Forrer, as "gay" in the sense that they propose a kind of love that transcends us, something whose form must be invented by each lover anew outside of social conventions. In his ongoing correspondence with Forrer, Rilke moves seamlessly from the defense of the "final and sweetest physical intimacy (also between women)" to a discussion of faith. Just as homosexual love was burdened with "ugly suspicions placed there by convention," so faith began to be seen "even from within the Christian belief" as "something difficult." Instead of experiencing interaction with God in "its most ecstatic dimension," Christians run up against "the attitude of communities and churches" which "cuts off" the individual's experience of God "with its formulations and promises."[40] In love and in faith, Rilke pleads that no one should follow a form sanctioned by any other authority than one's own imagination.

This notion is no longer a properly Christian thought. It may come from Rilke's intensive engagement during the time of his letters to Forrer with Samuel Abba Horodezky's *Religious Movements in Judaism*.[41] Brecht's suggestion that Rilke is "gay" in his attitude toward God can be made more precise in terms of this reading experience. Rilke's thought was not only "gay" in this new meaning of radically nonhierarchical faith, it was also unchristian and also possibly pre-Christian. If Rilke had been "gay," his name could have been Marcel Proust.

h
for Hair

A change of perspective can sometimes make it easier to recognize the significance of an experience or an object (objects, for Rilke, always contain the possibility of an experience). Rilke follows this principle in a series of poems where he upends the expected relationship between the subject to be closely described and the descriptive adjectives used to do so. He transforms this relationship in such a way that the description takes on more weight than the thing it is meant to describe. But the resulting poems are not poems about language, or poems that privilege their mode of expression over their content, subject matter, and message. Rilke isolates details so that the meaning of the whole emerges all the more effectively.

A poem in *New Poems* absorbingly develops over the space of eleven lines the metaphor of a cat's eye, until finally at the end of the twelve-line sonnet it becomes clear that the poem's actual subject matter is the stained glass "window rose" of a cathedral.[1] Rilke develops the rhetorical figure of the descriptive simile—in this case the cat's eye—so thoroughly that the figurative speech outgrows its role as ornament and description. The metaphor is no longer in the service of the thing, feeling, person, animal, or experience it is supposed to describe, the ostensible main concern of the poem, but comes to stand on its own.

"It is nothing but a breath, the void," begins a posthumously published poem in which Rilke then expands and unfolds the metaphor of breath, for outer space, in which we "are still the breathed-upon/today still the breathed-upon," until the unfathomable emptiness of space, through which our planet disconcertingly plunges, becomes practically palpable.[2] An incomplete poem describes a tiny bird, a tit, that "has fluttered" its way into a room, in order to develop from this tiny event the thought of how difficult it is for us to help others: for "even in the most helping hand/there's still death enough."[3]

The point of this rhetorical shift of emphasis from the subject back to the metaphor is for Rilke a "reversal of spaces," as he describes the empirical world of the senses and our experience of the world—which then constitutes another "space."[4] Through such a "reversal," which in Rilke's poems often takes the form of the inversion of an adjective or a descriptive metaphor and its subject, "inner worlds," that is, regions and objects we perceive, can coalesce "in the Open," that is, as something yet undefined or not yet experienced.[5]

In the small cycle of four poems in *New Poems* that deals with the death of a beloved person, Rilke uses this technique to describe the ungraspable experience of deep loss. Not only is the smallness of the metaphor he uses here emblematic of a central poetic technique of Rilke's—rather, it is also indicative because it deals with a normally unspoken part of the world we live in: It is about a single pubic hair. The shift of emphasis from the experience to be described to the metaphor that describes it further widens our perspective, since Rilke expresses something about the constitution of our existence in general through the radically singular experience of loss.

In the poem "Lament for Jonathan," which is based on the biblical legend, Rilke chooses the tearing out of single pubic hairs as a metaphor for deep grief. This construction is all the more striking and memorable because pubic hair is normally not the sort of thing discussed in public. But the most difficult experiences are also the most precarious; deep grief is so difficult because the pain can be neither grasped nor explained. Such experiences of grieving teach us how fragile we are. We are afraid to plunge into an abyss from which we may never emerge. This instability finds expression in "Lament for Jonathan" in the metaphor of pubic hair—just using the phrase is startling—for these hairs, like the grief of the heart, are unspeakable and hidden.

How does one experience psychological pain? In the Bible story, King David loses his beloved Jonathan and mourns for him with the words "I grieve for you, Jonathan my brother; you were very dear to me. Your love for me was wonderful, more wonderful than that of women."[6] As he learns of the death of his beloved, he cannot, as king, show his grief publicly: He "must contain himself and hear the tiding" without showing any reaction. He longs not to lament like a poet, but to cry out like an animal, saying,

> for here and here, at all my shyest places,
> you've been torn from me like the hair that grows
> within my arm-pits and like that which laces
> the spot whence sport for women rose.[7]

The death of the beloved hurts like having your pubic hairs pulled out, one at a time, endlessly, secretly. It is not a public pain that King David can talk about. It is not ritualized sorrow, but rather an intimate pain, inescapable and lasting.

With this "hair that grows/within my arm-pits and like that which laces/the spot whence sport for women rose," Rilke makes the poem so concrete that there is no room for sentimentality. He creates these remarkably strong images by shifting the perspective deliberately from the subject (King David) to his attributes (his pain, his pubic hairs). The pubic hairs that are pulled out one at a time are a "motivated" metaphor: They are not dropped after having deliberately rattled the reader, but are woven in the next stanza into a subsequent image, linking the pubic hair to the love affair between David and Jonathan:

> before you skeined up all my therein centred
> senses as one unpicks a tangled clew;
> my eyes looked up then and your image entered:—
> Now, though, they nevermore shall gaze on you.[8]

David's "senses" were "tangled" at "the spot whence sport for women rose." He did not understand himself, did not understand his own sense nor his sensuality, until he let Jonathan play with his fingers on this spot. Only then, with a glance at Jonathan, did David figure out why he, although a "sport" for women, felt himself to be a "clew."

In the commentary of the complete edition of Rilke's works, the editors write that Rilke "amplified" the "homo-erotic undertones" of the biblical story.[9] They want to save both Rilke and the Bible: This undertone is already present in the original text, the research says (David's love for Jonathan is not Rilke's invention), even if it is not explicit to the degree that it is in Rilke. But with the metaphor of the torn-out hair, Rilke does not "amplify" any suppressed "undertone" in the Bible. In fact he does the opposite: He returns to the biblical legend the poignancy that directly affects us as readers, by foregrounding the nearly inexpressible *experience* of the loss of a beloved person and not the nature of this affection.

With every single pubic hair that the abandoned lover tears out in his grief, Rilke tears from the poem the sentimentality that the commentators falsely ascribe to the story. He avoids the prudish stance that leads them to downplay the uninhibitedly erotic portrayal of this love as having a "homo-erotic undertone." The reader cringes when encountering the graphic image of pubic hairs being pulled out one by one, not because it is about two men, but because Rilke's image brings us closer to the unspeakable helplessness of such great pain. Rilke is not concerned here with who has loved and lost whom, but rather how the pain is felt.

The metaphor of the hair also breaks with the traditional poetic image of lustrous hair as a sea of voluptuousness, which Rilke uses in the poem "The Courtesan" (also in *New Poems*). Just as an individual word can assume a new meaning as soon as it is cut out of the text that surrounds it, so can an individual hair—as soon as it falls from its proper place—often cross the border from desire to disgust. The hair in a bowl of soup comes from a head you might like to nuzzle up to, another strand of which might well end up in a locket. Letting your hair down suggests disinhibition: In the original version of "The Tenth Elegy" Rilke regrets that he did not, "surrendering, lose [himself]/in your loosened hair."[10] In "Lament for Jonathan" he also evokes the fact that every lost hair marks a tiny step toward old age. Now that he "nevermore shall gaze on" Jonathan, King David ages, as expressed metaphorically through the loss of individual hairs.

Rilke brings about the reversal of metaphor and subject—in this case pubic hair and David's pain—through concrete images, in order to give the rhetorically amplified metaphor more weight. In an unfinished poem from the year 1915 the armpit hair and the sweat of the beloved are entwined in the form of postcoital "love-snakes" on the poet's inflamed body:

> Gray love-snakes I have startled
> out of your armpits. As on hot stones
> they lie on me now and digest
> lumps of lust.[11]

The poem—beaten, worn out, exhausted—succumbs to its own metaphors. As if not only the "love-snakes" made out of sweat and the finest kind of hair were inert, but as if even the poem had had its fill of its own rhetoric. The body of the poet that has turned into "hot stones" remains behind silently, so that Rilke's lines can digest their inspired, post-Edenic figures in peace. The armpit hair is not directly named. It shows that the strength of Rilke's poetry is sometimes as fine as the finest kind of hair.

1

for Inca

By inventing the seamless *Rainer Maria Rilke* as his signature and what we would today call "brand," Rilke put himself in the tradition of many authors' rechristening themselves, from Voltaire (born Arouet) to Mark Twain (born Samuel Clemens) to George Orwell (born Eric Blair). Such rechristenings are also well represented in the history of German writing, with such figures as Novalis (born Georg Hardenberg), Klabund (born Alfred Henschke), Theodor W. Adorno (born Wiesengrund), and, after Rilke, Paul Celan (born Antschel). The binding of many editions of Rilke's works sports an understated, embossed metallic *RMR*, and the reader can rest assured: The brand name guarantees quality.

But ultimately Rilke experiences this forging of his identity into a brand name as a limitation, which he keeps trying to undermine with pet names and nicknames. His name is supposed to promise absolute singularity, but it soon locks him into an ever-tighter carapace. In many poems Rilke invokes a "nameless" element that promises a freer, more expansive experience and stands in contrast to those experiences he names precisely elsewhere. By means of his finely wrought poems Rilke aspires to enter into a "nameless" reality that is no longer mediated by language. In *The Book of Images*, the poet grasps with greater accuracy that which we often call the "unconscious":

And again my inmost life rushes louder
as if it moved now between steeper banks.
Objects become ever more related to me,
and all pictures ever more perused.
I feel myself more trusting in the nameless.[1]

Und wieder rauscht mein tiefes Leben lauter,
als ob es jetzt in breitern Ufern ginge.
Immer verwandter werden mir die Dinge
und alle Bilder immer angeschauter.
Dem Namenlosen fühl ich mich vertrauter.[2]

A poem in *The Book of Hours* describes a monk who, in search of deeper contemplation, does away with his worldly name, which is "like a light that plays/on foreheads shadelessly" where it blocks his view. "Now you have me, but you don't know whom you have," the poem continues.[3] To reach deeper awareness, Rilke proposes a balance between inner absorption (that is, a heightened subjectivity and thus the invention of a singular name) and anonymity (the giving up of a name and the loss of self).

This dual desire both to determine and to lose the self is matched by the dexterity with which Rilke's publisher Anton Kippenberg, like a contemporary talent agent, handled the name of his author. Kippenberg protested as early as 1914 against the cheap "exploitation" of the brand name "Rilke":

> My dear friend!
> Just now I've looked at my mail, which contained this open letter. So in this manner that name, which for many years—as best I could—I had sheltered from being sucked into anything that looked like advertising & could have contributed loudly to the literary noise of our time, is being ruthlessly exploited by another publisher as propaganda for something repugnant! I am ashamed, even discredited in my efforts of working [on your behalf] . . .[4]

The occasion for Kippenberg's outraged letter was an advertisement in the newspaper *Berliner Zeitung am Mittag*, featuring handwritten contributions from various authors, including Rilke. Kippenberg feared that this advertisement ran the risk of devaluing the name "Rilke," as if by inflation: "By contributing here you are endangering, let me say this openly—your name. You, the most reticent of poets, suddenly involved in such an enterprise! [. . .] Just think that your handwriting, which is so dear to so many and prompts such great and quiet joy for them when they receive it from time to time, just think that your handwriting will now land each Sunday morning in facsimile on 260 coffee tables."[5]

Some of those who considered Rilke's writing "so dear" were already hawking it during his lifetime. Thus already in 1916 handwritten letters by Rilke were sold at auction, just as it is possible today to purchase letters and postcards with Rilke's handwriting for less than a few thousand Euros.[6] But Kippenberg warns against a practice that had existed already at the beginning of Rilke's career. For Rilke pursued a carefully managed career, a decidedly modern, twentieth-century career, by playing the idealized early-nineteenth-century type of the serious, solitary, and quiet poet, complete with gloves and overcoat, so convincingly that he eventually became it. Rilke settled into this and all of his subsequent incarnations, just as he settled into all of his many names. His next effort was to free himself from each of these names in turn.

As a seventeen-year-old Rilke had distributed free copies of his magazine *Signposts* (*Wegwarten*, also a play on the German word for the chicory flower) in Prague. He dropped off free copies at hospitals and community organizations, and sent his publications unsolicited to established writers who might promote them, such as the poet Stefan George. To try to get his plays staged, he contacted as many cultural figures in Berlin as possible and did not miss a chance to get close to the influential purveyors of culture of his day. He managed to obtain a recommendation to apply for a position with the French sculptor Auguste Rodin and was hired as his secretary. That Rilke later denied ever having been Rodin's secretary fits perfectly into this picture of a deliberately staged career: The bumpy and often crudely opportunistic beginnings must be erased in order to cultivate in retrospect the myth of the poet's poet who fell fully formed from the skies, as his editor Kippenberg demanded.

As far as a writer's beginnings are concerned, Rilke's desire for a poignant name is not very different from the self-naming of other poets. The invention of "RMR" can be understood today, now that advertisement has become the ecosystem of modern life, as just another instance of branding, by which a product receives a mark of quality to cultivate customer loyalty.

But to Kippenberg's dismay, Rilke keeps "endangering" the self-made myth of *Rainer Maria Rilke*. But Rilke's effort to compromise his own name is not simply a threat to his marketability. It is also a genuine effort to break free of any convention, even that imposed by himself. The clearest instance of his attempt not to let himself and his work be ruled by a single name—although he created that name—can be found in Rilke's correspondence. In his countless letters, Rilke's willingness to take on the nicknames and pet names of friends, lovers, and admirers knows few bounds. With each of these designations he frees himself deliberately from the name "Rilke," in order to recognize in this newly carved-out space, under a different name often not of his own choosing, something new in the world and in himself. The more successful Rilke becomes, the more tightly he locks the "RMR" around his work like a well-wrought clasp, and all the greater becomes his need to elude this name and open up space for the unnamed, the unknown, the nameless.

Rilke calls this free space the "blessedness," which is hidden beneath and behind the name and which he granted himself over the course of his life. Occasionally Rilke sidesteps his elevation to a properly sealed and stamped authorial presence through his love for nicknames, between which he locates this "blessedness."

The midwife of the name "Rainer Maria Rilke" was the thirty-six-year-old Lou Andreas-Salomé in 1897, who bestowed on her lover, fourteen years her junior, the talented and ambitious and also, "at the beginning of his 20's," disoriented René, a more masculine name.[7] "René" was too weak for Lou, too feminine, too indecisive; "Rainer" on the other hand is masculine, strong, determined. And "Rainer" constitutes a nicely memorable contrast to "Maria," whose middle letter "r" so harmonically balances the subsequent R in "Rilke" that a typesetter would be proud. With this branding, Andreas-Salomé becomes Rilke's antimother: She transformed the little mama's boy, whom his biological mother had dressed up in girls' clothes during the first years of his life and "tried to transform one little Renée" (where the "-ée" signals a girl's name), into Rainer.[8] He became a man.

But even a man must write neatly. Lou criticized Rilke's sloppy handwriting, causing him to practice until he could cast onto the paper the uninterrupted line of *Rainer Maria Rilke* with the elegance that adorns his books today. The strict lessons with his muse bore fruit. Shortly after meeting Andreas-Salomé, Rilke's style changed: The flowery rhymes of the early poems, such as those in the 1889 work "To Celebrate Myself," gave way to the more precisely formulated poems of the later publications.

In light of this deliberate creation of a stylized poet-personality it may come as a surprise that in her memoirs Andreas-Salomé insists on the "authenticity" of Rilke. For it was actually through her coaching that he became "authentic"; before their fateful encounter, her young friend was only one among many talented middle-class kids, most of whom blossomed in the hothouse atmosphere of the Austro-Hungarian Empire but withered away quickly. The beginning of Rilke's career is marked by a renaming, which seems to contradict the ideal of authenticity and originality.

In fact the renaming is a central gesture in Rilke's attempt to grasp his inner life. For he considered inner life inseparable from what he calls "the nameless." For example in "Progress," from the year 1902, in *The Book of Images*: "Objects become ever more related to me,/and all pictures ever more perused. I feel myself more trusting in the nameless."[9] It is that which can be found only outside of the determination of a person by means of his or her name.

Rilke received several names over the course of his life; others he chose himself. On December 19, 1875, he had been baptized René Karl Wilhelm Johann Josef Maria, and "since Friday was turning into Saturday," as his mother, Phia Rilke, later wrote to her son, "[he] immediately became a child of Mary!—and [was] dedicated to the merciful Madonna" (hence "Maria").[10] Some early poems are signed with "René Caesar Rilke."[11] As soon as the friendship between Princess Marie von Thurn und Taxis-Hohenlohe and Rilke began to deepen in 1911, a new name became necessary: "I," writes the princess, "cannot call you *dear Herr Rilke*—that does not at all sound right for you—I still have to invent a name for you."[12] After Phia and Lou, another muse, another mother, another name: Soon Rilke is rechristened by Princess Thurn und Taxis as "Dottor Serafico." He accepts this affectionate nickname and begins signing many of his letters "D.S.," "D. Serafico," and so on. But starting only in 1912, as Rilke was beginning *Duino Elegies* with the motif of angels, the name "Dr. Angel" is "*non più mai provvisorio, ma certamente e perfettamente Serafico*" (no longer just provisional but surely and perfectly Serafico).[13] As with the brand name "RMR," Rilke grows into the nickname "Serafico" as if it were his fate, for at the beginning of the friendship, "Serafico," as Princess Thurn und Taxis noted later, "was not yet quite right."[14]

Marina Tsvetaeva, who fell in love with Rilke purely through letters, was seduced by the magic of this first branding effort and did not christen him with a new nickname:

> Rainer Maria Rilke!
>
> May I call you thus? You, as poetry incarnate, have to know that your name alone is—a poem. Rainer Maria, that sounds church-like—and child-like—and knightly. Your name does not belong to this age—it comes from earlier or later—from *beyond*. Your name wanted it, and you chose the name. (We choose our names, whatever comes after—follows on its own.)
>
> Your baptism was prologue for your entire self, and the priest who baptized you probably did not know what he was doing.[15]

In fact, Rilke was christened by Andreas-Salomé, and she knew what she was doing: His author's name is androgynous, and therefore a bit confusing, erotic. Lou fused the sex appeal of the brand name with the childlike, churchlike, chivalric nature of her creation and achieved what not only Tsvetaeva found irresistible: Rilke as an express amalgamation of intimacy and sovereignty.

In the correspondence with Princess Thurn und Taxis Rilke keeps giving himself new names, in an attempt to escape this seal and to emphasize the seductive incompleteness and unending potential of his identity. This is remarkable for a poet so concerned with the public's response. During a depressing visit to his native city of Prague in the year 1911, he describes himself as a "rocket that got entangled in the bushes, [he] huffed and puffed, and nobody got anything out of it."[16] Elsewhere Rilke describes himself as "the tree [. . .] on the outside all silence, trunk and twigs, with not even the tiniest word-leaf," "a parrot jerking its beak right and left (wasting who knows what)," "the deaf mountain, quite stony," "the photographic plate that was exposed for too long."[17]

Then there is Rilke the caterpillar, "in his cocoon [. . .] Indian summer reigns in my study, enveloping me in everything that I spin out day and night until I'm no longer recognizable."[18] Rilke's willingness to surrender his own tried-and-true name for any new nickname or term of endearment stems from the wish to be free from what he had created. It is only once this freedom has been reached again and again, by breaking out of the hulls of used-up names, no matter how lucrative and solid they are, that Rilke's dependable "capacity to capture" the unknown and not-yet-spoken, as he describes his poetic gifts in a retrospective poem, becomes a true "endowment."[19] "Rainer Maria Rilke," this "beloved, blessed name," which his first critics had hoped to "pronounce in a prophetic, promising manner," is supposed to be shed like a layer of skin.[20] Rilke views what he has written not as a revelation of the self, but rather as a pupation from which he must break out again and again; he understands himself as a parrot, casting words and names about like seeds and nuts. His own work, which is identical to the name "Rainer Maria Rilke" insofar as both the work and the name were deliberate creations, is supposed to create a free space under the layers of what is written, in which Rilke is "no longer recognizable." This is Rilke's wish, the meaning of his creation: to be nameless.

The ready acceptance of names that others give him attests to his wish to create not a "self" with his writing, but rather the possibility of change and, in every incarnation, a new name: "Please be patient for the next butterfly. You saw for yourself, last fall in Berlin, how pathetic and repulsive the caterpillar had been, a horror. [. . .] I am an abominable bird, squatting on my rod, completely molted and dingy, with feathers flying into my own beak."[21] In the poem "Narcissus," written in 1913 in Paris, we see that for Rilke a fully coherent, self-reliant figure leads to the impossibility of being itself. As soon as Narcissus captures his effusive beauty through the sight of his own reflection, he can no longer be:

> Whatever escaped him he loved back in,
> and was borne no longer in the open breeze
> and closed raptly the radius of forms
> and self-annulled and could exist no more.[22]

> Er liebte, was ihm ausging, wieder ein
> und war nicht mehr im offnen Wind enthalten
> und schloß entzückt den Umkreis der Gestalten
> und hob sich auf und konnte nicht mehr sein.[23]

By always seeking a new name, Rilke took not Narcissus but the ever-changing figure of Orpheus as his myth. And in letters to Dory von der Mühll, Rilke suddenly signs with "Inca."[24]

The urge to describe himself anew, to take on new names, to accept, transform, discard, is somehow immature; that is why many of us lose our childhood nicknames when we enter our adult lives. A nickname turns a person into, or keeps her forever, a child. A term of endearment on the other hand is born of a moment of great intimacy; it baptizes us in a bath of strong emotions. We do not always choose terms of endearment for ourselves. But often we grow into them right away. Dottor Serafico! Out of Rilke's nicknames speaks the poet's urge to open up the world and himself again and again. But to willingly grant to another the right of renaming—to allow himself to be rechristened by Mama Lou as "Rainer," and by Mama Taxis as "Dottor Serafico," and then to become René again for his friend Elisabeth Dorothea "Baladine" Klossowska (who also goes by "Merline" and "Merly" and "Mouky"), attests to this wish to be unfinished, i.e., a child-poet.

Andreas-Salomé, with her compulsion to be a savior, and Kippenberg, for purely economic interests, treated the adult name "Rainer Maria Rilke" as a closed unit. For Rilke his name is the passage to something entirely different, still unknown: passage to the self that has not been written. Rilke welcomes and invents new names for himself, only to forget them again, leave them behind, let them be spoken and written as just what they are: names. None of Rilke's nicknames stuck; the luxury brand RMR suppressed the affectionate (self-)ironic and ephemeral names. They are not viewed as signatures of the work, but rather as anecdotal marginalia. But it is their frailty that makes Rilke's nicknames into *real names*. They are born of a particular encounter with their bearer and dissipate at just the moment when they direct our gaze toward something we did not know about Rilke and that Rilke himself had to see within himself for the first time. Someone chooses or invents a nickname to set something free of another person, something that, in spite of—or because of—the proper name, remains hidden: the unnamable uniqueness of a person, which can never be identical with a name. Rilke's many nicknames reveal what is masked by his brand name. But they can do so only when they are forgotten (which has been their fate in the reception of Rilke's works); for every "name has to be traversed, in order to encounter the person whom this name names, and who carries it."[25]

Rilke was aware of the influence of names. He once facilitated the purchase of a picture, which later turned out to be by a different artist than what he had thought. "But is this certain *Marini* equally desirable?

Of course, [the pictures] remain what they are either way, but something small comes and goes with proper names, if not inside the images, then in the way we look at them."[26] The "something small," as Rilke well knows, is not only a minor matter: A picture by Marieschi is simply worth a different sum than one by Marini. Names create value and unlock a world; we set up our perceptions in accordance with how we name things and people. The name "Rilke" signals a specific quality (to some ears, for example, a cult of childhood and kitsch). As the product of editor Kippenberg's publicity campaign, in which the poet's name was elevated to a "trademark" of literary quality, "Rilke" is just the kind of creation that corresponds to Rilke's understanding of the role of names in his poetry—as long as one understands this quality as the openness of his poetry onto something "nameless."

For critics like Theodor W. Adorno, himself the product of a self-baptizing, this intersection of brand names and individuality—the branding of authenticity—was more than an atrocity. It signals, Adorno said, art's increasing inability to redeem our regulated lives. Rilke did not believe in such a possibility of salvation. One must *go through* everything, including one's own name; only in this way is something new and nameless possible.

The only promises that Rilke makes us is that the name "Rilke" will not last forever, and that all he wrote under this name must be named anew. If his poetry offers access to something, then it is to that which in us, too, has no name and should not have one. In an unpublished love poem for Baladine (or Merly or Mouky or Merline) Klossowska (did Rilke love four people in one person? Did he love a woman, who lived among four names?), Rilke calls this intimate space between the names "blessedness":

> as everything in you, my still embrace,
> was nevertheless nameless,
> out there, things first were named,
> named after doubts and after time
> but we place blessedness
> suddenly between the names.
> (An "Interior View"
> For Merly
> Oktober 13th [1921] in the afternoon.)[27]

wie war in dir, mein stiller Schooss,
alles trotzdem namenslos:
draußen erst heißen die Dinge
Heißen nach Zweifel und heißen nach Zeit,
aber da legen wir Seeligkeit
plötzlich zwischen die Namen.
(Die "Innenansicht"
Für Merly
13. Oktober [1921] nachmittags)[28]

Rilke transcribed this poem alongside a watercolor showing him taking an afternoon nap in a suit, nestled on a big rose-colored sofa. The watercolor is attached to the volume of Rilke's letters to Klossowska published in France in 1950, as a colorful fold-out with the handwritten poem. The pretty page constitutes literally the unconscious (sleeping) center of Rilke's great love correspondence. Rilke here offers a confession: Naming things is not a godlike gesture, with which we create the world. Instead we name things to overcome our uncertainty ("doubts") and consciousness of our own mortality ("time") for a few moments, and only in the space between the names is there a "blessedness," for in that space world and self remain unnamed, still open, pure motion. Between the names Rilke locates the interior of language itself, where in the absence of names and words, language points at something nonetheless. What is named there is the space in which not only existing—i.e., named—things are found, but also the possibility of something yet unknown, something that does not yet exist (and thus does not bear a name given in advance). The interior of language is this blank spot for which a name has yet to be found.

In this intimate poem, poetry is like Rilke sleeping on a rose, like a woman's "still embrace." There, in the middle of a wondrous experience of forgetting akin to that of Sleeping Beauty in the fairy tale, Rilke gives birth to "blessedness [. . .] between" the names, which he terms "nameless." Blessedness: That is René and Merly, Rainer and Mouky, beautifully intertwined, until this poem makes us forget all these names as the names of a great "blessedness."

The impetus for the name "Inca," with which Rilke signed a series of letters starting in 1921, came from the one-and-a-half-year-old son of the family Von der Mühll, with whom Rilke was on friendly terms; on a visit in 1920, the preverbal child called the visitor, "in a child's mishearing of his name, 'Inca.' [. . .] Rilke was delighted at this innocent alteration of his name. 'So after the Last of the Incas there is now a very last Inca!,' he said laughingly, and from then on he signed his letters to [Dory Von der Mühll] with 'Inca' instead of 'Rilke.'"[29]

Since the original invention of the brand name *Rainer Maria Rilke*, which the poet so gladly discarded for the name "Inca" (which would also not be his last), was the product of such a decidedly American-style public relations campaign, I read with American ears: Inca, close to an imagined English word, "inker." Rilke, who placed his perfect signature on flawless manuscripts and letters with an expensive fountain pen, and who, in a poem next to a rosy ink drawing of Baladine Klossowska, designated the interior of language as his deepest wish for namelessness; Rilke, in whose veins flowed not only being but possibly ink; Rilke, who again and again—oh, place "blessedness/suddenly between the names"—rechristens himself in this ink, the auto-poetic bloodletting, in ever-changing incarnations of namelessness.

"Inca": Rilke, the inker.

for Jew Boy

All poets are Jews.

—MARINA TSVETAEVA

"And you, as a Jewess," writes Rilke to Ilse Blumenthal-Weiß on December 28, 1921, in a letter he later entitled "Letter on Faith," "with so much immediate experience of God, with such ancient fear of God in your blood, ought not to be concerned with 'faith.' But simply *feel* His presence in yours. And where He, Jehovah, had wanted to be *feared*— there this fear arose in many cases only because there was no other means but fear available for a mutual closeness between man and God [. . .]—You have, and do not forget this, one of the greatest Gods of the universe in your heritage, one to whom one cannot simply convert at some point, as to that Christian god.—One to whom one *belongs*, based on one's people, because he made and molded you from the beginning through your fathers so that each Jew is implanted in Him (and in the one whose name nobody may dare mention), irrevocably implanted in Him with the root of his tongue!"[1]

A Jew, according to Rilke, can speak only *as* a Jew and is, even without meaning to be, a Jew, even when he speaks of what no one dares mention. In 1950 the editors of Rilke's letters still rely on what at that time, a few short years after the Germans committed the crime of murdering millions of Jews during the Holocaust, had become a problematic classification: The register of names for a volume of Rilke's correspondence lists "Blumenthal-Weiß, Ilse, Jewess."[2] No other person among Rilke's friends and acquaintances has their religion listed in the register to this volume.

Rilke's estimation of Judaism is based on a one-sided emphasis on religious elements—the "most immediate experience of God" and the "fear of God." In his letter to Ilse Blumenthal-Weiß, Rilke continues:

> I have indescribable confidence in those people who have encoun-tered God *not* by way of faith but who experienced God through the most authentic belonging to a collective, by way of their own tribe. Like the Jews, the Arabs, and to a certain degree the orthodox Russians—and, in a different way—the peoples of the Orient and ancient Mexico. For them God is origin and thus also future. For everyone else he is something derivative, something from where and to which they strive as strangers or as people who have become estranged—and thus they actually need him always again as mediator, as link, and as the one who translates their blood, the idiom of their blood, into the language of divinity.[3]

The Jew comes from God and moves back toward God. He has a belief in God in his blood, while the Christians, as Rilke puts it just as insight-fully as derisively in another letter, have to use "the telephone 'Christ,' [. . .] into which someone constantly calls: *Hello, who's there?*, but nobody responds."[4] In these letters Rilke idealizes the immediacy of the rela-tionship of the "God-original" Jews to God, and criticizes from this perspective the contemplation, reflection, and effort that are necessary for the Christian faith. The Jews—and here Rilke means Western European Jews, just as Kafka in his letters regarded Eastern European Jews as a figure for a specific way of being—exist for Rilke on the periphery of a once almighty, direct experience of God, which earns them his great admiration. Like all idealizations, however, Rilke's projections can at any moment turn into their opposite. The truth is that Rilke wrote some anti-Semitic things and mailed them off in his letters (just as he published decidedly philo-Semitic texts). No casuistry can excuse these remarks.

While in "Letter on Faith" Rilke relies on the image of the "Jew" as *the* figure of radical change and the mobility of human existence, elsewhere in his work he characterizes the poet precisely in this way. "For there is no place where we can remain," writes Rilke in the first of the Duino elegies, "*Denn Bleiben ist nirgends.*"[5] Here he insists that man can realize his full potential only by making a tremendous effort to move out of and beyond himself: "as the arrow endures the bowstring's tension, so that/ gathered in the snap of release it can be more than/itself."[6] The Jew embodies for Rilke precisely this potential. In another poetic image, as inspired as that of the quivering arrow on the bow, Judaism, as Rilke writes in a letter, is, "in the absolute greatness of the universe: a direction of the heart":

> Religion is something infinitely simple, simpleminded. It is not knowledge, not the content of our feelings (for any possible content is given already from the beginning, wherever anyone engages with life). It is neither duty nor renunciation; it is not limitation, but in the absolute vastness of the universe it is a direction of the heart. How a human being might go and err toward the right and toward the left, and get knocked around and fall and get up, and commit an injustice here and suffer an injustice there, and be abused here and over there himself abuse, mistreat and misunderstand others: All this is absorbed into the great religions and within them maintains and enriches the God that is their center. And man, living still at the farthest periphery of this circle, *belongs* to this powerful center even if he had turned his countenance toward it only once, perhaps in the hour of his death. That at specific hours the Arab turns to face east and prostrates himself, that *is* religion. It is hardly "belief." It has no opposite. It is a natural movement within a human life through which God's wind sweeps three times daily as long as we are at least one thing: malleable.[7]

To be "malleable" and "a natural movement within a human life" means for Rilke essentially: to be human. Only he who remains agile within being, only he who frees himself from himself (without the help of a savior), remains open to experience, remains in motion; only he remains *in* life. As "God's wind" blows through the believer, so the wind of inspiration blows through the poet.[8]

The portrayal of the moved, malleable, and faithful Jews and Arabs corresponds to Rilke's description of a human being who has been moved internally, as in the poem "Natur ist glücklich" ("Nature is Happy") of 1919:

> Who has a heart through which the wind can wail?
> Who holds the space birds fly through inwardly?
> Who is at once so supple and so frail
> as any branch on any single tree?[9]

> Wem geht ein Wind durchs Herz, unwidersprechlich?
> Wer faßt in sich der Vogelflüge Raum?
> Wer ist zugleich so biegsam und gebrechlich
> wie jeder Zweig an einem jeden Baum?[10]

Or in *Duino Elegies*: "Like dew from the morning grass,/what is ours floats into the air, like steam from a dish/of hot food [. . .] new warm receding wave on the sea of the heart . . ./alas, but that is what we *are*."[11] The enigmatic "alas, but that is what we *are*" in *Elegies* corresponds to the more direct picture in "Letter on Faith": "There is a natural mobility within a human life through which God's wind sweeps three times daily." Human life is moved. In another letter, Rilke anticipates Heidegger's concept of "thrownness" when he describes the poet's inspiration as the experience of "being thrown."[12] Our task is to go along with this movement, to become one with it. Even the elegy seems to be caught on a rush of wafting German sounds: the "*warme*" (warm), "*entgehende Welle*" (receding wave) blows into a simple "*weh*" (alas) in the following line. Everything is wafting. Breathe in. And *out*. And *in*.

In another letter to Blumenthal-Weiß, Rilke emphasizes "to what extent the Jew seems privileged—just like the Arab and the orthodox Russian, not to consider examples from further in the Orient—because of his innate union of nationality and religion, which provides him with an advantage that becomes apparent at every turn."[13] After bringing up the politically sensitive issue of a Jewish nationality, Rilke views dialectically the discrimination to which Jews have historically been subjected, which legally and politically anchored their "instability" in society, and which had made them social outcasts, often of precarious legal status, in many European countries at the time. But once Rilke writes of "the Jew" in the singular, anti-Semitism has already emerged in this text.

That [the Jew] had lost the soil beneath his feet and had to persist on a piece of borrowed land is both positive and negative; with a few great exceptions he has had to abuse his own best traits in order to survive in this contested and groundless realm,—and he mostly abused *himself* and others. With a kind of cunning which was forced upon him in order to survive, he turned this condition of being ungrounded from a misfortune into an advantage, and where he abuses this hard-won advantage in petty, greedy, or hostile ways, and where he—instinctively—takes revenge, he has become a pest, an intruder, a dissolving agent.[14]

For Rilke the "bad qualities" of the Jews result from the "abuse" of their dialectically achieved "advantageous" position. The Jew, for Rilke, is a figure of an authentic, that is, *malleable* existence, as long as he bends involuntarily, from within himself. In this way he becomes for Rilke the figure of true life in modernity. Like the poet, this figure transforms his unhappiness at his "condition of being ungrounded" into "an advantage." But Rilke's statements about Judaism flip into anti-Semitic stereotypes at the moment when "the Jew" misuses his "advantages," namely his inner flexibility, which for Rilke determines human existence; for nothing is more important for Rilke than that we use our power to transform something like "unhappiness" using our own free will, from within us, and not in reaction to external circumstances. Rilke adopts the anti-Semitic stereotypes of his time, which condemn the Jew as the "pest" and "dissolving agent" of the nation's ethnic and cultural unity, or "*Volk*," but traces these effects back to injustices within the community. Then he adopts the anti-Semitic figure of the rootless Jew, who constitutes a threat to traditional social structures, and—once more in his dialectical thinking—turns that into its opposite. The lack of a homeland turns into an "advantage," and the Jew—as long as he remains flexible on his own free will—becomes the model of "magnificence." "But where the same process, and the same survival of fate occurred in a *powerfully* resolved human being, there this same ruthlessness produced magnificence, of which *Spinoza* would be a famous instance."[15]

For Rilke, the Jew, on account of his ability to "turn to his advantage" external circumstances and himself within them, becomes an incarnation of the most expansive human existence, the figure of modern man, who aligns his flexibility—the figure that he adopts in life—with what he calls in "Letter on Faith" the "natural mobility within a human life." For Rilke, the Jew is at once the promise and the abyss of modernity:

> The mobility and changeability of one's inner center, its independence (but also its rootlessness, when this realization does not lead to one's rootedness in God)—the authentically movable spirit has entered the world through the fate of the Jews: an unimaginable danger and an unimaginable freedom of movement.[16]

"Unimaginable danger" and, at the same time, "unimaginable freedom": Rilke's regard for Judaism is grounded in his belief, which is crucial for all people, of the "mobility [. . .] of one's inner center," which determined Rilke's own empirical life, and which he (as Emmanuel Lévinas after him) equates with Jewish faith in the Diaspora. The "privileged Jew" is for Rilke the figure of "the mobility and changeability of one's inner center." And this flexibility is the true measure of humanity in all of Rilke's poetry. Ultimately, Rilke reverses the meaning of the internal flexibility through a rhetorical operation in which anti-Semitic stereotypes are turned into their positive opposites.

Rilke's rhetorical inversion of "rootlessness" has a tradition: The conservative French novelist Maurice Barrès attacked the metaphorical rootlessness of modern man in his 1897 novel *Les déracinés* (*The Uprooted*), which the critic George Steiner later—similarly to Rilke—reevaluated, when he ascribed an emblematic meaning to the "rootlessness of the Jews," since this "historically enforced condition" has a "greater meaning" for our modernity in recalling the "free play of the spirit and the anarchic discipline of its dreams."[17] Rilke lends the figure of the Jew the problematic authority of a dignified victim who has experienced a historical "misfortune"; this is how history, as Vivian Liska argues in another context, becomes myth.[18] Even Rilke's notion of a "movable" inner homeland is not new: Already the poet Heinrich Heine had described the Torah as his "portable homeland."[19]

In his remarks on Judaism Rilke identifies the ability to move one's "inner center" as a uniquely Jewish trait. Everywhere else in his work, however, this ability is identified as a general condition of human life in the modern world and evidence of a fundamental "being moved within existence," of which the movements of Orthodox Jews and the prostrations of Muslims in prayer are only outward expressions. Judaism is for

Rilke the *potential of the human*: Only when we can move our inner center and fully allow for "the being-moved within our existence" are we capable of growth, of change, of life.

But this potential is always ambiguous. The "mobility within a human life" also harbors the risk of what Rilke calls "uprootedness." Rilke is certain only that this ambiguity must not be understood in one concrete way, that is, as a threat that finds its response in an argument for the forced expulsion of the Jews from Europe. "Whether one puts emphasis on one or the other side of this escape from the Jewish dilemma, one will either fear or praise it; whereas it remains clear that everything that has been achieved in response to it, is indispensable for all of us and cannot be wished away."[20] The Zionist movement conjures, for Rilke, the disappearance of that which the Jews have created—this "inner mobility"—from the world of Europe. In Zionism as well Rilke finds two sides:

> The Zionist idea, which originates in a purely Jewish impulse, would constitute a beginning of this effort which is probably necessary. This reclamation of ancient, primal soil, this new sense of rootedness, will then have to be interpreted both literally and symbolically. If we, as is probable, know the Jewish people only in various disfigurations, in its helplessness, in its twisted and occasionally warped stubbornness, and when we derive a certain amount of force from its survival, then we are disturbed by realizing what kind of strength it would have to muster to create something autonomous, legitimate, and favorable!—The growth of these people who are so productive even in their uprootedness would then reach a limitless fertility in God—, the continuation of this story of passionate and portentous harvests that turn the Old Testament, wherever we open it, into a proper experience and microcosm.[21]

Rilke is "disturbed," but not simply by the political and human consequences of the "reclamation of ancient, primal soil," which depended in 1922 on the consent of the Turkish caliphate. He is more "disturbed" by the "limitless fertility in God," which for him makes spiritual existence possible. Rilke's attitude toward Judaism is always two-sided and refracted: Admiration and disturbance alternate with each other, depending on which of the ways "of the escape out of the Jewish dilemma" is emphasized. These two sides are: the deliberate and voluntary relocation of one's inner center, on the one hand, and the reactive change in one's position under pressure from external circumstances. In his account of Judaism Rilke shows the ability to relocate his inner center and invert existing stereotypes: He considers the topic from ever-changing perspectives but ultimately reaches no conclusion to the questions he has posed.

As in his reflections on freedom, Rilke emphasizes in these remarks on Judaism that the ungrounded dimension of existence (in equal measures promising and threatening), rather than our sense of a stable identity, is the highest human potential.

In 1907, long before his letters to Blumenthal-Weiß, Rilke had mystified Judaism. In an entry for a widely read anthology of essays published by Julius Moses, *The Solution to the Jewish Question*, with eighty-nine statements from major cultural figures, including Thomas Mann and Maksim Gorky, Rilke emphasized the considerable advantage the Jews had, in his estimation, over other minorities. Moses had started the survey after particularly brutal pogroms in Russia, since "the most recent bloody events in the vast Russian empire urgently require [us to find] a complete solution of the Jewish problem, and not only for the Russian empire but for all nations where Jews reside."[22]

Moses's collection differs from earlier volumes of its kind in that Moses directly addresses the question of anti-Semitism, which had previously been only "the mad idea of a few fringe individuals or, if one could not quite decide to dismiss so summarily the anti-Jewish movement, then with the clever joke (which avoids the problem) that there is no Jewish but only an Antisemitic question. It ought to be no longer necessary to seriously refute such shallow and immature thinking."[23] As proof of the seriousness of his attempt to understand even anti-Semitism, Moses invited a few self-identified anti-Semites to contribute. In addition to being a critical document of its time, *The Solution to the Jewish Question* is intended to be a book of dialogue and tolerance—toward anti-Semites.

The majority of the entries in Moses's volume deal with the topic of whether the "Jewish question" is a racial, religious, or political matter. The authors suggest assimilation and emigration from Eastern European countries but also invoke, as a necessary part of solving what Moses poses as an urgent problem, pride in Judaism. The Russian writer Maksim Gorky calls "the Jewish question [. . .] the saddest and most scandalous tragedy in history [. . .]. These two words reflect the ugliest blemish that stains human life right now."[24]

In his contribution, Rilke is decidedly philo-Semitic:

> Because the Jewish people is pressured, discriminated against, and defamed, it must be permitted to make use of its truly enormous advantage. It must base its existence with single-minded devotion on the fact that its race corresponds to an inseparable religion, or, to be more accurate, religiosity. Everyone for himself, at his proper place, must be concerned with finding a connection to the great and ancient God for this contact will transform whatever is distorted and concealed into an ornament, a sign, an expression of reverence and awe.[25]

Here again Rilke is concerned with "single-minded devotion": The Jew is to become a figure and a sign, even if that figure originates in whatever is twisted and distorted in Jewish existence. Rilke detaches the "Jewish question" from its touchy status as a political and cultural problem. Although Rilke begins his definition of the Jews with a potentially problematic yoking together of blood and religion (since that is also the thinking of anti-Semites), he ultimately moves away from a thinking of politics: "each individual for himself." The "Jewish question" becomes for Rilke a question for each individual Jew whose connection to the "great and ancient God" does not result in a collective movement or group identity, but at best an expression of "reverence and awe." Rilke weakens the argument of both Zionists and anti-Semites who would like to treat the Jews as a group and see them act as part of a collective.

But ultimately Rilke does not completely defang the anti-Semitic clichés. "There is not much needed, but only a single turn and this people will again be facing its own, unforgettable God, who had always been its hard home and stony refuge."[26] According to Rilke, this return to their faith would have little meaning for the actual life of the Jews; he does not address the themes of assimilation, exile, and political equality. The "return to faith" applies to everyone "at the spot to which he has been dispersed." Rilke's expression of the "hard home" and "stony refuge" attests to his familiarity with the rhetoric of the Zionists. He draws no political conclusions from his suggestion that the Jews should find their way back to their God. At best, this return creates a safe haven from the persecutions and exclusions of daily life: "By returning its fate to this spot [the Jewish people] and thus wresting it from the hands who would like to toy and gamble with it, [the Jewish people] would reclaim its own, powerful existence: within the tremendous fertility that results from maintaining a great god."[27]

Rilke could be accused here of being out of touch with reality and of appeasement (as some critics have done).[28] He recommends to the Jews that they seek comfort from God when the noose is around their neck, instead of organizing politically or fighting back (in Poland the Bund, the largest non-Zionist Jewish organization before the Second World War, owed its success partly to an effective militia that protected Jews from assault).

In a later letter, Rilke compares the "tact and propriety of the Jews during times when they do not use their God" to the propriety of aristocratic emigrants whose titles would have been inappropriate "in misery, poverty, and exile."[29] The letter contains a basic strain of anti-Semitic thinking: the resentment against the Jews, since, according to Rilke, they necessarily have to consider themselves superior. But this notion of propriety (of not being outwardly proud of their "enormous creative origin and distance at the source of their blood which lies there like a treasure at the bottom of the sea") is ultimately considered a kind of "dishonesty."[30] What is first described in this letter as "tact" finally turns into "affectation" when the Jews hide what Rilke considers their well-deserved pride. But Rilke conceives of the reticence of the Jews in public life differently in his short contribution to Moses's *The Solution to the Jewish Question*. There he characterizes the Jewish people as "pressured, discriminated against, and defamed," which explains the reticence regarding public declarations of faith among the Jews.

Even in his contribution to Moses's collection, Rilke turns his attention to the individual ("every man for himself"). In the letter to Blumenthal-Weiß it may strike us as strange, if not alienating, that Rilke assumes that his friend carries "the fear of God in her blood."[31] This stereotype has an equivalent in Rilke's contribution to *The Solution to the Jewish Question*, where Rilke refuses to consider the Jewish question as a political problem. At the same time he stresses the possibility of taking the fate of the Jews out of the often brutal and opportunistic hands of those "who toy and gamble with it." For Rilke, religiosity and faith—even when they are anchored in blood—are a matter of the individual. The "hands" for whom the Jews are the playthings belong to all of those who wish to define the Jews collectively: anti-Semites and Zionists, separatists and advocates of assimilation.

Behind these thoughts we glimpse Rilke's strong individualism and his doubts as to whether human beings may be considered as part of a collective at all: "The more human we become, the more different we become, too. It is as if all beings were suddenly to increase a thousand-fold, for a collective name that would be sufficient for millions in former times will soon be too narrow for just ten people, and we will have to consider each one individually. Just think: Once we will have instead of people, nations, families and societies just human beings, when it'll be impossible to combine even three in *one* name! Wouldn't the world have to become a bigger place then?"[32]

Rilke wants to restore to the individual the right to self-determination, which risks getting lost in a collective politics. This thought is in keeping with the thoughts cited above in the letter to Blumenthal-Weiß, where Rilke can marvel at a distance at the supposedly more direct relationship a "Jew" has to God—without addressing himself to the problematic aspect of such an attribution.

On account of these letters Rilke has been accused of subscribing to an "extreme individualism [. . .] in an age of mass movements and collective problems."[33] This is correct. But to posit individualism and political engagement as opposites relies on premises that Rilke rejects in every sentence. Individualism is his artistic credo, which rejects all political or moral criteria. In both Rilke's contribution to *The Solution to the Jewish Question* and his letters, the Jew is the embodiment of the very poetic principle that determines Rilke's artistic thought as well as his artistic existence: that of the "mobility and changeability of one's inner center." Curiously, the Jew takes on this feature often ascribed to and claimed by Rilke, which is also the one that invites the most political criticism.

The decisive difference between the inner "mobility" of the Jews and the flexibility that Rilke sees as the condition for an authentic existence can be described by his use of the term "mission." In the first letter to Blumenthal-Weiß quoted above, Rilke's images risk turning into anti-Semitic clichés depending on whether the "mobility and changeability of one's inner center" takes place of its own accord or in reaction to external circumstances.

Rilke concludes his brief essay in *The Solution to the Jewish Question* by considering the irrepressible strength of the Jews, which will impress itself on us like a "climate" or an "event." As soon as the Jews gain this strength "as something they impose from within themselves," they will garner nothing but admiration and respect from Rilke. The internal "mobility" that Rilke considers such a great potential among the Jews, but views as a "distortion" in their lived reality, must be *self-made*; it is a principle of life, which is not essentially different from his artistic credo. It must not be a response to external circumstances. In *Duino Elegies* this thought culminates in the following expression: "All this was mission."[34] For Rilke, the flexibility of human existence makes it possible to experience our existence as something dynamic. This distinction between a reactionary "mobility" and one chosen freely underlies Rilke's formulation of an authentic existence, for which the Jew becomes emblematic.

Already in the texts written to Jewish acquaintances or colleagues, Rilke in no way shies away from anti-Semitic arguments (Jews as "pests" and "dissolving agents"). What he calls the great "advantage" of the Jews that turns the "Jew" into a central figure for Rilke's poetics—"the mobility and changeability of one's inner center" as an "unimaginable freedom of movement"—becomes, in a letter written a bit later to one of Rilke's closest confidantes, Nanny Wunderly-Volkart, a reason for his "ultimate reticence" when it comes to the Jews. Rilke writes about why he has never had a close Jewish friend. The word "mission" changes to "transmission" and evokes fear of infection. Rilke explains why "we"—Rilke; the addressee, Nanny Wunderly-Volkart; and apparently all non-Jews— experience the essence of Jews as invasive, since "the Jew is not the same as all of what he brings with him, transmits to us [. . .] that, which prompts him to be a kind of contagion. So that we finally keep what has been brought to us, if we can make it our own, with great joy, while we ultimately experience the messenger himself, since he is not identical with what he gives us (and could bring a thousand other things and tomorrow, possibly, even its opposite), and quite abruptly, as too much, as too close, as nothing but intrusive. I have never developed a close friendship with a Jew but could imagine that it would have taken only this course if I would have been closer to, say, Rathenau or Wassermann or anyone else who would have prompted such closeness."[35]

The "mobility and changeability of one's inner center," which Rilke considers the central mission of our existence, here becomes an occasion to wish away the Jew as the bringer of an otherwise "joyous" openness. Rilke likes the Jews for what they exemplify to the non-Jew in their lives: the transformation of their "ungrounded state of being from a misfortune into an advantage." At the same time he does not like the Jews, because they continually shift their "inner center" in reaction to external conditions—and "could bring a thousand other things and tomorrow, possibly, even its opposite."

The Jew is for Rilke the figure of the possibility of an authentic life, which for him includes the poetic and the creative as such. We keep what he has "brought to us, if we can make it our own, with great joy," and abandon the bearer of these gifts. This is also Rilke's understanding of creativity: All creation is born out of the encounter with something real as an external "pretext," which we abandon as soon as we have changed ourselves in the act of creation. Once we recognize that the Jews are an abstraction for Rilke, another fundamental principle of Rilke's poetics becomes clear. Throughout Rilke's poetry runs not only an indifference, but even a degree of contempt for the things he speaks about, the things he exaggerates poetically as a "pretext" for the transformation of our selves. This is precisely the role of the Jew in Rilke's thinking. In a different context, Rilke explains his disregard for all those who gather their inner strength "out of opposition" and "in defiance of obstructing circumstances." In a letter to Reinhold von Walter, he writes on October 21, 1907:

> Even the apparently most useless diversions can be a pretext for an inner concentration; one's nature might even instinctively seize upon such activities to distract an alert intellect's controlling observation and attention away from those mental processes which wish to remain unrecognized. One may do *anything*: only this corresponds to the full scope of life. But one ought to be certain that nothing is done out of opposition, in defiance of obstructing circumstances, or to impress others due to some kind of ambition. You must be certain that you are acting out of pleasure, strength, courage, or a sheer sense of abandon: that you *have to* act this way.[36]

This remark about poetry sheds light on why Rilke dislikes the Jews, whose flexibility comes (in his opinion) all too often as a result of external circumstances. Admiration for their inner "mobility" turns into contempt as soon as they show Rilke their potential for the "mobility" of his own "inner center." Immediately, the Jew is "too much," "too close," and "meddlesome," since as the messenger of this possibility, and a kind of booster rocket, he remains only a pretext that prompted the poet to shift his inner center.

The discrepancy between Rilke's abstract support of Judaism as a "preferred" group and his actual, regrettable behavior toward Jews finds its clearest expression in his description of his first encounter with Franz Werfel, as he reports it to his confidante Princess Marie von Thurn und Taxis.[37] Rilke greatly admired Werfel's poems and had advocated for him with publishers and potential patrons.[38] But then in October 1913 he met Werfel in person in Prague. After this encounter Sidonie Nádherný von Borutin described Franz Werfel, disparagingly, as "Jew boy" (*Judenbub*), a term that Rilke adopts "unhappily," since it does not seem "entirely wrong" to him: "'*A Hellerau et à Drèsden j'ai beaucoup vu Franz Werfel. C'était triste,* ein Judenbub,' Sidie Nádherný said (who had come over from near-by Janowitz, quite stunned) *et elle n'avait pas complètement tort.*"[39]

Rilke accepts the term "Jew boy." He seconds his friend's remark, which would have sounded different by the standards of the time. But as soon as he met Werfel in person, his goodwill was all gone:

> I had been wholly prepared to open my arms to this young man and instead of doing that, I folded my arms behind my back like someone who is entirely indifferent while taking a walk. Ten times a day I recalled to myself that he had created all of these miracles, and in his absence I could still get excited about him, but when he was there, I felt so embarrassed that I could not look him in the face. But he was not unlikeable, extremely intelligent, maybe too intelligent for his poetry which loses something when you imagine it as something that has been cleverly imagined, devised by a Jewish spirit who knows his merchandise all too well [. . .] For the first time I experienced the falseness of the Jewish mentality that is detached from everything which ties us together, and that nonetheless succeeds in speaking about it, fed by a nearly negative mode of experiencing things. This spirit that enters all things without owning them, like a poison that penetrates everything and exacts its revenge for not belonging to any organism.[40]

"For beauty is nothing/but the beginning of terror," declares Rilke in one of his most famous lines, from the first Duino elegy.[41] The admirable Jew, whom Rilke stylized into a poetic concept, and the work of Werfel, which only a few weeks before had "filled Rilke with conviction and happiest joy," begin to become terrible.[42] Instead of opening his arms to the young man, Rilke readily seconds his friend Sidonie's anti-Semitic cliché. It is a fact: During this encounter, and in his later description of it, Rilke behaved as a bigot and an anti-Semite. He turned Werfel, whom he otherwise admired, encouraged, and supported, into an emblem of falseness.

Maria von Thurn und Taxis feels encouraged by Rilke's use of "Jew boy" to express her feelings about Werfel even more clearly: "But you know, I was not at all surprised, really not at all, by your impression of Werfel—I was certain that he would be this way. Of course I have greatly admired what you gave me of his writings—but there was something that repulsed me immediately [*me répugnait*]—instinctively."[43] Rilke's distaste for Werfel's actual appearance was no doubt a reaction to his own overly high expectations, which no one could have met: "Did I mention to you," wrote Rilke in August 1913, "how very occupied I am at this moment with the young poet, Franz Werfel, whose work I just recently discovered? I am reading him almost exclusively; astonished, astonished."[44] In the same year Rilke composed a prose text, "On the Young Poet," for which he credited "as practically a prerequisite the wonderfully uplifting involvement with Werfel's poems."[45] The text is a mystification of the poet as a naïve "lad" in whom "God comes into awareness."[46] Rilke starts a hymn to the "great poem," which he had "until recently taken for granted as something in existence, while entirely removing from consideration the fact that it had been produced in some way."[47] Like someone who's thrown himself head over heels into a love affair conducted entirely through ever more grandiose written messages, Rilke has a slight premonition that the actual encounter with the empirical person will result in disappointment. In "On the Young Poet," Rilke wisely keeps in check his own tendency toward idealization. Werfel's generation forces him to put an end to the dangerous elevation of the poem over the poet. "It has not been until a new generation of younger, rising poets have turned their own process of becoming into a not insignificant part of their poem's creation, that I try to take into account not only poetic achievement but also the conditions of the poet who achieved it."[48] But in the real world,

Rilke does not follow his own advice. He allows himself to be completely let down by the actual meeting with Franz Werfel, which is even more pitiful in light of the remarks in "On the Young Poet." Already in this indulgent text, Rilke has to force himself to even notice the poet behind the poem. Rilke, who could not open his arms to Werfel, wanted to think of poets—as we know from the letters—as elusive and ungraspable. "Thus the great poets of past and present have always remained absolutely ungraspable for me, each one replaced by the tower and the bell of his heart."[49]

Shortly after Rilke's encounter with Werfel, Alma Mahler-Gropius fell in love with the art of Franz Werfel. Like Rilke, she found the man Werfel (whom she later married nonetheless) less attractive than his art. Rilke lost himself in Werfel's artistic achievement but found the actual man unbearable. Rilke's aversion toward the Jewish body, which he views as a negative contrast to the artistic achievement and which thereby tears apart the unity of an artist's life and work, body and spirit, remains constant in Rilke's life. In an otherwise appreciative and otherwise affectionate remark about his penultimate typist, a Fräulein Wertheimer, Rilke writes "(I can't really say she is my third hand, since she is too small and Jewish to become truly attached to me)."[50]

With the term "Jew boy" Rilke insists on Werfel's individuality, his empirical appearance, his body. Rilke's aversion and Marie von Thurn und Taxis's "revulsion" are not based on a figure transformed into a metaphor of the "mobility and changeability of one's inner center" that resists a collective name; they are rather reactions borne by the racism of Rilke's time toward a living person (who, as a poet, actually should have stayed "ungraspable"). The philo-Semitic thoughts in *The Solution to the Jewish Question* are no direct contradiction to Rilke's anti-Semitic outburst after meeting Werfel. In both cases, the Jew becomes the figure for mobility as such, which for Rilke is never inherently positive, but can turn out either positive or negative.

The term "Jew boy" plunges to the bottom of Rilke's work with the unbearable weight of that particularly German brand of anti-Semitism that led to the persecutions and annihilation of the Jews under Hitler's regime: It is a leaden word that drags part of Rilke's oeuvre along with it into an abyss. Precisely because it is not Rilke's invention, but rather Sidonie Nádherný von Borutin's, it indicates a particular moral weakness. For Rilke here adopts a bigoted and hateful cliché from a friend, without living up to his own highest mission of creating one's own language. And yet, as an anti-Semitic expression, "Jew boy" as a description of Werfel is not at all incompatible with Rilke's utopian political conception, where a "collective name that had been sufficient for thousands will soon be too narrow for just ten people, and one is forced to consider each person on his own."[51] In contrast to contemporary theories of singularity and difference, Rilke does not believe that the perception of an individual *as* individual will inevitably result in a positive evaluation of this person.

The persecution and near-annihilation of European Jews by the Germans, the Holocaust, makes it all but impossible today to hear the term "Jew boy," when spoken in German, as a term for an individual. And even if "Jew boy" in Rilke's work would not open up possibilities of expanding the world, possibilities that no longer exist, the term would still mark the limits of Rilke's world. Since his remarks about Judaism and the Jews are dependent on the distinction between the mobility that comes from within and that which is imposed by outside circumstances and used opportunistically, we cannot speak here of judgment or exoneration. Instead, perhaps we can understand the term "Jew boy" the same way that Rilke saw his own work: not as something we already understand, something our understanding and judgment condemns as dangerous, but rather as an obligation, mission, and task.

The fact that Rilke's correspondence with Princess Marie von Thurn und Taxis, with its sobering insight into Rilke's anti-Semitism and the terrible term "Jew boy," was published at all is the achievement of Franz Werfel. As early as 1929, Werfel recommended to Princess Maria von Thurn und Taxis, after reading the entire correspondence with Rilke, that it be published *in full*. He made this recommendation with the following incisive and surely somewhat ironic words:

> There is hardly a page where one is not stunned by the brilliance of Rilke's perception, of his insight, or his essence, and always again these absolutely unique comparisons, the terrifyingly gorgeous insights by your friend whom you so rightly call a "magician." These are not even letters but poems that have simply been subjected to a little less pressure, since otherwise they also would have turned into crystal. I feel that these 700 pages are not an accidental collection of letters but rather constitute an unconscious work by Rilke [. . .]
>
> I place an admiring kiss on your hand, and remain yours. Franz Werfel.[52]

k

for Kafka and King Lear

Rilke spent the winter of 1911–1912 in Duino Castle, a somewhat stark and somber residence owned by the Thurn und Taxis family that was usually locked up during the off-season but had been kept open for the poet. In January 1912, in the middle of solitary weeks filled with letter-writing and leafing through dusty volumes pulled off the shelves of the unheated library, Rilke heard a disembodied voice on the steep stairs leading down the cliffs to the foaming waters of the Mediterranean. In a letter written a few days later, he recalled this "dictation . . . so tumultuously recited to [him] here on Pathmos," and how he had written it with "both hands, to the right and to the left, in order to capture the entire inspiration."[1] The first stanzas of *Duino Elegies*, received as if against the poet's will in a state of acute receptivity, were complete. It would take more than ten years for Rilke to finish the "dictation" that begins with "Who, if I cried out, would hear me among the angels'/hierarchies?" in "The First Elegy."[2] The myth of this original moment of inspiration is completed by a second, similarly legendary scene in a small stone building in Muzot near the Swiss city Sierre, where Rilke lived from 1921 to his death in 1926. If something had been "tumultuously recited" to Rilke at the beginning of *Duino Elegies*, at its conclusion he encounters in a "nameless tempest a hurricane of the mind (just as once in Duino)"[3] and says, "I did not know that it was possible for *such* a tempest to come over the heart and mind."[4] Rilke's many attestations in his letters about the great breakthrough in 1922 are shot through with metaphors of a tempestuous storm that link the completion of the elegies with their beginning: "It was a hurricane just like the one in Duino: everything in me, every fiber and thread in my whole body creaked and bent."[5] Between the elegies' genesis in a Mediterranean storm and their completion in a "hurricane of the mind" and "storm of work"[6] lies a quiet period. Scholars habitually refer to this decade, from 1912 to 1922, as the period of Rilke's traumatic speechlessness during the war years, and of a "waiting in silence."[7] That is a simplification. Between 1911 and 1922 Rilke wrote more than one hundred fifty poems and thousands of letters. But more important for an understanding of Rilke's account of how the greatest poems of the twentieth century were "dictated" to him as if out of thin air is a short prose text written in 1919. This small piece serves as a key to understanding the two storms at the beginning and end of the elegies. From the lull between these storms, Rilke explains that his poetry is nothing but the decoding of the traces of a text written *on his body*.

The text is called "Primal Sound" ("Urgeräusch") and first appeared in 1919 in Rilke's publisher's journal, *Das Inselschiff*.[8] It is the childhood memory of an experiment in physics class, in which the students piece together a tube of cardboard and wax paper, a bristle, and candle wax to create a primitive gramophone designed to receive and transmit the human voice. Rilke describes the building of the gramophone and the attempts to record and play back the pupils' young voices, which one could "easily imagine," in breathless, rushed sentences, as if he were literally transcribing the sounds of the voices of his old fellow students rather that recalling a memory from his school days.[9] "The effect was profound every time."[10] The students stood "facing a rather new, still infinitely fragile piece of reality, from which there spoke to us children something long since contemplated and yet brand-new and in need of help."[11] The uncanny encounter with one's own voice and the recently invented technology made a lasting impression.

But there is a memory with a more profound effect: It was not the recording of his voice but the "traces inscribed on the cylinder" that Rilke found "much more unsettling."[12] Years after finishing school he received a human skull for some anatomical investigations. As if by chance one evening he remarked in the flickering candlelight that the seam of the skull, which marks the suture at which the skull grew together over the fontanelle during infancy, reminded him of something: of "that unforget-table trace that was once inscribed on a wax cylinder by the tip of a bristle!"[13]

Rilke does not put his flash of recognition of a similarity between the traces of a voice and the seams in the skull into action; he does not place a needle on the seam of the skull. In such an experiment the skull "would have to produce a sound, a series of sounds, music . . ." This music would be superhuman, unknown and undecipherable to a human being, but nevertheless come directly from him. "Disbelief, shyness, fear, awe . . . keep me from suggesting a name for the primal sound that would have come into the world . . ."[14] This is the birth of poetry out of technology, a belief in the spirit life (Rilke attended numerous séances), and necro-philia. The "series of sounds" to which Rilke does not want to give a name is based on the ghostly voices that are etched on our skull. This recog-nition becomes the key to understanding poetic creation. Poetry is not new creation, but rather the transcription and copying down, the quite literal "dictation," of a trace written on a person.

This poetic "primal sound" uncovers the hidden meaning of a person, since it is read off his body. Rilke was terribly proud of his hypothesis of the "primal sound" and hoped that it could be proven scientifically.[15] But his claim is more than a thought experiment. Rilke gives as a source a "unique rhythm of his imagination" and "a stubborn perseverance" for his obsessive thinking about this experiment, which "again and again suggests itself" to him, he is presenting his own creativity and his own text, "Primal Sound," as the repetition of a trace that was already there.[16] Just as if his pen were only rendering visible an imminent trace, the text is the transcription of a thought independent of Rilke's will, which he only confirms by transmitting into language the thesis of the primal sound.

In "Primal Sound," Rilke does away with the belief in genius or divine inspiration and replaces it with a conception of poetry as a workmanlike copying of a bodily trace. The metaphorical language of the poet is for him no longer the flash of insight overcoming the discrepancy between the short human lifespan and the immense and enduring task of artistic creation, which Rilke's great admirer Boris Pasternak once described as the "stenography of the soul."[17] Rather, the language of poetry follows the soft spot that once marked the open border between body and world: the fontanelle, the part of the human skull that does not close off until a few months after birth. Just as the baby's head is exposed, with only a thin layer of skin, to the world, the poet is exposed to the world through his body. He becomes a recording gramophone; his body is needle, cylinder, and cone at once.

This idea of a bodily analogy for poetic inspiration does not come to Rilke out of nowhere. It seems as though he is following other writers with similar thoughts. In 1916, Franz Kafka had read "In the Penal Colony" in Munich, a story in which the wording of a death sentence is inscribed on the body of a condemned man with hundreds upon hundreds of needles, until he expires (in the story, the machine breaks down when its designer ultimately tests its mechanism on himself).[18] Rilke was probably present at the reading, but there is no doubt that he heard about it in great and enthusiastic detail from his friend Max Pulver, on whom Kafka made a strong impression. Rilke was a great admirer of Kafka: "I have never read a line by this author which did not speak to me or astound me in the most unique way . . . I am, I may confirm, not his worst reader."[19] His "Primal Sound" was written in August 1919, when Kafka's "In the Penal Colony" was already available in book form. And as early as 1911 the French poet Henri Barzun had published a manifesto on "simultaneanism" as the basis for a new, and modern, poetry. In it Barzun explains the simultaneous recoding and transmission of multiple voices as the model of a new, superpersonal lyric poetry. Paul Valéry, Rilke's great idol in the twenties whose poetry he sought to emulate in his French verses, was long fascinated by phrenology—the measuring of the skull. The thinkable connection between radio, poetry, and body, between the recording technology and a human-inhuman voice, was almost palpable in the air: In addition to these poets, others such as Filippo Marinetti, Walter Ruttmann, Bertolt Brecht, and Ezra Pound propagated the possibilities of an art made by mixing voices and sounds, man and technology.

The conception of poetic creation that lies at the base of these practices stands in striking contrast to the idea of artistic creation that Rilke unfolds, famously, in *Letters to a Young Poet* and as a first attempt in the *Malte* novel:

> Ah, but poems amount to so little when you write them too early in your life. You ought to wait and gather sense and sweetness for a whole lifetime, and a long one if possible, and then, at the very end, you might perhaps be able to write ten good lines. For poems are not, as people think, simply emotions (one has emotions early

enough)—they are experiences. [. . .] You must be able to forget them [. . .] Only when they have changed into our very blood, into glance and gesture, and are nameless, no longer to be distinguished from ourselves—only then can it happen that in some very rare hour the first word of a poem arises from within their midst and takes off on its own.[20]

You notice right away, even in Rilke's prose, that no word "arises" from what was in Rilke's blood. Instead it starts only once he is writing. A later passage in the *Malte* novel unmasks this idea of artistic creation as outdated and dishonest, and announces a harder poetics, which will be the "time of that other interpretation":

But the day will come when my hand will be distant, and if I tell it to write, it will write words that are not mine. [. . .] In spite of all my fear, I am still like someone standing in the presence of something great, and I remember that I often used to feel this happening inside me when I was about to write. But this time, I will be written.[21]

Rilke is not writing about words that are retrieved from long-forgotten experiences. The poet becomes passive, receptive, and abandons himself. These are words that not he but his body and "his hand" write. "When I was about to write": that was the time of his poems rooted in experience, the time of waiting for the word that emerged "in some very rare hour," at the center of a verse. Now, after shedding these youthful, romantic notions, he works differently, more truthfully, authentically: the poet *will be written*. On October 21, 1913, Rilke visited a fortune-teller, who recognized a "fluid" in him, thanks to which he—the poet as word processor—"can write automatically, at any time, without needing anyone."[22]

In her memoirs, Princess Marie von Thurn und Taxis-Hohenlohe, Rilke's mentor and confidante, and the generous owner of the Duino Castle, explains the stormy "inspiration" of Rilke's elegies as follows:

Outside a bora [strong wind] was blowing, but the sun was shining, the sea was a brilliant blue [. . .] Rilke was climbing down to the bastions [. . .] The rock face there drops off steeply, easily 200 feet straight to the sea. Rilke was pacing up and down, deep in his thoughts, occupied with the reply to a letter. Then, all at once, in the middle of his musings, he stopped short, for it was as though a voice had called to him out of the wailings of the storm:

"Who, if I cried out, would hear me among the angels' hierarchies?"

He stood still and listened. "What is that?" he whispered softly . . . "what is coming?"

He [. . .] wrote down these words, and a few more verses that formed themselves without his help.

Who was it? [. . .] He knew it now: it was God.[23]

The princess was a wealthy person, and according to Rilke, who knew how to recognize people who helped him, the proper "owner" of the elegies. Indeed, the Duino elegies are not simply dedicated to the princess but are inscribed, by Rilke, as "her property," as if to underline that this inspired work just passed through his mind and heart and soul and pen but that he never really owned it. But Princess Marie did not really understand her beloved poet. Rilke knew that there was no "God" in his inspiration. The "primal sound that would have come into the world" in his poetry is something "that is born naturally of itself."[24] It is not a translation of the divine into the human, but rather a dictation of what exists on its own, a transcript of bodily sensation taken down in a storm.

A final passage from one of Rilke's letters helps us understand the "primal sound" as an explanation of the stormy "dictation" of the elegies. A few days before he received, on the storm-whipped stone steps a few feet above the gushing, cold sea and below the castle perched atop a craggy promontory jutting into the blue Mediterranean, the "tumultuous recitation" of the elegies, Rilke was reading "a bit of Shakespeare," as he remarks casually to underplay the bard's influence on him.[25] Rilke knew only a little of the English poet (in 1896 he had seen a performance of *Troilus and Cressida*) and could not get proper footing in the text, since Shakespeare was "too much of a mountain, too steep, too amorphous" for him.[26] We do not know what Shakespeare text Rilke read at Duino. I suspect, however, that he was reading *King Lear*, in particular the third act, where the king faces off against the elements in a storm on the scraggy heath. Duino Castle stands on a formidable rocky projection. On the heath, in *King Lear*, there is no God who speaks to the shaken king or who inspires Shakespeare, as the princess later claims of Rilke. There is nothing there but a terrible storm, which roars all around a completely exposed body, on which the pouring rain makes an inscription. The raging elements are the external image of the storm that wreaks havoc in Lear's soul, and the scraggy heath is the objectification of the alienation and exile endured by many characters in the play. On the heath Lear, as a naked, exposed, mortal body—as "the thing itself"—and no longer as the bearer of political or worldly power, wrestles with language.[27] Without his crown, even the king is nothing more than "the thing itself:/unaccommodated man is no more but such a poor, bare,/forked animal." When King Lear faces the elements, as Rilke would a few days later on the steep stairs, the storm rages in and around his body, on and through whose nakedness Shakespeare writes down in his language the truth of the universe. *In* Lear's body the storm is fiercer than the one around it, and it is only *in* this figure that Shakespeare takes form, that a language takes form that in spite of and because of the storm is able to surpass the simple observation that when we go out on a limb, we are nothing more than "the thing itself:/unaccommodated man": this dictation of existence, so mountainous, so steep, so amorphous, so godless.

"Primal Sound" has been read as a rejection of romanticism: as Rilke's irrevocable step into the media-dominated modern age.[28] But for Rilke our skull's seam is not the break between soul and body, spirit and matter, poetry and reality, erotic and stochastic. Shakespeare's *King Lear* is a tragedy, since the end of the kingdom does not coincide with the death of the king: The king, as Ernst Kantorowicz has shown in his important study, always has two bodies—a political and a creaturely.[29] With the "primal sound," Rilke points out that the modern poet experiences the same thing: He does not suffer from the separation of spirit and body, but rather faces the task of aligning his two bodies with one another. The body of Rilke the poet, the one we can approach biographically, corresponds to the political body of King Lear, which is separated from his natural body and stripped from him on the heath. The seam of the skull marks Rilke's point of contact with his second body, which cannot be grasped, only experienced.

Existence can be copied down only if both of these bodies speak. When the poet writes love poems, he touches the seam in the skull between experience and language, so that the resulting sounds say more than that we are bodies. K stands for Kafka, King Lear, and Kantorowicz, but also for: "When were these kisses ever words?/These words were kisses once."[30]

1

for Larean

In a letter to his Polish translator Witold Hulewicz, Rilke remarks on a historical change in the relationship between man and his surroundings: "What has been lived, what has been experienced, the *things that know us* are vanishing and have no way of being replaced. *We are perhaps the last ones who will have known such things.* The responsibility rests with us, to preserve the memory not only of *them* (that would be inadequate and irresponsible), but of their humane and larean value. ('Larean' in the sense of household deities)."[1]

With the epochal discovery that with his generation, the first to consider itself truly "modern," there has come into the world a new responsibility to remember and preserve the "humane and larean value" of things, Rilke puts his finger on a fear that was moving through Europe at the time. The loss of "things that know us" constituted a crisis for European self-understanding, since such a loss would lead to the disappearance of the singularity of individuals. At least it would seem this way from the melancholy choir of European thinkers, who all, though from otherwise widely divergent perspectives, lamented the fate of things at around the same time that Rilke wrote the letter quoted above (November 13, 1925). Sigmund Freud, Walter Benjamin, Martin Heidegger, and, a bit later, André Breton and then Jacques Lacan dedicated their own analyses to the status of the thing as a sign of a grave transformation in modern existence. (One exception is Ludwig Wittgenstein, whose thoughts on this topic are generally free of melancholy.)[2] All of these thinkers ponder the changing essence of objects in daily life (brought about by the circulation of mass-produced objects) to pose anew fundamental questions about perception, reality, and humanity. "Larean" is a rare word, referring to the house deities that, in Roman times, lent protection to the members of a household. In a lexicon from Rilke's time one finds the following definition (most modern dictionaries no longer carry an entry for the word): "Lares, described as the sons of the old-Roman goddess Lara (or Larunda) and Mercury, are Roman Gods of a lower order, but of great meaning who provided protection for families, houses, streets, rural and urban quarters, etc."[3]

For Rilke, "larean" means a nontransportable and irreplaceable uniqueness, which is threatened with extinction. An equivalent expression would be "auratic," but such a substitution entails the risk of losing the singularity that Rilke is concerned with. For he positions the (already in his days) extremely rare word "larean" in his letter just as people once used to place the statue of a minor deity at a particular spot in a house (for instance on a mantel or near the entrance) to create an irreducible, nontransportable atmosphere. With this word Rilke establishes a specific context that cannot simply be replaced by a different set of references. In other words, Rilke's reflections on the disappearing singularity of things cannot be subsumed under other discourses of the time initiated by thinkers such as Benjamin, Heidegger, Freud, Wittgenstein, Breton, and Lacan. It should be noted, however, that Rilke's remark on the changing essence of things was explicitly taken up by Heidegger, who, in contrast to my reading here, considered Rilke's thoughts to be nostalgic and culturally pessimistic.

But Rilke's remark about the new responsibility that has entered the world is not just a nostalgic sigh. On the contrary, Rilke realizes that the disappearance of things with "larean value," which bound generations of our ancestors to their homes, also sets us free. This liberation from the weight of tradition signals for Rilke an opportunity to change the world. Rilke hopes that the historical situation will allow radical changes. He celebrates "the invisible vibration and excitement of our nature, which introduces new frequencies into the grand vibration of the universe. Since the different materials in the universe are merely different orders of vibration, so in this way we prepare not only intensities of a spiritual sort, but who knows, new bodies, metals, nebulae and constellations [. . .] And this activity is being uniquely supported and forced by the increasingly rapid disappearance of so many visible things which will not be replaced."[4]

The historical change of a rapidly modernizing world results in not only the task of remembering and honoring things with a "larean value" but also an opportunity, "uniquely supported" by the disappearance of those things, to prepare "new bodies"—that is, to change the world.

Rilke's attitude toward things with "larean value" is ambivalent. Such objects stand in direct relation with humanity, since we humans create, use, grasp, and endow them with meaning. A poet does this by naming things. He positions things in the middle of his reflections "until, born by us/they move into the center of tension."[5] Things become truer, according to Rilke, when they come into existence a second time, invisibly, in our consciousness. But Rilke's affect in these lines is hard to determine. The figure of the angel, who can hold the vanishing things on a higher level and therefore more permanently, remains "terrible" for us, since we "still remain attached to the visible."[6] And the pathos of the generation that Rilke calls "the last ones who will have known such things" seems, as Heidegger's commentary on Rilke suggests, to correspond to the Spenglerian cultural pessimism of a fear of the decline of the West.

But ultimately the loss of these things opens for Rilke new possibilities. The change that arrives when mass-produced consumer goods replace handmade, unique objects with a value beyond their material components prepares new "intensities," whose extent and effect remain immeasurable. When Rilke insists on the "larean value" of things, he only conditionally aligns himself with the incipiently neurotic, if not slightly hysterical, discourse of a generation of European men who feared that their traditional, privileged way of life was being swept away in a deluge of factory goods. Unlike many of his contemporaries, Rilke regarded the irreversible loss of the uniqueness of things not necessarily as a sign of the looming loss of the uniqueness of individual people, but rather as a possibility to free ourselves of our dependencies on the visible world. It is an occasion to see that our possibilities—precisely what is invisible to us—are as valuable as our realities, that is, as what is visible in the world. Rilke expresses these possibilities, always with startling, unsentimental directness, as a way of thinking that does not separate death from life.

Behind the gentle sound of the word "larean" lurk Rilke's radical meditations on death, as well as the complex and polyphonic philosophical, artistic, and political discourse about the status of the object as a symptom of a loss and a downfall. Things with a "larean value" assure us that we are at home in the world. If these things vanish from our lives, the world becomes unworldly, inhospitable, uncanny. We no longer know what things we can hold on to. But here Rilke executes one of the conceptual "reversals" that characterize many of his poems, where he flips the concrete and the abstract, the detail and its context to achieve a new perspective on things. As soon as the things have disappeared, we are held in place only by the invisible, and thus all the *more* firmly. Rilke writes this in the same important letter in which he laments the disappearance of the "larean" things that grounded our lives in our belief in the durability of human creation: "this life suspended over an abyss . . . is ultimately affirmed" if "a higher level of reality" becomes recognized "in the invisible." Thinkers such as Heidegger diagnosed this as a crisis. But for Rilke it offers the unique opportunity to think of ourselves on a "higher level of reality" than that which can be seen and touched.

Rilke opens the discourse about the fate of objects in the modern world when he characterizes the ever-faster disappearance of man-made things with "larean value" as an instance of a grave historical change capable of bringing out something unknown from *within* us. This unknown, which cannot be linked to any visible thing, is the invisible cause of "the vibration and excitement" of our nature, which distinguishes our being from that of mere objects.

When Rilke, as a poet who wrote thing-poems (descriptions of such things as balls, carousels, fountains), is one of the last to "have known such things," that is also a liberation. For Rilke's fetish for things originated with the deep disappointments of his childhood and in particular his traumatic experiences in the Austrian military academy where he received a good part of his schooling:

> When I was a child [. . .] and people were still strange to me, I was drawn to things, and they enveloped me with great pleasure, a pleasure in being which was always uniformly gentle and strong, and which never contained any hesitation or doubt. In military academy, after long and anxious struggles, I gave up on the Catholic piety of my childhood, extricated myself from it, in order to be even more alone, even more devoid of comfort. But things, in their patient, waiting permanence, later provided me with an even greater and

more pious love, a faith without fear or limit. Life is also part of this faith. O, how I believe in it, in this life. Not the life that is made out of time, but the other life, the life of small things, the life of animals and open country.[7]

It is our responsibility to recognize the "humane" value of things in their ability to release us. The young Rilke extracted the "pleasure in being" just from his interactions with inanimate things. In his complicated relationship and conflict with his revered mentor Auguste Rodin he sublimated his youthful traumas and disappointments into a poetics of self-sufficient things that have their own life, as alive as our lives but apart from them since they are subjected differently to time. We, unfamiliar as we are with the word "larean" and what it meant for generations of Rilke's forebears, inherit the responsibility to recognize life as a totality, as the life made up of time and "the other life, the life of small things, the life of animals and open country." To stop dividing up life.

When with Rilke's generation all those who "will have known such things" died out, a responsibility was transferred to them even before it came to us, a responsibility that weighed heavily. These people felt that their "pleasure in being" depended on things, which were irretrievably "vanishing." With the collapse of received structures arose the possibility of experiencing the "pleasure in being" differently and independent of such structures—and of the things that held them together.

Instead of leading to melancholy, the disappearance of things and the subsequent extinction of thing fetishists enable us to free ourselves of their traumatic associations. We become free to think and live with others, no longer thinking only of things—to believe, in a phrase both with and against Rilke, in a "life made out of time."

for Mussolini

In a letter to Duchessa Aurelia (Lella) Gallarati-Scotti in 1926, Rilke expressed his admiration for "Mister Mussolini." In subsequent correspondence Rilke attempts to justify this political gesture, which he quickly recognizes as a mistake, with an uncharacteristically naïve account of that process by which his own words come into the world. When the recipient of Rilke's letter, an Italian aristocrat, criticizes his stance on Mussolini, the poet appears surprised by the effect of his words, which had taken on an unexpected "firmness" when he set them on paper. Rilke's failure to anticipate this reaction by his close Italian friend, who not only takes his words seriously but actually criticizes them, stands in sharp contrast to his often-expressed and fervent hope that his linguistic creations would have a lasting meaning.

Rilke's expression of surprise at the unexpected "firmness" and impact of his own words is, first and foremost, an evasion. Yet when Rilke tries to escape from what he willfully regards as Gallarati-Scotti's misreading of the impact of his writings he arrives at a quite different misunderstanding. For in his letter he had expressed only admiration for Mussolini's rhetorical abilities and the "beauty" of his language, without taking into consideration the effects of the fascist language and, as Gallarati-Scotti insists, the resulting "terrible violence [. . .] which carries with it so much hate."[1] For many admirers of Rilke, set in their beliefs about the favorite poet's otherworldly goodness and his role in offering solace from the world, Rilke's explanations are hardly comforting. But the position he takes on Mussolini, as unpalatable as it is and as unwelcome as it may be to fans of Rilke, reveals in an exemplary fashion a central paradox in Rilke's work, and in poetry in general. It reveals that a poet's unshakable faith in the power and effect of words is balanced out by a childish naïveté about that same power: that faith in the impact of one's language does not keep one from being surprised by one's language.

> Even in Italy: what an improvement, not only in literature, but also in public life! What a beautiful address delivered by Mister Mussolini to the governor of Rome! During my stay in Paris I learned to admire especially Ungaretti among your great poets. These are the many topics I wish I could have discussed with you . . . And many more . . . But I must force myself to stop. Yours always, my dear countess.
> Rilke.[2]

The strange thing is that Rilke "must *force* [him]self to stop" ("Ich unterbreche mich *mit Gewalt*") from singing the praises of Mussolini, since obviously he is not put off at all by Mussolini's use of actual, physical force. Tearing himself away by *force* from Mussolini's muscular rhetoric, he places the *duce* as an aesthetic phenomenon in the lineage of great Italian poets from Dante to Ungaretti. What do we make of this? A few critics have taken Rilke to task harshly, among them some of those leftist critics who regarded Rilke, who was not an explicitly political poet, as a forerunner of fascist ideologies who turned a blind eye to politics in favor of unicorns and angels. Those critics read Rilke's cult of interiority (including the "*Weltinnenraum*" discussed in the chapter "E for Entrails") as an irresponsible turning away from reality and its problems. Other critics have searched Rilke's biography to unearth the first seed of this political position. A third group has rendered the worst possible verdict for a poet, in the context of postwar German intellectual life: that he is at once apolitical and protofascist.

Rilke, politically correct critics maintain, was mired in the "problems that lead people to literally rip apart their fellow man."[3] After examining his early diaries, in which Rilke adopts a Nietzschean tone to sharply criticize the press, the mediocrity of public taste, the watering-down of all norms and values through mass culture, some critics concluded: Rilke was "protofascist."[4] His *Five Songs*, which he composed in Munich in August 1914 to celebrate the outbreak of World War I, valorizes self-sacrifice for a greater movement, which (some critics assert) "thirty years later would lead so many into National Socialism."[5] As a final piece of evidence, these critics point out, somewhat off-key, that nowhere in Rilke's letters do we find "the slightest indication that would allow the suggestion that Rilke would have disapproved of the persecution of the Jews by a fascist regime."[6] This is not criticism, but rather the impossible demand that even before the Shoah, writers should have imagined its possibility, identified what remains difficult to imagine to this day, and rejected this hypothetical years before it became reality.

Another group of critics has tried to minimize the import of Rilke's momentary enthusiasm for Mussolini by all but burying Rilke's confession about Mussolini in a diligently edited, seven-hundred-fifty-page scholarly anthology of the poet's letters on politics. Flanked by two hundred twenty-five other letters, almost two hundred pages of studious commentary, a detailed report on the composition of the text, and a carefully judicious afterword, the relatively brief confessions about Mussolini (from the letter cited above) are softened and relativized in the diligently prepared scholarly edition that few individuals outside of the academy are ever at risk of reading. The "Milan Letters" with the statements about Mussolini, the editors dispassionately state, are "in no way the high point of Rilke's articulation."[7] The imposing volume is meant to attest to Rilke's long-lasting and nuanced interest in politics but downplay his enthusiasm for Mussolini (which he shared with Churchill, Ungaretti, Marinetti, and until 1925 even Benedetto Croce) as the short-lived episode of a man deep in the throes of a terminal illness. The editors present a seven-hundred-fifty-page brief in Rilke's defense, including his full correspondence with "predominantly democratic or even radical" leftist addressees, with the intention of balancing out the "remarks on Mussolini, which occupy only a short period."[8] Rilke's leftist sympathies allowed a "fair presentation" of the pro-Mussolini letters. Eventually these letters are excused by Rilke's "own deprivation," and the "alienation due to illness" in his final years, as "an unforeseeable intellectual danger at the end of his life."[9]

Yet Rilke's enthusiasm for Mussolini is canceled out neither by his support of the imprisoned dissident Ernst Toller nor by his sympathies for Rathenau, Landauer, Luxemburg, and Liebknecht, all of whom were assassinated for their radical (leftist) politics. Such efforts to exculpate Rilke are as dubious as the self-righteous verdict of Rilke as a "proto-fascist" poet issued by critics who sit with the infallible benefit of historical hindsight, in complete knowledge of what kinds of political involvement, in 1926, should be criticized in what way. But both the full-fledged condemnation of Rilke as protofascist and the apologists' readings are inadequate. Great creative achievements do not insulate an artist from conservatism or great mistakes. But does the support of a repressive politics constitute an "unforeseeable intellectual danger" for an artist? All of Rilke's critics as well as his defenders share the belief that art is not compatible with repressive politics. But even momentary enthusiasm for repressive politics, as we see in Rilke's case, does not necessarily compromise artistic achievement.

Rilke did not glorify freedom as an abstract greatness to be defended at any price. His passionate support of rhyme in a correspondence with a young poet is an example of this; there he considers rhyme not a hide-bound, conservative straitjacketing of poetic license and freedom, but rather a "very great God, the God of the oldest and most secret patterns and structures."[10] Rhyme limits the freedom of the poet, yet just this limitation gives rise to more exact expression.[11] Unlike some of his critics and apologists, Rilke never reflexively believed in freedom in art. For freedom is never an end in itself, but only the opening of as-yet-unknown and thereby truly "free" possibilities. Since he fosters such skepticism toward freedom, Rilke manifests an astonishing tolerance for dictatorship:

> This is my problem with what is called 'freedom': that it can only bring people as far as what they understand, no farther [. . .] Is this not what dictators, the true dictators, understood when they made use of benevolent and steady force [. . .] In any case, the Italy of 1926 has admirably demonstrated a life ready to take charge and a renewed goodwill, while the surrounding countries foster a level of confusion that undermines and destroys this life. This is a fact to which I would not hesitate to sacrifice a few of my thoughts and feelings, so great and impatient is my wish for order. Only this vital sense of overall agreement, which has galvanized your country's forces for some time now, could save us from our indecision and pointlessly arbitrary inclinations; even if the foundation of this

enthusiasm is bold and provisional: what does it matter if it makes the hearts beat faster and the spirit rise up![12]

In light of Rilke's opinion, it means quite a bit that "the foundation of this enthusiasm" of a new Italy may be a bit "bold," for this boldness also ushers in the violence that the fascists introduce into daily life. From his house in Muzot, near the Swiss city of Sierre, where he had been living in relative isolation from the world since 1921, Rilke observes Mussolini and his "élan," or enthusiasm, as an aesthetic phenomenon and an abstract instance of order as such: The movement of the masses seemed to him merely ornamental. But he warns of limiting the monstrous potential of "freedom" by formulating it as a right or an article (in the sense of legally guaranteed liberties) that can be issued and withdrawn as necessary. For Rilke, what is decisive about freedom is that it leads us only to the edge of our understanding, where we then do *not* automatically know what we are capable of or what we want. His support for dictatorship is consistent in this context, since the dictator, like the poet, opens to us what we had not yet known nor understood. Nevertheless Rilke here mixes up wholly incompatible categories, if one can formulate it that way: Politics means taking the long road, not reordering social and political relations in dictatorial bursts.

As readers of poetry, it is difficult to acknowledge that the poet is more complex than his writings, especially since we are interested in his political views only because of the complexity, beauty, and depth of these writings. Both critique and defense of Rilke remain bound by the same logic. They do not explain what made Mussolini so attractive in 1926 to so many writers, both intellectuals and artists (who are not the same thing). To put it differently: The hand-wringing about Rilke's "entanglement" in the political questions of his time assumes a complete understanding of what fascism has been and what it is. But it is far from clear that we have completely understood fascism even today, and why fascism appealed to seemingly progressive minds in the 1920s. Instead of pursuing this question, most of the participants in this principally inner-German debate about Rilke's politics (with German scholars debating questions of German guilt) rely on the idea, expressed in 1944 by Benedetto Croce, that Mussolini's fascist regime was a "parenthesis," or an exception in the otherwise continuous Italian history; that it was not supported by most Italians; and that it could in no way be reconciled to art.[13] Given this definition of fascism as the interruption, bracketing, and opposite of culture, Rilke's enthusiasm for Mussolini is offensive. How can this poet, the epitome of European "culture," succumb to fascism? But the question of what prompted Rilke to make his statement about Mussolini ultimately avoids the possibly weightier question of what fascism actually is. Fascism in Italy, contrary to Croce's views, had a culture and was a culture—which is why numerous intellectuals and artists attached themselves to it for a time. It was a culture in the sense of a social movement, the expression and the enactment of individual wishes and desires in and through a collective.

Rilke's critics on the left as well as his defenders see fascism as an interruption of history in the form of a parenthetical anti-culture. In the German context, critics implicitly place culture and fascism as antitheses of each other to allow for the view that even though culture was over-powered by fascism, it had been preserved in some surreptitious, clandestine, but true, authentically German way. In this spirit Anton Kippenberg emphasized, at the opening of an exhibit featuring Rilke manuscripts, first editions, and the like in 1947, that Rilke, as a German poet, embodied the humanistic tradition that had survived through and in spite of Europe's catastrophe.

But we are not concerned here with the tenability of Croce's thesis that Italian fascism was a "parenthesis" that had nothing to do with culture. What matters is that all commentators interpret Rilke's support of Mussolini in a way that safeguards a particular understanding of both politics and culture, and indeed saves culture from being contaminated with totalitarian ideas. The possibility of a fascist culture is ruled out in order to save the concept of culture—for or against Rilke—and to dismiss fascism as something else entirely. In this way Rilke's enthusiasm for Mussolini becomes a scandalous misstep, an "unforeseeable intellectual danger," or proof that he was a "protofascist" at heart. This strategy allows the critics to avoid thinking about how the word "Mussolini" must be interpreted in Rilke's work as the opaque signature of a cultural movement, to which Rilke, even Rilke, attached himself for a time.

The debate about Rilke's enthusiasm for "Mussolini" rests on an understanding of Rilke's text that limits itself to the truth value of the work and the intentions of the author, without understanding the effects and structure of the text. The "riddle" of fascism, as Jacques Derrida put it in another context, consists of the question of how the "reactive degeneration [of Fascism] could exploit the same language, the same words, the same utterances, the same rallying cries as the active forces to which it stands opposed."[14] In Rilke's case that means: How can the wish for order, the praise of rhyme, the desire for limits, the reverence for high rhetoric be reconciled with the affirmation of the violent destruction of all order? How can Rilke, as an educated European with a fine-tuned linguistic sensibility, be taken in by Mussolini's language, without recognizing the effects this language has in the world? How can a poet so vastly underestimate the effect of his own words in a letter to a friend, while assessing the influence of Mussolini's words? Can a poet actually question the value of freedom because it does not automatically lead us beyond the limits of our own understanding? Rilke wants his language to speak in this space beyond freedom. But how can a poet's language be at once in the service of two opposing agendas: the protofascist program of the culturally conservative admirer of Mussolini and the progressive program of cosmopolitan, pan-European consciousness? Here is another reason why Mussolini is and remains a question: Fascism managed a great surge of modernization in the twentieth century, but this surge is bound to the movement's barbarity. To separate the developments from the inhumanity of fascism is possible only when the nature of fascism—and Rilke's attitude toward it—remains an open question.

Rilke cannot be saved. And even if that were possible, such a rescue mission would be highly suspect, after fascism's messianic promises to rescue the masses—from the decline of culture, from bolshevism, from the Jews, from capital.

The commentaries on Rilke's Mussolini letter make a strict distinction between letters and poetry, political engagement and lyrical language. This separation considers language an expression of definitions that already exist and are already understood. Yet, in Rilke's work, language is a potential with no previous conventions that can be enlisted for a political position. "Mussolini" is taken by the Rilke critics—with the postwar generation's self-satisfaction of historical hindsight—as an *answer* and not as a question: as if we knew with certainty how to think about fascism, and as if we actually understood the effects of its language on the world.

Rilke's letter to Gallarati-Scotti did not remain without a response. The countess rejected Rilke's interpretation of the state of affairs: "You will not hold it against me that I cannot manage to see in [Mussolini] the dictator you desire for modern humanity! . . . [Your] words [gave] me the impression of a reality and a level of refinement which, I regret to say, is precisely what we don't have."[15]

Rilke's response to the countess's disagreement attests to his willingness to learn, as well as to an understanding, surprising in light of the rest of his work, of the effects of his own language. In Rilke's Mussolini letters the political ignorance of the poet coincides with a rare and decisive expression of doubt as to the efficacy of his own words:

> You have given my dilettantish letter too much credit. Your kind reception has caused my thoughts to mature, and now they return to me more valid; corrected by your concern they have achieved something like a preliminary firmness, which was meant more as a wish than a comment on this foolhardy and opaque reality whose dangers you feel every day. Yes, this merciless nationalistic excess is begging for something to parry it, but it is precisely carried out with such force in order to preempt any such attempt. The question of national sentiment is one of the most delicate questions there is.[16]

Anyone who has ever held in his hands one of Rilke's breathtakingly gorgeous manuscripts or a page from his letters, always painstakingly rewritten if so much as an ink stain or a crossed-out word threatened their elegance, knows that not a single word here is an accident. When Rilke calls his statements about Mussolini provisional, unreflected, "dilettantish," and only partly true, this is a poor attempt at an excuse. Behind such a statement lies a notion of language that runs through Rilke's whole body of work and connects to his skeptical attitude toward freedom.

As a poet, Rilke believes on the one hand in the potential of language to lead us to the limits of and possibly even beyond what we understand. On the other hand he maintains an astonishing naïveté, so characteristic of poets, when it comes to the effects of language in the world. Only on account of this naïveté can Rilke talk about words this way, as if every word contained the potential to open up an unknown world. It is the belief in this power of words that makes poetry possible. But it depends on the poet's astonishing naïveté about the effect of his words on the status quo, for if he knows the effects of his statements in advance, his words will not open something new. A less naïve person uses language not to write poetry, but puts it exclusively in the service of communication. This is the fundamental paradox at the heart of all poetry. This naïveté is the Achilles' heel in Rilke's statements about politics.

In the same letter Rilke laments as a catastrophic political development the fact that in his native Prague, the "inquisitive and clever nation [the Czechs] had disavowed themselves in such a senseless way that they had lost all pleasure in their own language" and that they "accepted what was cast off from the German way of speaking" simply because it was something new.[17] The cultivation of a strong language, the letter asserts, is a condition of political freedom. But since Rilke considers freedom only as potential, never as a final goal, a strong language must be a language whose effects remain unknown. The effect of Rilke's own language, which takes on an unexpected firmness once his recipient responds to his letter, cannot be completely known in advance. Rilke's explanation of his grave misunderstanding of Mussolini remains an evasion. Behind it rests an understanding of language that gets closer to the question of how to think about fascism. For Rilke's statements about Mussolini directly address the quality of the fascist leader's language as potential.

Rilke's evasion suggests a particular concept of the role of language in political reality. Is it possible to say something without letting your own words develop an unexpected "firmness," through which they take on a life of their own? When the generous Countess Gallarati-Scotti gives "too much credit" to Rilke's words and takes them at face value, then she reads Rilke exactly as he wants to and ought to be read as a poet. It is likewise appropriate and fair that later critics take Rilke to task for the political implications of his writing. The difficulty arises when the paradox at the heart of Rilke's poetry—and at the heart of all poetry—goes unnoticed. It is a dangerous paradox, but it also conceals the only hope of grasping with words something like fascism, whose appeal to millions upon millions, in spite of its horrific record of destruction, still has not been fully understood.

In his reaction to the *duchessa*'s criticism, Rilke demonstrates an ability to learn that is greater than that of his critics or apologists. For they persist in trying to understand what the word "Mussolini" means in the work of a poet. We cannot do any more than follow Rilke's example and continue to treat the question of nationalist sentiment—"one of the most delicate ones"—as an open question, instead of burying it, as if already answered, in polemics or anthologies.

n
for Nature

"Never nowhere without the No" ("*und niemals Nirgends ohne Nicht*"), it says in "The Eighth Elegy," in which Rilke focuses on the difference between human and animal.[1] All of the elegies seek a space where we can be truly ourselves, since we are woefully lost in a universe with strangely elusive, angelic messengers of redemption in whose embrace we would instantly "expire." Animals live in such a "pure space" without concepts, expectations, and projections. Man, on the other hand, recognizes the world around him only when he can conceptualize it with the aid of thought. We, as humans, are aware of the constraint of death and see everything as if in reverse, from this final limit of what we can know. For us there is always only the world, which Rilke understands as the surroundings as they are grasped (and *experienced*, not merely mediated) by our bodies, language, and consciousness. A "never nowhere without the No" would be a utopian, "unseparated" space of pure possibility, extending around us free of concepts, desire, or calculation. Such a space exists according to Rilke only for very young children and for animals, who live in a world without longing and for whom there is no such thing as past and present, only the "pure condition." The world in which we live is for Rilke a product of our self-conception and self-determination, on which we rely to give meaning to everything. What we long for is a moment of respite from this world that is not the stillness of death but unmediated nature as experienced by children and animals.

Philosophers such as Martin Heidegger, Maurice Blanchot, and Giorgio Agamben have interpreted Rilke's "The Eighth Elegy" as a treatise about the ontological difference between human and animal. According to Agamben, "Heidegger returns to this concept and traces a summary genealogy of it. That it arose out of the eighth *Duino Elegy* was, in a certain sense, obvious; but in being adopted as the name of being [. . .] Rilke's term undergoes an essential reversal, which Heidegger seeks to emphasize in every way."[2] Maurice Blanchot, on the other hand, praises Rilke for considering the existence of "never nowhere without the No" for animals and children: "they play for hours and even lose themselves in the game, for this is the space of wandering."[3] But these readings turn Rilke's poem into a philosophical tract (which ultimately fails the strict philosophical standards applied by Heidegger and Agamben in their respective analyses). Rilke's formulation of the animal most likely refers back to Nietzsche. Placing the principle of reflection as the basis of human existence, Rilke's insight into the difference between subject and object is, as another critic notes, "not fundamentally new."[4] For Rilke's formulation of nature can be traced to the Romantic poets, for whom space, after the departure of religion in our disenchanted and enlightened age, can only reemerge *as* space through the application of human consciousness—as, for instance, in the explicitly a-religious and unscientific genre of landscape poetry, where the landscape becomes a phenomenon of secularization par excellence and a meaningful site only with the help of our mediating consciousness. Nature *as such* cannot be grasped by human understanding according to either the Romantic poets or Rilke, since only once nature has been mediated in this way (and thus does not occur "as such") does nature become the basis of our world. The "never nowhere without the No" would be the pure space in which there is neither assent nor negation, neither wish nor rejection. There we would not "stand opposite" our environment, but rather we would be a part of the whole—if our understanding did not depend on such an opposition and on the differentiation of space into (us as perceiving) subjects and (perceived) objects. Yet, Rilke is not concerned with the originality of his thoughts. Instead of that, his poems seek to reveal the nontranscendental basis of subjectivity—the gap between pure or "empty" space and world—as something that has to be created ceaselessly anew.

According to Rilke there occur rare opportunities in life to see the unthought-of space, that "infinite space/we dissolve into" behind the intricate webs of our concepts and thoughts.[5] The figure of the angels in the elegies announces this possibility that the emptiness around us might harbor a meaning. For lovers, this possibility offers itself "as if by accident" in the selfless moments of intimacy that are then immediately obscured and literally blocked by the actual sight and presence of the beloved.

Rilke considers the loss of this openness to be a fundamental human experience, which in the following lines is opposed to the concept of the world: "Lovers, if the beloved were not there/blocking the view, are close to it and marvel . . ./[. . .] But neither can move past/the other, and it changes back to World."[6] Children lose access to this openness in the moment in which—paradoxically, through the disappearance of the beloved parent—they learn to look upon their own condition and thus gain access to the world. They proceed innocently toward the openness but are then forced to see "objects."

"The Eighth Elegy" draws, in addition, on Catholic doctrine, according to which our existence on earth is only a "second home" after the fall. When Rilke locates even the animals in an "ambiguous and drafty home," however, he leaves the Christian schema and disposes of all received religiosity. That "never nowhere without the No" that we cannot access is not a paradise, where everything would be healed. For we no longer know who has brought us into this position of alienation. In the poetic universe of Rilke's elegies there is no longer the sort of God a believer would recognize. Human life plays out not only before the background of nature, but as a process by which we repeatedly separate ourselves from this background, which we cannot recognize until we have seen it before us and in so doing contrasted it to us. Human existence consists of the fact that the grounds or premises of our understanding are not part of this understanding. Nature, it seems, is this unthinkable space of "never nowhere without the No" that we can see only in flashes of revelation, "as if by accident." But the nature Rilke evokes is not just trees, lakes, and birds. It is the nature that is in us and cannot be anywhere else. Nature, for Rilke, is when you *have to go.*

In Rilke's early book from 1902 about a group of painters at the artists' colony in Worpswede, in northwestern Germany, Rilke disabuses himself and his readers of the romantic belief of a well-meaning nature that is interested in us. "Granted, someone could invoke our kinship with nature, from which we are descended, as the final fruits of a vast and growing family tree."[7] This naïve and despairing belief that nature has something in common with us, only because "you can cultivate a field, clear a forest, and make a river navigable," is a fool's illusion. "[Nature] knows nothing of us. And whatever mankind has achieved, it was not so great that nature shared our pain or joined in our joy."[8] Not only is "nature" not benevolent, it isn't ever even horrible and strange. Every relationship between us and nature is a projection. The degree to which "nature" takes no interest in us is impossible to grasp, since we all think of it as coming from us. So "nature" for Rilke gives rise to a negative foil, which, like an inverted kind of transcendence, provides the grounding for human existence, without ever being grasped by thought or experience. "Nature" is just there; we are the ones who divide this existence up into presence and absence, subject and object. The distance from nature to us remains immeasurable in this schema, since the unit to measure this distance would have to come from nature and therefore be beyond our grasp.

Exactly at this point in the elegies Rilke becomes remarkably concrete. Everything that we have assembled so far about nature in Rilke speaks to a skillful blending of Platonic, Christian, Romantic, and pantheistic thought, in which nature grounds everything as an absolute metaphor, without itself needing to be thought. In "The Tenth Elegy," however, in which Rilke evokes as the conclusion of his cycle of poems the spectral realm of the dead, "nature" is not absolute, nor beyond grasping, nor the original cause of our existential homelessness. The poetic attempt in "The Eighth Elegy" to no longer name and differentiate the "never nowhere without the No" does not open a language beyond reference, a pure language à la Mallarmé, or empty yet meaningful space à la Malevich. It also does not abandon the concreteness of language for that quasi-mystical unity of all things that endears Rilke to New Age readers. In the final elegy Rilke finds a language of immediate concreteness. "Nature" is what dogs do when left alone in a meadow.

In the first part of "The Tenth Elegy," Rilke bluntly comes to terms with the diversions of the modern world, which distract us from ourselves: "the streets of the city of grief/where, in the false silence formed of continual uproar,/the figure cast from the mold of emptiness stoutly/swaggers: the gilded noise, the bursting memorial."[9] We, Rilke writes, stagger at the shooting gallery at the "carnival" of life between "cheers and chance," and watch how "naked" money multiplies with its "genitals" and leaps over everyone and everything with its peculiar logic of limitless fungibility. With graphic images Rilke writes angrily about our addiction to distractions and comfort, which are gladly accommodated and provided by church and commerce. But suddenly a vista opens up beyond the crass hype of our daily existence, "beyond the last of the billboards, plastered with signs for 'Deathless,'/that bitter beer which seems so sweet to its drinkers,/as long as they chew fresh distractions between sips" ("*hinter der letzten Planke, beklebt mit Plakaten des, Todlos',/jenes bitteren Bieres, das den Trinkenden süß scheint,/wenn sie immer dazu frische Zerstreuungen kaun*"). And "just in back of the billboard, just behind, the view becomes *real* [*ists wirklich*]."[10] Real? Is it *real*? After Rilke has cleared the distractions and garbage of the inauthentic modern world out of the poem, we arrive at the point where all his poetry wants to go.

And what is "real"? A simple picture of paradise, replete with images of innocence, harmony, simplicity, and genuineness. "Children are playing, and lovers are holding hands, to the side / solemnly in the meager grass [. . .]" So far, so homey. But then: "and dogs are doing what is natural" ("*Hunde haben Natur*").[11] They are doing precisely *what*? What does it mean to follow one's nature, when the point of the poem is to discover that realm prior to consciousness? Again:

> Children are playing, and lovers are holding hands, to the side,
> solemnly in the meager grass, and dogs are doing what is natural.

> Kinder spielen, und Liebende halten einander,—abseits,
> ernst, im ärmlichen Gras, und Hunde haben Natur.

Either dogs are carrying on with their "genitals," as Rilke has had money do a few lines before, or they are doing their business on the grass—and now we see what makes it "meager." Either way, nature here is no inexplicable abyss of human existence, the unformed "freedom," the "never nowhere without No: that pure / unseparated element which one breathes / without desire and endlessly *knows*." Whatever the "nature" of these dogs is, it is "nature" that—not even when taking into account the readings of Heidegger, Blanchot, and Agamben—cannot be arranged in categories and concepts beyond formulation, like Heidegger's "*Bezug*" (a term that defies direct translation) or Agamben's "the open." "Nature" *is* what dogs "have" (or, in the English idiom, *what* they do—"what is natural"). "Nature" is copulation, urine, scat. Rilke's unusual formulation "*Hunde haben Natur*" ("dogs do what is natural") has either been ignored or dismissed as "almost insulting" by most interpreters of the elegies.[12]

"Nature" is what dogs *follow* when they *are* dogs: They do what is natural. Rilke chooses dogs here because they are, for him, beings with a two-sided access to nature, "neither man nor animal," and because they "have lost that attentive depth of instinct, which we discover in the gaze of wild animals."[13] "Neither excluded nor assimilated," the dog stands between a version of nature that has been tamed by man—"expending his reality" on the world as interpreted by humans—and the untamed nature that it nevertheless "has." The dog cannot completely go over into the world of humans, in which it holds its face "almost with a pleading, on the verge / of comprehending, close to an agreement," for then "he wouldn't be."[14] Man, "The Eighth Elegy" implies, cannot give himself completely to "nature," which he nevertheless follows, since this "nature" would hinder the consciousness of his being. Indeed, the dog provides Rilke with unique access to a consciousness without consciousness, a kind of awareness that fails to be aware of itself:

> I love gazing into things. Can you imagine with me how glorious it is, for example, to see into a dog, in passing—into him . . . to ease oneself into the dog exactly at his center, the place out of which he exists as a dog, that place in him where God would, so to speak, have sat down for a moment when the dog was complete, in order to watch him at his first predicaments and notions and let him know with a nod that he was good, that he lacked nothing, that no better dog could be made. For a while one can endure being in the middle of the dog, but one has to be sure to jump out in time, before the world closes in around him completely, otherwise one would remain the dog within the dog and be lost to everything else.[15]

This playful passage from a letter, not atypical for Rilke when he was in love, reminds us that his poetry always stays on this side of mysticism. "This side," in this context, refers to the side of human consciousness, and also the communicative, rather than incantatory, dimension of language where words refer to the world of sensory impressions—to human reality.

In the elegy, "nature" is something that is in us and that nevertheless overcomes us, that we have and yet do not completely possess. "Nature" is what *really* exists and at the same time offers the possibility of experiencing reality as such. From Rilke's book about Worpswede we learn that nature is indifferent. It is not, however, a measureless emptiness that surrounds us still and strange and that we try to control with our longing and projections. "Nature" is the strangeness we have inside ourselves and it is also all we are, not unlike the dog in the meadow. We can reach Rilke's paradise only through this "nature." The promise of salvation in Rilke's poetry is anchored in this concrete "nature," which cannot be sublimated and therefore has been either primly overlooked or dismissed as offensive by many interpreters.

Other critics unpack what Rilke describes so very concretely as our bodily nature as the unknowable ground of human existence. They uncover this unknowable ground by arranging philosophical arguments and metaphors around a center that is then identified as a purely linguistic proposition, as a place made up of a language that forgoes reference.[16] Especially postmodern readings insist that Rilke exchanges the "original meaning of language as the reproduction of a reality external to it" for a deconstructive use of language in which the signifier moves completely free of its function as a sign.[17]

With the "nature" of the dogs in "The Tenth Elegy" Rilke undercuts such astute interpretations. "Nature" is not simply a metaphor, concept, reality outside of language, or free sign, which Rilke's unconventional language ultimately sheds entirely. Such interpretations open up large parts of Rilke's work but conceal the fact that Rilke does not want his poem to be understood only as a referential series of written signs, but also as a play on the "meager" grass. "Nature" is also what dogs do.

O

for

p

for Proletarian

And like a gown, the honor of that man
sank from his breast, and swarms of children ran
in terror from the proletarian . . .[1]

Und seine Würde war wie ein Talar
von seiner Brust gesunken, und es scheute
ein Kinderschwarm sich vor dem Proletar . . .[2]

A group of children hardly has any idea what a "proletarian" is. In the
cycle of poems *Visions of Christ*, Rilke borrows the word "proletarian"
from the often unpoetic and demystifying discourse of Marxist class
analysis. "Proletarian" comes from "*proles*," Latin for "offspring"; in
ancient Rome the word referred to the portion of the population whose
only value—as opposed to that of the ruling class—rested in the children
they bore. The word was first used in the German context in 1826 by
Joseph Maria von Radowitz. Since Karl Marx, "proletarian" (Hegel used
the word "*Pöbel*," "the mob," instead) has been used for the group of
exploited workers, whose class consciousness is steadily developing and
who will ultimately overthrow the unjust relations in the proletarian revolution. This will be followed, according to the grand narrative of orthodox

Marxism, by the rational "dictatorship of the proletarian," where the means of production will be owned and controlled by the workers.

The word "proletarian" first appears in Rilke's work in the first part of *Visions of Christ*. These poems were written in 1896–97 and all but irredeemably drip with kitsch. In these rhymed vignettes Christ appears in continually new contexts. One of the poems' recurring themes is the biblical idea of material poverty as boundless spiritual wealth. But Rilke interrupts these biblical images and ideas, and the high style that goes with them, with the word "proletarian." It is his wish, as in several other works, to desentimentalize the figure of Jesus.[3] The word "proletarian" does not rise to the level of the transfiguring language of religious visions since it originates in the decidedly antireligious, enlightened, Marxist social critique. As such, the word "proletarian" effects a break in the style of the poems, and thus becomes an exemplary word for what Rilke calls the "dictation of existence."[4] By using the incongruous word "proletarian" in a poem about Christ, Rilke juxtaposes words from two distinct rhetorical discourses, or traditions, to highlight the original sense of these two guiding myths. Rilke's objective is to make something appear in the ensuing contrast that had remained unsaid until now.

Just as in the Christian tradition the name of Christ promises salvation from the conditions of our earthly existence, so does the word "proletarian" function in the vocabulary of Marxism as the key to the hidden mechanisms of modern society. "Christ" promises salvation on a spiritual level. "Proletarian" promises "salvation" on a material level. The "invisible" words of the dictation of existence (as explained in the introduction to this book) have the potential for Rilke to turn "everything that has been carefully learned and grasped . . . into majestic sense."[5] Rilke aims to reach the point where words flip into another meaning, and not where explanations elucidate their deeper meaning. With the word "proletarian" this abrupt reversal from invisibility into sense is not described but rather carried out, by means of the stylistic break. For with this term, unexpectedly surfacing in a Bible story, Rilke does not mean to explain the poverty of Christ as an effect of his social conditions. Instead, he juxtaposes elements from the two great eschatological discourses of salvation from earthly suffering and the overcoming of poverty in order to highlight poverty all the more poignantly between these two strategies for overcoming it. The unexpected use of such a practical, politically charged, and quotidian word as "proletarian" in this cycle of poems marks poverty as something in the poem that cannot be quite excised by either of the great divergent antipoverty discourses.[6] What is poverty then, other than a word?

The word "proletarian" illuminates what Rilke carries out in the different themes and variations of the eleven poems in *Visions of Christ*. Yet he does not offer an explanation or elucidation: The intention is to get rid of the received, in this case Christian, understanding of poverty. On the thematic level, all eleven texts describe the unexpected, abrupt unveiling of a marginal or suspicious figure as Christ: a difference that is experienced in the world and that then changes the world. A break in the style like the use of the word "proletarian" in one of the eleven poems is therefore not a lack of style (or an anachronistic use of a modern word to describe an ancient event) but rather a marker of a difference that changes everything. Rilke does not explain or point to this difference but rather performs it. It doesn't mean; it is.

With the abrupt introduction of an element from Marxist discourse, for which the world "proletarian" is a metonymy, Rilke changes the meaning of "Christ" in his poems. For Rilke borrows this "proletarian" from a discourse that aims all its metaphorical weapons against the elevation of "poverty" as the condition for spiritual wealth. The proletarian does not hide a spiritual wealth in this sense, but rather he is supposed to achieve salvation from his empirical situation, first by reallocating the means of production and ultimately through revolution.

What happens with a word from the "dictation of existence" like "proletarian" after Rilke has put it in this poem? Does it return unchanged into Marxist discourse? Or is it, by virtue of its short appearance in Rilke's poetry, enriched by an additional layer of meaning? To put it differently: If the word "proletarian" breaks with the received image of Christ, does our understanding of "proletarian" change after reading Rilke's poem? The poem has a function that reaches beyond itself: if not a social revolution, then a transformation of language.

A good number of commentators are troubled by Rilke's systematic attempt to reevaluate poverty as spiritual wealth: "For: poverty is a great radiance from within," Rilke quotes himself in a letter from September 1907.[7] This line, "poverty is a great radiance from within," has "admittedly [been] a bit jeered at by realistic thinking."[8] It appeared, to the consternation of a whole generation of critics, in the section "On Poverty and Death" in *The Book of Hours* in 1903.[9] In a rare reply to his critics, Rilke writes that he finds his "conscience clean as to the charge that I am being evasive when I cite the right to neutrality of the artistic expression for my poem where I juxtaposed the terms 'rich' and 'poor' . . . But it may well be that for a while I was tasked with taking stock of wealth and poverty on their own terms. And why shouldn't it happen, even in this context, that one ends up praising each of these terms once they have been recognized properly."[10]

Some of Rilke's sponsors complained about this sort of mystification from a poet whom his publisher called a "real problem child" because of his chronic financial trouble.[11] Later, Marxist critics disputed the possibility of the "taking stock" of poverty on its own terms that Rilke espoused. In reply to the class-conscious critiques of Rilke, such authors as Herbert Marcuse praised just such a stock-taking as Rilke's "[i]mage . . . of joy and fulfillment . . . ; the gesture that gives and receives, the deed that is peace, and the end of the hardship of conquest, [this] is the emancipation from time, which unites man with God, man with nature . . . the redemption of desire, the cessation of time, the end of death, stillness, sleep, night, paradise—the nirvana principle not as death, but as life."[12] Neither side can lay claim to a subtle literary touch: Marcuse's claim that Rilke's poetry evokes a nirvana principle in life is just as crude as the Marxist anger at the privileged and entitled poet. The question, passionately argued by both sides, of whether it is acceptable to put poverty into a poem overestimates the sense and the influence of Rilke's work. Whether or not Rilke criticizes poverty or celebrates it, damns it or "praises" it—this has a limited influence on whether actual poverty is being addressed. Rilke is a poet; his stylizing of poverty as the image of a poet who is afraid lest someone "see him as a beggar" is at once offensive and, as part of a long tradition in which poverty makes way for spiritual wealth, easily decoded.[13] The more meaningful question seems to be what happens to a word like "proletarian" when it, as the point of contact between two discourses in the poem, opens a new line of sight onto two very powerful salvation myths.

Strangely, the numerous critiques of Rilke's cult of poverty have in common that they *defend* poverty against Rilke's assault, even though their intention is the *elimination* of poverty. In fact, various critics hold on to that particular conception of poverty (as injustice, social problem, suffering, a political problem), as opposed to Rilke's "neutral" attempt to understand poverty as an ontological, spiritual, and psychological condition. These critics are troubled by the "vagaries and contradictions of Rilke's text" in his attempt to "glorify and romanticize" poverty, because they want to reduce poverty to a single meaning that is not so "lacking in history, and remote from society" as Rilke's "lack of concreteness" and "almost indulgent aestheticization . . . [his] transformation of the social-historical into the natural" seem to make it.[14] These critics *defend* poverty doggedly against being taken up by a poet, and they defend the poor as "patient victims of [the poet's] unbridled imagination"—although their own aim is the fight against poverty.[15] What makes Rilke's poems about poverty and the poor so troublesome is that he broadens the concept of poverty metaphorically. It is therefore less astonishing that the same commentators who offer such critiques consider the "concept of the proletarian" in this critique to be "quite appropriate," since in Rilke's work, "even if momentarily, the existence of two classes is recognizable."[16] The "concept of the proletarian" seems to be perfectly self-evident: It is precisely the description of a "concrete-material" condition.[17] So the word "proletarian" in these commentaries summons the entire Marxist social analysis, without any need to understand it further.

Is the appearance of "proletarian" in *Visions of Christ* an enrichment of the semantics of "poverty" or, on the contrary, its impoverishment? The remarkable change in tones in *Visions of Christ* results from the juxtaposition of "proletarian" with the vocabulary of Luther's Bible in the preceding lines:

> He stood there like a traitor in the rout,
> a Nay-sayer, who rued his love, no doubt;
> no hint of grandeur did his hair suggest.[18]

> Er stand wie ein Verräter in der Schar,
> stand wie ein Leugner, den die Liebe reute,
> und ohne all Hoheit war sein Haar.[19]

Rilke's mixture of the "crassly economic with the religious into a strange conglomerate," as some interpreters have called it, has been described as "strange and remarkable," but also as "gleefully capitalistic."[20] With "proletarian" Rilke makes it "remarkably" clear how limited and ultimately how poor Christian and Marxist understandings of "poverty" are.

If one truly wants to eradicate poverty, then one would also have to accept the disappearance of the term "poverty." And this is what Rilke is aiming for: that poverty no longer be understood as poverty, that poverty, as soon as the word changes, also changes on an ontological level. With the use of the word "proletarian" in the poem he simply shows that the Marxist theory shares its thoughts on salvation with the Christian discourse. In *Visions of Christ*, which Rilke's interpreters rarely discuss, he introduces this not in the form of an argument but rather as the "strange conglomerate" with which he deliberately interrupts the style of his own poem. The break in style takes two discourses committed to salvation and opens them onto one another. But Rilke doesn't know about that: With "proletarian" he closes the door on the Christo-Marxist promise of salvation.

Rilke wanted to believe that his poetic use of certain words rendered them unfit for the critical or other discourses they had been in before: "*No* word in a poem (I mean here every 'and' 'but' and 'the') is identical with the same-sounding word used in everyday conversation; the more pure purposiveness, the grand relation, the constellation which it takes on in a verse or in artistic prose, transforms it deep into its core, renders it useless and unusable for normal speech [. . .]."[21]

We do not have to follow this poetic megalomania. Yet, Rilke is unconsciously writing down a consequence of the Marxist and Christian salvation myths: that once transformed "to the core of its nature," poverty would become completely foreign and unintelligible to us, as soon as the word itself either achieved heavenly salvation or was dissolved in the dictatorship of the proletariat.

for *Quatsch*

"Vladimir, the Cloud Painter" is one of Rilke's finest prose texts. Like a cloud, it lingers in your memory after you read it, and then drifts away. In addition to the pleasure of reading it, the text offers another layer of meaning: It is a piece of experimental prose, in which Rilke with subtle irony presents his poetics of the autonomy of words and, as if in passing, marks a historical shift in the European artist's relationship to his work.

One dreary Prague afternoon, three world-weary and deliciously bored artists leave their habitual café and go "out for a dusk visit," that is, to drop in on the studio of the painter Vladimir Lobowski, who can be reached "only through his work. Since he smokes all of his pictures."[1] Vladimir, as the little story's title says, paints clouds—but like the words of Rilke's story, which take on a new life past the story's end, Vladimir's pictures are not representations of clouds, but are in fact clouds themselves. "The whole studio is full of fantastic smoke. You can consider yourself lucky if you can find the shortest path through this primordial fog to the old, worn-out daybed where Vladimir lives—day in, day out."[2]

Sitting on his throne of clouds, Vladimir is a quasi-divine artist who knows nothing besides what he has created. At first the artists cannot even discern him through the smoke that clouds their vision and fills the studio like low-hanging clouds. Only his voice is heard, drifting in and out with strange declarations, while the visitors partake of some liquor they find and wait for what will happen next. Words rise up in the smoke only to dissipate again.

Smoke, smoke, smoke and then lovely, leisurely words that pass through the world and admire the things from a distance. The clouds lift them up. So many clandestine ascensions.

For example:

Smoke. "Here it is: Humans always look away from God. They search for him in the light that grows ever colder and sharper, up there." Smoke. "Meanwhile God waits elsewhere—waits—at the very bottom of it all. Deep. Where the roots are. Where it is warm and dark—." Smoke.

And the poet starts walking up and down, suddenly.

The three think of the God who lives somewhere behind the things—who knows where.

And later:

"To be—afraid—?" Smoke. "What for?" Smoke.

"For you are always above him. Like a fruit under which someone holds a beautiful bowl. Golden—shiny in the leaves. And when the fruit is ripe it lets go—"

Then the painter tears apart the smoke with an impetuous gesture: "By God—" he exclaims, and encounters on the daybed a little pale human with large, peculiar eyes. Eyes, shiny eyes, behind which lurks eternal mourning, shiny and glad, like the eyes of women. And very cold hands.

The painter stands there, a bit helpless. He doesn't quite know anymore what he had wanted.

It's good that the baron joins him now: "You have to paint this, Lubovski—." What, this the baron does not know exactly. At least he repeats it. "Really, Lubovski." It sounds almost a bit patronizing, though he does not mean it.

In the meantime Vladimir has gone on quite a journey: from being frightened through a dark sense of astonishment. Finally he arrives at a smile and dreams quietly: "Oh, yes. Tomorrow." Smoke.

Suddenly there isn't enough room in the studio for the three of them. They bump into each other. They all leave: "Good-bye, Lubovski."

Already at the next corner they shake hands with unnecessary vigor. They can't wait to get rid of one another.

They part quickly in different directions.

At the end of Rilke's short and nearly plotless story, the "cloud painter" bolts his door and sits "small, on the edge of the daybed and cries into his white, icy hands. His tears come gently and easily, without effort and without pathos." This undramatic ending, with neither self-pity nor explanation, turns Rilke's story about the picture-smoking cloud painter Vladimir into a literary-historical response to Honoré de Balzac's "The Unknown Masterpiece." In Balzac's story, first published in 1831, the famous painter Frenhofer shows two artists visiting his studio a painting that he has been working on for the last ten years, to the exclusion of all else. In his search for the absolute meaning of art, Balzac's fictional painter has transformed everything on the canvas into a "chaos of colors, sounds and vague nuances, a kind of fog without form."[3] The two visitors in Balzac's story, Poussin and Probus, render their verdict based on the swirl of colors and forms on the canvas: "This is the end of art on earth," explains one, and the other adds: "from now it will be lost in the heavens."[4] The fatal blow is Poussin's bitter discovery that Frenhofer "will have to recognize sooner or later that there is nothing to see on this canvas!" Looking back from our contemporary vantage point, we recognize Balzac's account of the fictional Frenhofer's picture as the birth of abstract painting. But in Balzac's story the incomprehension of two colleagues at a painting that does not represent anything sends Frenhofer into a crisis; the following night he burns his masterpiece and kills himself. This pathos of the misunderstood artist, driven to despair by the reaction of an ignorant public (plus an unhappy love affair, which Balzac also weaves into the story), who then kills himself, is just what Rilke's story dissolves. In contrast to Balzac's Frenhofer, who "has erased art with art" using his "shapeless fog"[5] and hopes for his colleagues' recognition and approval of this radical gesture, Rilke's cloud painter retains "the only thing that he has not yet betrayed, that belongs to him alone. His solitude."[6]

By comparing Rilke's to Balzac's story we gain insight into a historical argument about art's transition from the world of shapes and appearances into pure form. To get to the bottom of this perplexing process by which absolute form is supposed to triumph over forms, and absolute color over colors, we may thus ask, along with contemporary philosopher Giorgio Agamben, "has meaning erased the sign, or has the sign abolished the meaning?"[7] In the period that stretches from Balzac to Rilke, the relationship between the artist, the work of art, and the audience has changed. The birth of abstract art coincides with the birth of modern art, an art to which the artist dedicates himself for its own sake (rather than in order to represent something). While Balzac still portrays this birth as a dramatic struggle that ends in crisis, Rilke does away with the pathos and instead celebrates solitude, giving it the peculiar name of "his lonely" ("*sein Einsames*"). Frenhofer's abstract canvas inaugurates an age when art will "from now on be lost in the heavens," according to Balzac's story. In "Vladimir, the Cloud Painter" Rilke does nothing but take literally Balzac's metaphorical description of the end of art, when it no longer fulfills man's (in the form of fellow artists') need for understanding. Vladimir "smokes all his paintings," writes Rilke, and by describing as fogged-up reality an artistic praxis on earth (i.e., in the studio) what Balzac described metaphorically as art dissipating into the heavens, Rilke blurs the distinction between image and representation, form and formlessness.

Nevertheless, Rilke's story dissolves as quickly as it aspires to be an implicit comment on the changed role of art in his historical moment. "Cloudiness," as Rilke wrote in a letter, "*das Wolkige*," this "flowing forming of the self and giving up of the self," meant a great deal to the poet.[8] And so "Vladimir, the Cloud Painter" is neither an art-historical argument nor a philosophical thesis, neither the biography of an artist nor Rilke's poetic credo. "Smoke, smoke, smoke and then lovely, leisurely words that pass through the world and admire the things from a distance. The clouds lift them up. So many clandestine ascensions."[9] The smoke, mists, and fog continue to billow, like the words in Rilke's story.

Smoke. Smoke. Smoke. *Rauch.* This word appears nine times on a single page in Rilke's micro-fiction, with no explanation, no adjective, no article. It seems to be nothing more than: smoke.

But Rilke's word does describe something. It describes the state of the studio, and does so without itself becoming smoky, cloudy, vague, or imprecise. Before visiting Vladimir's studio, the three men sit for a long time in a café, and one of them, the poet, expresses a longing for quiet, a desire to simply clear the table. He expresses his wish to invalidate all that has been said and thought, or at least not to have to consider any further opinion.

> Quiet, they only want some quiet. The poet says it as directly as onomatopoetically.
> "*Quatsch*," he says after another half an hour. "Hooey."
> And again the others agree fully.[10]

Quatsch. Hooey. Gobbledygook.

Onomatopoeia is painting with sounds. With the expression "*Quatsch*," Rilke proceeds just as Vladimir does with color and brush. He uses a word whose entire meaning comes across in its sound (you don't need to know German to get it; just try voicing it and you'll get that it makes no sense), in fact whose meaning consists entirely in this vague sound. Just as the meaning of Vladimir's pictures of clouds consists of nothing but their cloudiness, so "*Quatsch*," hooey (which developed from the actual sounds made by soggy clothes, shoes, or things, through the adjective *quatschnass*, "completely saturated with moisture, wet through and through," to mean "linguistic nonsense" in the nineteenth century), means nothing but *Quatsch*. In a text, "*Quatsch*" is just what Vladimir's visitors see on his canvas, and what, earlier, in Balzac's story, Frenhofer's visitors had seen on his canvas: something that means nothing but itself, just as Vladimir's and Frenhofer's colors and forms aspire to mean nothing but themselves. For Frenhofer's visitors in Balzac's story, this means that they may in fact not have an opinion, that they have nothing to say but wish to say precisely that, this absence of meaning. The word used by the bored poet after long reflection in a café in Rilke's short story becomes an empty spot, meaningless and cloudy, in the compressed center of the story, in which sound and meaning, representation and object, coincide in this one moment—"*Quatsch*." "*Quatsch*," like "hooey," is an autonomous word, which corresponds to the smoke rising up from a painter who "smokes his paintings" in this story, without describing the smoke. By putting the word in the mouth of the poet in the group and characterizing his statement as absolutely precise, Rilke underlines the irony of his poetic method. He does not want to say anything more in this story than that there is nothing more to say: that Vladimir's art is not concerned with the public.

"*Quatsch*" says that there is nothing to say. It characterizes the silence of the acquaintances in the café by simply interrupting it—but in doing so is still a part of language, only a part that doesn't say anything. The interruption isn't about anything and states nothing except itself. An onomatopoetic word is a word whose sound corresponds to its meaning ("quack," "fizzle," "pop"; Rilke's use of "*querren*" in the chapter "E for Entrails"). Such a word is also the opposite of the smoke that winds its way through the story and enshrouds the whole thing. Because "*Quatsch*," as an onomatopoetic word, is not supposed to reveal anything else and does not enshroud anything; it's nothing but *Quatsch*. When Rilke uses the unusual technical term "onomatopoetic" in the otherwise simple story, he practically offers the reader instructions on how to read the story and thereby marks precisely the empty middle of this airy, light, ascending story. For "*Quatsch*" is not one of the "dear, slow words that go through the world and wonder at things from afar."[11] "*Quatsch*" has no reference except itself, since it contains everything.

This word, whose sound Rilke so clearly emphasizes, finds an echo when all three men arrive in Vladimir's study (which we may imagine to resemble the attic scene in Orson Welles's adaptation of Kafka's *The Trial*). "He smokes all of his pictures. The whole studio is filled with fantastic smoke [*Qualm*]."[12] From "*Quatsch*" to the German "*Qualm*," a kind of thin smoke as from a stove or pipe, it is a small move. But while "*Quatsch*," being onomatopoetic, says nothing but itself, the "smoke" in Vladimir's study is the smoke from which the whole story rises. *Qualm* and smoke prompt the process of reflection in the story, the condensation of the story into its meaning, the meta-level of the story, which succeeds in characterizing itself as smoke. Smoke is what makes Rilke's story, in contrast to Balzac's tragic story, a self-reflexive and thereby modern story.

And while the smoke enshrouds and releases everything in "Vladimir, the Cloud Painter" (internal events and their reflective commentary), *Quatsch* remains *Quatsch* and smoke remains smoke. The story describes Rilke's attempt to write the artist's solitude and his art's meaning—"the only thing that he has not yet betrayed"—without *describing* and therefore destroying it. The resulting text floats between *Quatsch* and *Qualm*, hooey and smoke, between empty space and the smoke that fills and enshrouds it. "*Quatsch*" evokes smoke, without discussing, poeticizing, or tearing it into pieces, or letting it dissipate before the story's end. (One ought to read "Vladimir, the Cloud Painter," even if this splendid text of barely five pages has only recently been translated into English and is not included in recent German editions of Rilke's works.) To let the "smoke" hover until it has dissipated into that word beloved of poets and children, "*Quatsch*," which Rilke applies here with technical precision and which flies in the face of its own meaning to become the weightiest word in this light little story—that is poetry.

r

for Rose

Oh rose, pure puzzlement, desire
to be no one's sleep beneath so many
eyelids.[1]

Rose, oh reiner Widerspruch, Lust,
Niemandes Schlaf zu sein unter soviel
Lidern.

This is the inscription on Rilke's gravestone, which he wrote in 1925, one year before he died of leukemia in Switzerland on December 29, 1926. In Rilke's will, which he entrusted to his friend Nanny Wunderly-Volkart on October 29, 1925, the poet dictated that these lines be inscribed on his tombstone. "It may be possible to get hold of an *old* stone (something of the Empire style) [. . .] If you rub off the older inscriptions, then this can be in their place: my family coat of arms [. . .] my name, and, set a bit apart, these lines of verse."[2] Rilke wanted to be put to rest under a used, weather-beaten stone, suggesting not only that the ages and influences to which the stone had already been subjected lived on, but also that death itself is only one more phase in the course of human existence within the greater context of stones, and things, and time. It is a beautiful, peaceful expression, in which so much of Rilke's work seems to find its way back to its origins. Emptiness is described here as sleep within a rose, around which the petals group. First, they stand for the closed eyes of the dead, and second, they represent poetic creation, from whose timeless dreams songlike poems (the German word for "song," "*Lied*," is a homophone of the German word for "lid") unfold like "so many eyelids" ["*soviel Lidern*"]. "Rose" is an anagram of "Eros," and with the notion of the "desire" (the forceful "*Lust*" in German) of sleep without a sleeper, Rilke links Eros to death and turns the rose-petal "lids" into the metaphorical cover of night, under whose protection the unspeakable experiences of love and death are consummated.

On the level of sound, the first few syllables of the verse converge into a pattern similar to that of the rose: From both sides the sound "ro" symmetrically surrounds the "se" in the middle, if you read backward through the "oh" like this: Ro—se—ohR . . . In spite of its harmonic sounds, the inscription is described as a "puzzlement" for death and as sleep without a sleeper.

When I was teaching a freshman seminar on German poetry at New York University a few years ago, and all but soliloquizing on these and other nuances of Rilke's poem, a student who had learned her excellent German in Vienna interrupted me. With distinctively velvety vowels, which surely had also colored Rilke's Prague German, she read these few lines that I had written on the board. It's crystal clear from the first line onward, she remarked, that this was a gravestone epitaph, without heeding my attempts at explaining Rilke's intricate wordplay. For up on the board was the name of the deceased: "*Reiner*," the German word for "pure." "*Reiner*," "pure," which I had stared at but seen only as "pure puzzlement," to her (and anyone with ears to hear) sounded identical to: "Rainer." Of course, now I heard it too. And yet before that class I had never seen Rilke's name in this line before.

Other interpreters have also read quickly past the "*reiner*," a homophone for the name that Lou-Andreas Salomé gave to Rilke when she decided that his given name, "René," was too effete.[3] Those critics conclude, among other things, that the inscription does not amount to an "unambiguous" statement.[4] Perhaps my student in New York recognized what was unambiguous about the epitaph so quickly because she read Rilke's poem from the distance of a native English speaker. The word "*reiner*" appears in Rilke's poems in at least twenty-three other spots, sometimes in its comparative form meaning "more pure" (as the concordance to his work points out). For a native German speaker it's quite possible to read all of these lines purely, so to speak, without hearing the name "Rainer" even a single time.

On Rilke's gravestone his name thus appears twice: once engraved below the family crest, as he specified, and once hidden in plain sight in the rose, in his last poem. In the fifth sonnet to Orpheus Rilke writes that a gravestone would be unthinkable for Orpheus, the archetypical poet:

> Erect no gravestone for him. Only this:
> Let the rose blossom each year for his sake.[5]

> Errichtet keinen Denkstein. Laßt die Rose
> nur jedes Jahr zu seinen Gunsten blühn.

To let the rose bloom does not mean to get excited about flowers. Instead it means to read a poem aloud to honor the memory of someone, "for his sake." If you read aloud the poetic inscription each year on December 29, the day Rilke died, without a "gravestone" and far away from his resting place in Raron, you say and hear the name of the poet every time.

In the inscription *"reiner"* ("pure") refers to the "puzzlement" in its obvious meaning. In its other meaning, as a name, it no longer *refers* to anything, but rather separates itself from the poem and stands alone, a primal linguistic form. The irony of this poem, which so many readers have overlooked, consists of the word *"reiner"* no longer being *"rein"* or "pure," but rather split into two different meanings. One of them *is* in fact pure, the name "Rainer," while the other one only *says* that it is *"rein,"* or "pure." The following sentence, written by Walter Benjamin in 1916, is revealing in this context. (Rilke knew Benjamin fleetingly in the 1920s and passed on to the budding intellectual the assignment of translating Baudelaire's *Flowers of Evil*.) "The name is that *through* which, and *in* which, language itself communicates itself absolutely."[6] For the tombstone inscription of a great poet, the transformation of a word *into* "language itself" creates a final resting place. Nothing more is transmitted.

It doesn't get purer than that.

S

for Stampa

Have you imagined
Gaspara Stampa intensely enough so that any girl
Deserted by her beloved might be inspired
By that fierce example of soaring, objectless love
And might say to herself, Perhaps I can be like her?[1]

Hast du der Gaspara Stampa
denn genügend gedacht, daß irgend ein Mädchen,
dem der Geliebte entging, am gesteigerten Beispiel
dieser Liebenden fühlt: daß ich würde wie sie?[2]

Forget it. Give it up, let it be, don't even think about it. Rilke idolized, fetishized, and elevated unsatisfied, abandoned old maids who lost themselves in their love for a man. O yes, some of these mystics of unrequited love became almost holy because of their ostentatious abstinence. As near-saints they furnished a compelling model for the existence of the *poet's poet*: Everything—especially great suffering, great pain—is sublimated. S stands for Stampa, the saint, and for suffering and sublimation. The catch is that Rilke consistently formulates the artist's existence as exactly the opposite of sublimation: as acceptance and affirmation of existence, as intensification and letting go of resistance and being-in-the-world. "You know it yourself: it is wrong to be tired / in the face of life," Rilke writes to Erika Mitterer on October 30, 1922.[3] Therefore: *Forget it*. Gaspara Stampa, an Italian poet from the sixteenth century, who created in her poetry an immortal monument to her unfortunate love for Count Collalto, is such a "fierce" (read: hysterical) example that no one could possibly turn to her for inspiration. Rilke did not. When he makes Gaspara Stampa a model of the abstinence that overcomes itself, the kind seen in unlucky lovers like Louïse Labé, Marceline Desbordes-Valmore, Marianna Alcoforado, Hildegard von Bingen, Bettina von Arnim, and Teresa of Ávila, he does so in spite of himself and because he himself cannot "abstain," although in a letter he warns against "'interpreting' the incomprehensibility of bodily pain . . . to which we seem to succumb with our entire being, even though it is only a misunderstanding, a contra-diction, reluctance, and a desperate desire to allow our joyful nature which supports our life so wholeheartedly to stay in charge."[4] But in spite of this admonition to himself, Rilke turns Stampa into a figure of abstinence and begins to "interpret" pain, in the form of her unrequited love. And this in spite of his own insight, in reading Stampa and through his own later experiences of illness, that pain does not tolerate our interpretations (as though pain itself were sick, sensitive, and vulnerable). It is "our task not to dissolve pain in our consciousness; it does not tolerate being inter-preted. You have to, so to speak, let it burn itself out in its particular spot, without examining in the light of its flickering blaze any object of our spirit or of the unaffected parts of life. Pain is reasonable only on the side where it faces nature, on the other side it is absurd, raw material, unhewn, without form and surface, ungraspable . . ."[5]

Rilke first mentions Stampa in *The Notebooks of Malte Laurids Brigge*. She considers everything in the "flickering firelight" of her unrequited and unremitting love. But her "fierce example of soaring," or, literally, her "heightened example," just like physical pain, cannot be dissolved in our consciousness by applying our cognitive powers. Rilke hopes that our own internal movement, triggered by unrequited longing for the beloved person, can lead to something beyond this person, so that the absurd "raw material" of unrequited longing can take shape. But those are accidental occurrences, unintended consequences, rolls of the dice that mostly end up blank. You cannot count on results here: We tolerate pain just as little as pain tolerates being interpreted. And just as seldom as we transform pain into an image as beatific as Rilke's image of Gaspara Stampa (for in

Rilke's stylization Gaspara Stampa becomes a figure for a *general* approach to life), will we become "fierce examples of soaring" and "heightened examples" in our own lives.

What could it mean to commemorate Stampa "intensely enough," to carefully hang her sublime image over a lace-covered, lily-white bed, and underneath this paean to sublimation promptly forget life, love, lust, longing, suffering? Our tender memories of missed chances and unrequited loves prompt us to forget life itself. We toss and turn sleeplessly, thinking of what we could have had, instead of recognizing the next chance, the thing or person right in front of us, which is what life actually is. And we succeed in transforming these memories of what never happened into a "beautiful model" or an "inner source," as Rilke writes in the *Malte* novel, in only the rarest of cases. And yet, the example of Gaspara Stampa can teach us a few things. First, this figure of a female suffering poet can teach us how we can lift ourselves out of ourselves *without* the object of our desire and *without* exemplary models. Gaspara Stampa did not forget, but rather sublimated and heightened her life, her love, her lust, and her desire in her boundless solitude. Her love detached itself from the object of her beloved, and as a lover she remained constant, or, if we were to add up the balance sheet of this love, she continued to have a surplus of love long after it should have faded. But she had no precedent for this and did not see herself as a model. She wrote. Wrote beyond herself and made her pain immortal through language, instead of recalling someone else, especially not Count Collalto, who had dismissed her love. Completely buried in her own pain, she remained alone, so intensified by this negative experience that she lived with no precedent and thus became a model. So let us not deprive Rilke of his fetish, but let's put it in the right light, instead of imitating it.

Rilke immersed himself in the poems of Gaspara Stampa starting in 1908. When reading her poetry, as Rilke said, the "fate and blessedness" of this and other abandoned women affected him greatly. Their fate was "so heavy in [his] heart . . . that [he] thought that the angel inside [him] was breaking out and [he] had a hard time restraining him from suddenly bursting into full blaze in plain sight."[6] To be abandoned and to be blessed are one and the same for Rilke, who hesitates to characterize his own unhappy loves as such in another letter, "for they are indeed the most blessed ones."[7] "Blessed" means that the object of love is consumed by love itself and thus overcome: that the movements of one's soul become independent of all external circumstances, that the act of loving becomes independent of the beloved person. Blessedness lies in frustration, in being confronted with nothing but yourself by having your desire rejected. In response to her rejection, Gaspara Stampa wrote poems that limned her inner life more fully, more creatively than all but a few others before or after. In this way Stampa becomes the signifier of an immeasurably large "instead of"; life becomes a noble act of abstinence and renunciation; love becomes, through sublimation . . . a poem. Rilke elevates this Italian poet to the stature of a myth of the sublimation of love as defined by Roland Barthes: the combination of "the Socratic myth (to love means 'to give birth to many beautiful and splendid words and thoughts') and the romantic myth (I will bring forth an immortal work by describing my passion.)."[8]

Rilke identified with the "fate and blessedness" of these unlucky women to such a great degree, as he wrote in a letter, that he had difficulty "restraining [the angel in him]." But he was drawn to these women precisely because they understood how to "restrain" their own love and longing: to deny themselves something because they couldn't have it, and turn this renunciation into great art (to add "emptiness [. . .] into the spaces," to deepen our (non-)experience of naught, as suggested in "The First Elegy"[9]). Stampa becomes an idealized figure because her creative accomplishment makes up for her abstinence. The decisive thing is that Rilke himself, as his remarks reveal, is incapable of such abstinence, measure, and restraint; the narrator in the *Malte* novel points out, speaking of "those strong girls, still unused in their innermost selves, who have never been loved,"[10] "I would be straining and overvaluing myself, if I tried to be like them."[11] On the one hand, Rilke boundlessly admires these women, while on the other hand, he cannot love them (or anyone else) in equal measure, and with the same degree of selflessness. The tension between this admiration for these women and his inability to achieve their state of heightened selflessness becomes a major impetus for Rilke's poetry. For in his engagement with Gaspara Stampa his "angel" erupts and "bursts into full blaze in plain sight." A name for the eruption of this guiding angel is, strangely, Gaspara Stampa.

The achievement of Gaspara Stampa consists of taking the pleasure of desire itself, that is, a pleasure in experiencing pain, and stretching it to infinity: to hold oneself in a condition of eternal "pre-desire," as Freud called it, or a kind of perpetual foreplay. Rilke, too, behaves this way when

he translates the poems of Gaspara Stampa, the Portuguese letters of
Marianna Alcoforado, and the sonnets of Louïse Labé into German.
Then he overcomes, with the help of what he calls the "Ange des mes
affirmations" (angel of my affirmations), these icons of great lovers both
rhetorically and substantively: Gaspara Stampa is duly forgotten for the
remainder of the elegies.[12] For Rilke's angel of affirmations does not
abstain, does not sublimate, does not deny himself for the sake of
becoming a "heightened example," in spite of Rilke's persistent idealizations of the frustrated lover. Rilke's angel always wants to have it both
ways:

> Yet, God never shows two faces,
> and takes no joy in betrayal,
> only: he brings, and also denies,
> and his mouth has affirmed them both.[13]

> Doch der Gott zeigt niemals zwei Gesichter
> und hat nicht Gefallen am Verrat,
> nur: er ist ein Bringer und Verzichter,
> und sein Mund hat beides gleich bejaht.

To bring *and* deny (because no man or woman can do both at the same
time), but not to betray life, love, and desire for poetry. In the years in
which Rilke created icons of great lovers and wrote the poem quoted
above, "The Lovers," James Joyce conceived the character of Molly Bloom
in his novel *Ulysses*, who says yes to both at the same time: "I asked him
with my eyes to ask again yes and then he asked me would I yes to say yes
my mountain flower and first I put my arms around him yes and drew
him down to me so he could feel my breasts all perfume yes and his heart
was going like mad and yes I said yes I will Yes."[14]

Surprisingly, Gaspara Stampa ultimately also says only *yes*. Yes. Yes.
Yes. But unlike Molly Boom, whose happiness Joyce is trying to describe,
Gaspara says yes to love *beyond* the beloved and in spite of his lack of a
response, even if she does not forget the rebuff she suffered at his hands.
In doing so she becomes a key figure for Rilke's poetry. Don't be fooled:
Stampa is insatiable, only wants more, never gives up. For this reason she
is "heightened": She burns her whole life long, "burns up in her pain,"
rather than flaring up even once with Collalto. "Because I never held you,

I hold you fast,"[15] as Rilke writes in a great love poem that erupts near the end of *The Notebooks of Malte Laurids Brigge* as a song about the delusions of love. Trapped forever as an unworthy object in the poems by Stampa, the beloved count didn't escape at all.

But Rilke deceives himself with Stampa—just as he lies to all of the women in his life, and eventually also to his readers with the idea that such ever-burning but unrequited love is our only opportunity for surpassing ourselves. "To be loved means to erupt in flames. To love means: to shine forth fed by inexhaustible oil. To be loved means to tenderly vanish, to love means to last."[16] Rilke knows very well that a sudden flaring up is neither less than nor even comparable with the long, slow burn, that an instant of ecstatic pleasure must not be contrasted with the duration of time. For we cannot hold on to either of them. Gaspara Stampa represents the insight that it is impossible to contrast the lived moment with perpetuity. At this point Rilke's magnificent metaphors tend to turn into their opposites. "Isn't the entire world, in fact, created by you? For how often have you set it on fire with your love and watched it flare up and burn out and then secretly replaced it with another one, while everyone was asleep."[17] Love endures, but the world that it sets on fire, and thus opens up for us for the first time, is constantly new. Or else just the opposite: The world abides, and the experience of love is constantly unprecedented and new. Rilke wants to have it both ways: perpetuity and ever-new experiences.

Rilke's concern, in his reflections on female mystics and in all of his love poems, is with the way in which we actually live our loves. This concern runs parallel to an essential question about modern poetry. That is the reason why the figure of Gaspara Stampa appears in central positions in both the long, epic *Notebooks of Malte Laurids Brigge* (in the sense of a lengthy, albeit manipulated, narrative chronicling an individual's fate as an allegory of his culture or time) and in the imagistic and artfully disjointed *Duino Elegies*. For Rilke she is an essential figure for the tension between perpetuity and the present moment, between time as we experience it in ecstatic moments and as we experience it as duration. The nature of desire, in the figure of Gaspara Stampa, is the key to this tension, which is the reason why Stampa occurs in both Rilke's narrative prose and his long letters as well as his more immediate, focused poems.

Love offers us the illusion that we will persist, that we may withstand our own decline and demise. The enormous exertion Stampa makes to hold on to a love that has no object, long after the object of her affections has disappeared, becomes a lie in defiance of time: I continue to love, just as strongly as before, continue to long, on and on, "fed by inexhaustible oil." For otherwise the beloved person would be exactly as great as her love. But in the story of Gaspara Stampa it is not Count Collalto but her intense experience of her unrequited love that becomes a model: a model of all that passes away, of our decrepitude and thus of how we are bound by time. Stampa forgets the count who has rejected her, and with him her own mortality—this is what is at stake. She should be a "heightened example of soaring" to us, since she is an outlier, living on beyond rejection (of which the count is only an instantiation, since it is not about contingent subjects but rather love itself). In order not to resign himself to melancholy in the face of the fact that there is nothing but the here and now, Rilke crafts his hyperbolic sentences, which seem to know that we—the readers exactly like the women to whom Rilke told the same thing—*want* to be taken in, and even fooled, by them. "To be here is splendid" and "to love is to last." It isn't, it isn't, it isn't. Or: It isn't always, since nothing lasts forever. Or: It actually is, for what else should be glorious if not the "here and now"? It actually is, for how else can we love, even only for a moment, if not in the belief that the love will last? How else can we love, if not by making ourselves independent of the reaction of our beloved and forgetting him or her as well as ourselves in the moment of love?

"To love means: to shine forth fed by inexhaustible oil." But when Rilke writes about Stampa, then her pain erupts "so intensely in [his] heart" that his inner angel has a hard time "not to burst suddenly into full blaze in plain sight."[18] The full blaze stands here for duration, in contrast to burning up in the moment. What ultimately shines for Rilke is poetry itself, in which he creates his icons of great love. Gaspara Stampa is therefore Rilke's great image of deceit: the consoling deceit that confounds our knowledge that there is nothing but the here and now.

Love, understood in this way, even "the deception of high romanticism and the deceit of these remarkable women [in Rilke's life] (who understood this deception and still wanted it and needed it)"—as literary critic Harold Bloom puts it—"this seems to me to be poetry itself."[19] Following Bloom's thesis, poetry is the promise that love can last: a deceit, which we recognize as such and which we nevertheless want and need. And of which we can keep convincing ourselves and those we love—this is the unbelievable achievement of poetry. Rilke deceives himself with Gaspara Stampa, since not only does he not practice her kind of abstinence in his own life, but he also doesn't hold back, doesn't sublimate anything. And he deceives us too by using this very figure, this "heightened example of soaring," as the fundamental thought of his lyric poetry and a project of deception that we want because it consoles us in the face of our mortality. Not to believe this deception means not to believe in perpetuity, but to resign oneself to the indifferent passage of time. Gaspara Stampa teaches us this. And still she is always outdone in Rilke's work by the angel of affirmations—that is, by the poetic imagination with which he creates such figures. Rilke makes pure, objectless love the basis of poetic insight and elevates the pure love into the center of his poetry, but this is self-deception, for Rilke is always desiring something. To tell the truth with a lie: I love you, I am loved—that is poetry.

It is thus less important that abstinence, in the case of the women whose unrequited love Rilke fetishizes, is always the result of their lovers' rejection. This is how things are, Rilke writes, with love: Men are incompetent, while women do all the work themselves. And since men are so incompetent in love women have all the more opportunities to sublimate the frustration of unlived, unsatisfied love.

"What a pathetic figure man cuts in the history of love. He has almost no strength but the superiority that tradition ascribes to him, and even this superiority he bears so carelessly that it would be outrageous if his distraction and absent-heartedness were not, on occasion, partly justified by important events. Yet nobody will talk me out of what is plain to see between this most intense lover [the Portuguese nun Marianna Alcoforado] and her shameful partner: that this relation definitively proves how on the part of women, everything has been achieved, endured, and accomplished in love, while on the part of men, there is only an absolute incapacity to love. She receives the highest diploma in the art of love, to use a banal analogy, while he lugs around a basic grammar book of love from which, at best, he has picked out a few words to construct an occasional sentence, as gorgeous and thrilling as the well-known sentences on the first pages of a language primer."[20]

Abstinence assures women guaranteed admission into heaven; in life, however, they continue to flounder about in desire and joy. As if they themselves were bent on getting that admission, many critics have

elevated Rilke's ideology of sublimation and abstinence to a poetic principle. The "hypothetical negation becomes a means of affirmation," they
write (identifying a major poetic principle), and praise the withdrawal in
Rilke's poetry. The insight into Rilke's poetic technique is crucial.[21] But
does Gaspara Stampa, as Rilke's muse, truly deny? *No, no, no!* I have to
spell it out: The angel of affirmations does not hypothetically negate, it
says yes. Yes. Yes. Yes. Incessantly. One more time: Stampa's desire never
flags. Love, as another critic writes, "should be selfless for the 'I' as well
as for the 'you,' and each one should be given to the other not as something 'opposite' but rather as the freedom of an open-ended act of love."[22]
So it's all about freedom and "an open-ended act of love." Instead of that,
I keep reading Rilke. And immediately following the long list of sublimating sisters, I find an enigmatic and seemingly unmotivated childhood
memory in *The Notebooks of Malte Laurids Brigge*. This passage could not
make it any clearer what Rilke is thinking about, in addition to his great
gospel of abstinent love and its sublimation, when it comes to these
women, who became "inner sources." He is not thinking about these
women's abstinence and self-loss for the sake of freedom and an abstract
openness, but rather about a fan-shaped jewelry box with "a border of
flowers" and "a little mound of light, a slightly worn velvet," through
which runs a groove.[23] In order to decode the following image from
Rilke's 1910 novel, there is no need to refer directly to Freud's interpretation of the casket choice in Shakespeare's *The Merchant of Venice*, his
case study of Dora, Luce Irigaray, Hélène Cixous, or Elfriede Jelinek, or
their profound inquiries into female sexuality:

> I still remember exactly how, one day long ago, at home, I came
> upon a jewel-case; it was as wide as two hands, fan-shaped, with a
> border of flowers stamped into the dark-green morocco. I opened it:
> it was empty. I can say this now after so many years. But at that
> time, when I had opened it, I saw only what its emptiness consisted
> of: velvet, a small mound of light-colored, slightly worn velvet; and
> the groove to hold jewelry which, empty and brighter by just a trace
> of melancholy, vanished into it. For a moment this was bearable.
> But when considering those women who are left behind as lovers, it
> is perhaps always like this.[24]

Instead of elevating the "open-ended act of love" into a category, as his
interpreters do, Rilke wants to linger in front of a faint groove found in a

velvet-lined jewelry box. It was Rilke who bragged that he spent several days preparing for the night of an "act of love" and then set this term loose with the following metaphor: "I want to take off into you . . . like the rocket at the loneliest star. I want to be you."[25]

Following Rilke's alternately progressive and problematic statements about the misery of erotic relationships, we begin to understand why he makes a woman into the figure of unhappy, disappointed, and *true* (in his view, objectless and unrequited) love, but as a man was not himself capable of such love. For he is a man after all, and from the beginning he wanted to be a man, as an early letter to the writer Theodor Fontane confirms: "You have been misled by my second given name [Maria] and seen a woman in me; this is not the case—I am of the male gender and hope that in my life I will always comport myself as a male, in the best sense of the word."[26] While he declares renunciation as the right path for women, Rilke the man continues to love women—and many of them.

The concept of the "fierce example" of Gaspara Stampa, from which young girls are supposed to learn abstinence, thus contradicts everything for which the figure of Stampa is supposed to stand. For her life after being abandoned, to which Rilke is seeking access in his poetry, is a life *without* models, a life *without* examples, a life lived into pure space, into freedom, into the open. As soon as we remove all that is negative from an unhappy, unsatisfied love, so that "the most ancient of sufferings finally become/more fruitful," and the inner movement of being abandoned is reevaluated as pure becoming (and creating), then there is no more figure, no face, no beloved, and no counterpart.[27] In such cases there can be no more examples, for this dispossessed, objectless love must be radically reinvented. Rilke's fascination with the "unhappy women in love, the abandoned ones," rests on the tremendous achievement of becoming something new, without precedent, and still managing to write it down.

This isn't all quite right. There is a vast difference between fetishizing an abandoned woman and Rilke's ecstatic poems about love. And Stampa doesn't want anything other than to abstain from abstinence; she wants to push away all her longing, she does not want to become an example, she wants not to want anymore. Taking Stampa as a "heightened example" only projects one's actual longing onto a literary figure. As a model, Stampa herself becomes the object of desire. But precisely this displacement of desire is not necessarily sublimation. For the displacement of the signifier of desire does not necessarily lead to the end of desire or the satisfaction of one's longing.[28] In other words: We could fall *in love* with Stampa out of narcissistic love.

This is not about resolving Rilke's contradictions. It could also be shown that Rilke himself forgets Stampa (and she is after all a figure of memory that loves beyond the object, instead of preserving the ability to love in forgetfulness), for already in "The Third Elegy" Rilke proceeds with "It is one thing to sing the beloved. Another, alas/to invoke the hidden, guilty river-god of the blood" ("*Eines ist, die Geliebte zu singen, Ein anderes, wehe,/jenen verborgenen schuldigen Fluß-Gott des Bluts* [*zu singen*]") and brings it to a head by "summon[ing] the night to an endless uproar."[29]

The relation between poetry and life can be defined more closely when the poeticized figures are recognized as examples that are so intensified that they admonish us to turn ourselves into fierce examples of soaring. A love poem for Lou Andreas-Salomé traces the unresolved tension between lived love and sublimation:

> As one would hold a handkerchief in front of
> one's piled-up breath . . . no: as one would press it
> against a wound from which life, all in one spurt,
> is trying to escape—I held you close
> till you were red with me. Who can describe
> what happened to us? We made up for all
> that there had been no time for. [. . .]

> [. . .] It's not that I
> discover you at the sad, cooled-off places
> you left; the very fact that you're not there
> is warm with you and realer and is more
> than a privation.[30]

> Wie man ein Tuch vor angehäuften Atem,
> nein: wie man es an eine Wunde preßt,
> aus der das Leben ganz, in einem Zug,
> hinauswill, hielt ich dich an mich: ich sah,
> du wurdest rot von mir. Wer spricht es aus,
> was uns geschah? Wir holten jedes nach,
> wozu die Zeit nie war. [. . .]

[. . .] Ich erfinde
dich nicht an traurig ausgekühlten Stellen,
von wo du wegkamst; selbst, daß du nicht da bist,
ist warm von dir und wirklicher und mehr
als ein Entbehren.[31]

Rilke never sent Lou this poem. In the first stanza a masterful metaphor spreads like blood soaking a bandage: The reddening of the beloved person ("you were red with me") is described with such strong images that the actual reddening practically fades from view behind the metaphorical descriptions of longing. This intensification of a metaphor, behind which the actual thing or action being described almost disappears, is a method perfected by Rilke. On the linguistic level the rhetorically created pre-desire is heightened in terms of time and intensity to such a degree (from handkerchief to bandage, from breath to life, from air to blood) that it might be the high point of the poem. This poetics of intensification matches the theme of this poem: Rilke wants to show that direct contact with the beloved person does not overshadow all other dimensions of the love experience. In the second stanza, where Rilke writes that Lou's absence was "realer and [. . .] more/than a privation," we find a clue to how to read the figure of Stampa. In the poem about and to Lou, Rilke wants simply to make himself *aware* of the pain of the separation and the loss of the beloved body. And this pain is "realer" and "more" than only the imaginary impression of the beloved on the pillow, on the cheek, on the leg: It has a weight, which has all the intensity of the experience described in the first strophe. Just as Rilke wants to experience love in its entirety, without letting himself be distracted by the pros and cons, he wants to experience the pain of separation in full. Pain is experienced without anger or resentment. Experience, for Rilke, can be measured only in intensity: There is no distinction between "good" and "bad" here.

The distance between Rilke's love poems and the idealized figure of Gaspara Stampa, for whom the absence of the beloved is ultimately "realer and is more," does not rest on a value judgment. If experience is measured without regard for good and evil, easy and difficult, as either intense or lifeless, then abstinence can be as strong as love. When experience is measured in intensity—when rejection and solitude are experiences just as intense as love—no norm can be drawn from it. The sublimated spinster does not offer an example, but rather remains a radically singular figure.

In a letter where Rilke explains the intentions of *Duino Elegies*, he writes: "I [am] more and more concerned in my work with correcting everywhere our habits of repression, which have removed and gradually alienated us from all of the secrets that would infinitely allow us to live fully."[32] The figure of Stampa is Rilke's effort to correct our habit of repressing what we cannot understand. We should lose our morbid fear of loss. The great self-deceit of love enables us to do this, according to Rilke—a deceit that we do not *want to recognize* as such. But we should live out this experience with the help of the fierce example of soaring, in order to move beyond it, not into sublimation, but rather "to live forever and in full." On the rhetorical level, Stampa is a model for the overcoming of models: a transitional situation and border case, but never the goal.

The unreadability and unlivability of the example of Stampa turns her at once into an envoy of excess and a figure of disorder. With the army of other great lovers, she guards the entrance to Rilke's poetic creation, in order to provide a way to separate excess from disorder, cosmos from chaos. "It is only one step from the surrender of the woman in love to a lyric poet's act of surrender," writes Rilke.[33] In order to take this decisive step from surrendering to having surrendered, he makes use of his sublimating messengers. Their "surrender," of which Rilke is simply incapable, opens up the space where excess and disorder are no longer distinguishable. There he creates iconic figures that deal with a life in full, that is, a life *in* reality.

Forget it. Recall Gaspara Stampa as an example of how there is no path from poetry back into life. We have heeded Rilke's warning in *Duino Elegies* and now "imagined" Stampa "intensely enough." Now we can forget. Remember the "girl/deserted by her beloved" as a figure of the deception that we know to be deception but still need and want. In her incoherence, Stampa stands for the fact that Rilke's poetry does not sublimate or abstain from life.

t

for Tower

When Rilke describes his conception of art, he names two seemingly mutually exclusive tasks for the modern poet. First, the poet is to grant each individual word such weight that it stands on its own in the poem and ultimately becomes autonomous. Yet, at the same time, each word is to contribute to a greater meaning that surpasses everything else. These opposing tendencies in Rilke's poetics underline the main concern of his poetry, which is the question of how to live truly in the modern era. Rilke is absolutely convinced that we can move beyond ourselves entirely *on our own* or *from within ourselves*, or, as he also writes, that from within us a kind of nonreligious "superabundant existence" ("*überzähliges Dasein*") may rise up.[1] For Rilke the following paradox must be expressed again and again in new ways: that we are capable of becoming more than we are even without relying on a transcendent or divine authority; that individual experience can lift us up out of our life. This is the parallel between Rilke's instructions on how to write good poetry and how to live a good life: Just as individual words relate to the meaning of the whole poem, so do individual experiences, in Rilke's understanding of our being, relate to the meaning of our life. Individual experiences transcend life, yet they can be experienced and understood only within life.

In his poetry, Rilke tries to express this potential to live more (not simply more intensely but actually *live more*) than we already do in every moment, without recourse to any higher, transcendent authority.

Perhaps we are *here* in order to say: house,
bridge, fountain, gate, pitcher, fruit-tree, window—
at most: column, tower . . . But to *say* them, you must understand,
oh to say them more intensely than the Things themselves
ever dreamed of existing.[2]

Sind wir vielleicht *hier*, um zu sagen: Haus,
Brücke, Brunnen, Tor, Krug, Obstbaum, Fenster,—
höchstens: Säule, Turm. . . . aber zu *sagen*, verstehs,
oh zu sagen so, wie selber die Dinge niemals
innig meinten zu sein.

These lines in "The Ninth Elegy" name the opposing principles in Rilke's poetry. It is our task to give expression to the world in our particular manner, in order to nurture its reality more lastingly within us. This happens, says Rilke, when the value of an individual word increases until it outweighs the world. It can help to understand Rilke's poetry if you think of this strange relationship between word and world, which is constantly reversing itself, as an allegory for the place of human beings in the modern world. When we express ourselves in our own way, that is, live our life after a model of our own making, or, as Rilke says, do not merely repeat the words we use, but rather make them more our own; when we take the sentence as the measure of the world; when a word gains particular meaning due to its sound, then we are making a world through our being. But as long as we experience the world at hand as the source of this authentic expression, we cede this being back to the world.

The lines quoted above, from the ninth of the *Duino Elegies*, about the special place of "column, tower," follow this paradoxical logic. Every word in Rilke's lyrics should have its own value, and as an autonomous unity stand out above the line, the sentence, the stanza, or the whole work the way a "column" or a "tower" registers above the surrounding terrain. On the other hand, the larger meaning of the line, the stanza, and ultimately the entire poem or even book must be borne by all of the words used, as if by supporting (and even concealed) columns. The poem should transcend the words used in it, yet even the smallest word should outweigh the poem as a whole and hold its ground against being subsumed into the larger context.

In the workshops of the sculptor Auguste Rodin, Rilke observed how a single sculpted piece of clay—a hand, a toe, but also simply a surface, an edge, a depression—could entirely unexpectedly take on a life of its own, which outweighed that of the whole sculpture. In his poems Rilke imitates with language what Rodin does with clay and stone. He isolates individual words (akin to a small surface area of a much larger entity sculpted by Rodin) as if they have a quality that has nothing to do with their function of conveying meaning or being subsumed into the grammatical structure. Rilke wants to grant every word he uses the status of a thing and actual object that can unlock the whole world. When Rodin and Rilke treat everything—every edge in the sculpture, every word in the poem—as self-sufficient, and as if unrelated to the greater whole, they grant each of these units the meaning of a world. This corresponds with other attempts by European thinkers to deconstruct the metaphysical opposition between this world and a more meaningful one beyond it, an opposition that deeply influenced the philosophy of the nineteenth century. As Ludwig Wittgenstein writes, at the same time when Rilke and Rodin were making modern art in their respective media, "as a thing among things, each thing is equally insignificant, but as a world, each one equally significant."[3] For there should be "no place that does not see you," as Rilke puts it in "Archaic Torso of Apollo": There should be no spot that is less alive and expressive than any other.[4]

When a word is grouped together with other words into a poem, its autonomy remains preserved in the line, the stanza, the cycle. Every word introduces to the world sense and meaning, which in Rilke occurs as creaturely experience. Every word should make its contribution to the sense of the poem, but it should be a glad, voluntary task. It is lifted up out of the everyday use of language, and it stays there. This creates the impression that every word is part of the world, rather than merely describing the world or dissolving into allegory. Rilke learned from Rodin that even the smallest, most unremarkable word must be reimagined at its most fundamental level: It should not sound different or be used differently, but rather it should *be* different. If a word is used to describe the world and is not fundamentally changed as it does so, it will simply vanish when its task (of communicating) is finished.

Rilke saw such potential for the world to be imagined anew in the word "*création*," which acquired significance for him because of Rodin. Rodin had discovered as the basis of his art not the depth, weight, and mass of the bronze and the stone, but rather—a revelation for Rilke—the surface. And so "all the received notions of sculpture had become useless for

[Rodin]. There was neither the pose, nor the group, nor the composition. There were only innumerably many, living surfaces, there was only life . . . Rodin took hold of the life he saw everywhere he looked. He took hold of it in the smallest places, he observed it, he pursued it. He . . . caught up to it wherever it occurred, and he found that in every place it was equally large, equally powerful, and equally captivating. There was no insignificant or minor part of the body: it was alive."[5]

Rilke shared Rodin's wish to engage with everything and to discover everywhere with astonishment that there is nothing that means less than anything else. Yet Rodin's conception of a world in which everything has a meaning, which is everywhere "equally large, equally powerful, and equally captivating," changes in Rilke's hands from a Gnostic *belief* to a contradictory *task*. And this *task* underlies his poetry, as he terms it in "The First Elegy": "All this was mission [*Auftrag*]." Taking his cue from Rodin, he wrote: "It is the artist's task to make a single thing out of many things, and out of the smallest part of a thing, a world."[6] Here lies a great and productive contradiction in Rilke's poetics: The world is supposed to arise from the smallest fragment, yet all these parts are to add up to a single thing.

In *The Notebooks of Malte Laurids Brigge*, Rilke writes: "The time of that other interpretation will dawn, when there shall not be left one word upon another, and every meaning will dissolve like a cloud and fall down like rain."[7] As early as his book about Rodin, written in 1902, Rilke suggests the same deconstruction of language. With this book begins the "time of that other interpretation"; it is the modern age that Rilke sees arriving with Rodin and that he wants to help fashion. "And now? Hadn't we once again come to an era that longed for this kind of expression, for this powerful and insightful interpretation of all that was unspeakable, confused and mysterious in it?"[8] From Rodin Rilke takes the idea of an impersonal art, in which the self no longer portrays itself, but rather where the self is created in the act of creation, in the finding of an authentic expression and of the right word. The resulting works of art and their constitutive words are no longer judged according to their meaning, but rather by the fact of their existence.

In this study, Rilke describes an as-yet-unbuilt, column-shaped sculpture of Rodin's, which was meant to represent and celebrate work as such:

This will be the *Monument to Work*. On this slowly rising relief a history of work will take form . . . for this monument to work will be a tower. Rodin did not want to portray work in one great image or gesture; work is not visible from a distance. It precedes itself into the studios, into the studies, into the heads; in the dark [. . .]

Perhaps the tower of work is already rising in one of these studios. But at the moment, since its realization is still in the future, it is necessary to speak of its meaning; and its meaning seems to lie in the material realm. When this monument has taken shape, one will feel that even in this work Rodin wanted nothing beyond his own art. The working body showed itself to him, as the loving body had before. It was a new revelation of life. [. . .] In the final sense, new life meant for him simply: new surfaces, new gestures. [. . .] With this development Rodin has given a signal to all the arts in this helpless time.[9]

Rodin does not hope to achieve a particular meaning with his art; rather, he puts the work of art into the world as something existing, just like a tower. Rodin's "signal . . . in this helpless time" consists of his art no longer setting down a sign, but rather, as a modern work of art, being nothing but formed materiality. The "tower" points to nothing but itself. Rilke seeks to transfer this godlike gesture of creation into his poetry. The written word should be recognized in its materiality instead of disappearing into its function as signifying or representing some imagined reality.

In the *Malte* novel Rilke expressed this notion thus: "But this time, I will be written. I am the impression that will transform itself. Only very little is missing for me to understand all this and assent to it."[10] What is missing? What does Rilke need before he can "understand all this and assent to it"? "Very little" is missing, "just one step, and [his] misery would turn into bliss."[11] So we turn from the study on Rodin back to Rilke's language. What is missing for Rilke is a word. But not just any word, not just anything, but rather some "small, imperceptible object": perhaps the word "word" itself. Rilke programmatically proposes a kind of impersonal writing that is called "modern" these days, since by dissolving a central narrative perspective it both deepens consciousness and reflects the alienation and groundlessness of modern man. When Rilke elevates writing and what is written above the writer, and the word above the sentence, sound above meaning, the tower above the poem, he charts new possibilities for literature to convey and create meaning. This act of liberation through the exaltation of the word is nevertheless still a loss: "but I cannot take that step; I have fallen and can no longer pick myself up because I have been broken."[12] The fragmented subject—Rilke, still young, poor, and unknown during his time with Rodin—places his hope in individual words, which, although only pieces, are supposed to outweigh the whole. It is an attempt to think of the word on the level of its *being* in the world and not on the level of its *meaning*. The word should do no more than be here, but in this "being here" it *is* everything that it ever can be: It *is*. Only when what is written has become self-sufficient in this way does it acquire the power to give the sense back to our existence. "I am the impression that will transform itself": The words in Rilke's poetry transform something on the level of being, not of meaning.

To turn this around (against Rilke's understanding), it is helpful to understand Rilke's "word" as an allegory: as an allegory for man in the world. In a letter of July 24, 1904, Rilke writes: "the word must become man!" which means that words should take on a life of their own, and moreover that man can be changed.[13] What Rilke intends to transform, in each of his poems about zoo animals and houseplants, about old maids and dogs, about falconers and orange-boats, is not the *meaning* of these words, things, or people, but rather the very being of each word, thing, or person in turn.

The constitutive paradox of Rilke's poetics, as mentioned at the beginning, reveals itself here. From the smallest word a world is supposed to take shape that not only *expresses* what is "unspeakable, cloudy and mysterious" in the world but *is* it. But at the same time every word is supposed to only "copy down" what is already there in the world: Poetic creation is nothing but the carrying out of a dictation. The artist is at once God and secretary; Rodin's "tower" is nothing but a tower, but at the same time it is the entire world created by Rodin's hands. It *is* labor and a monument to it. This tension is born of Rilke's aforementioned belief that man can be changed in his existence, but that this change comes from nowhere but within his own being.

In *The Notebooks of Malte Laurids Brigge* Rilke tries to counteract the decline of the author and of the self, with which writing suddenly develops new possibilities, by copying something down. "Until now I have always believed that help would come. There it is right in front of me, in my own handwriting [. . .] I copied them from the books I found them in, so that they would be right in front of me, issued from my own hand as if they were my own words."[14]

"The time of that other interpretation," announced in the *Malte* novel as the dawning of a new age, depends on something very small, through which everything changes its sense. This "small thing" cannot be created by Malte or Rilke; it must be something completely independent of the writer's intentions. Otherwise the author would only be endorsing himself, would only indulge in the myth of an authentic statement, but would hardly come any closer to the *effect* of the "subject" as author that Rilke is pursuing here. But for all its independence the "small, imperceptible object" cannot have its source in a sphere beyond human existence. For then the "time of that other interpretation" would no longer be a moment in history. The *Malte* novel is explicitly characterized by its time and place—Paris at the beginning of the twentieth century, first entry: "September 11th, Rue Toullier." So what is missing is no particular word, but the word that is nothing but a word: "that small and possibly inconspicuous word which all at once transforms into magnificent sense everything we had struggled to learn and everything we had failed to understand."[15] A word that is like a thing: no longer decodable and not hiding any greater sense. A word that is just as insignificant as a word among words as it is significant as a world. Our existence wants for nothing, and yet, according to Rilke, we can *be* more. It is possible to live "more"; like a word, life can be more.

Thus we return to Rilke's allegory of the smallest word and to the tower. Only one word is missing, which opposes Rilke's great promise of transcendence—the whole rigmarole of angels, unicorns, tragic maidens, and the "soul of a future time," in Paul Valéry's description of Rilke. For in the lines where poetic creation is described as the transcription of a dictation and where human existence is explained as exceeding itself, there Rilke offers poetic images only of human constructions: only "columns" and "towers." That word which is a world and at the same time reveals the meaning of the existing world is man-made, in Rilke's view. When he describes his attempt to grasp language as existing material, instead of placing it in the service of communication, not every word bulges with meaning.

"At most [*höchstens*]: column, tower," in "The Ninth Elegy" names our task: to speak the greatest, highest, farthest, and longest-lasting things *made by men.* No natural beauty is evoked, not heaven, tree, mountain, moon, star. "At most: column, tower" are the words that manage to express the world and, as individual words, to do nothing more than be "highest" [*höchstens*]—there is nothing higher.

The construction of the tower of Babel is one of our oldest images of the human desire to achieve and to surpass divine heights through our own power. It is the poet's task to bear witness to the ruined effort to reach transcendence through language. In "The Seventh Elegy," we read:

> But a tower was great, wasn't it? Oh Angel, it was—
> even when placed beside you? Chartres was great—and music
> reached still higher and passed far beyond us.[16]

> Aber ein Turm war groß, nicht wahr? O Engel, er war es,—
> groß, auch noch neben dir? Chartres war groß—, und Musik
> reichte noch weiter hinan und überstieg uns.

The work of man passes "far beyond us": This is the credo of a modern poet. Even the list of words preceding "column, tower," which do not yet express our highest task, contain nothing that is not touched by human hands: Rilke there places a "fruit-tree" as an example of nature that is tamed and bred by man. But "at most: column, tower" also means simply: The "highest" that I saw were "columns" and "towers" like those of Chartres, which out-reach everything, even a figure like the angel, who is supposed to contain and surpass everything. "Highest" means simply what it is.

In 1922, living in what he stubbornly called the "tower" of Muzot in Switzerland (actually a modest stone house), Rilke completed *Duino Elegies*, which he had begun eleven years earlier in the castle near Duino of the aptly named family Thurn und Taxis (Italian "Torre e Taxis"; French "Tour et Taxis"). God is an "old tower" in one of Rilke's widely known poems, around whom the poet circles in widening gyres ("I live in expanding rings").[17] In Rilke's erotic poems and in his book about Rodin, the phallic meaning of the tower is evident. To say "tower" "more intensely than the Things [*Dinge*] themselves/ever dreamed of existing" means to treat "tower" as a word and to make it into something real. As soon as the word "tower" appears in a poem, it is no longer a word, but rather something "higher" than the words before and after. A word before which one stands in awe or in fear, or which one can climb for the sake of the view. Or that was simply piled up, with no relation to anything else. A thing, one of Rilke's *Dinge*, emerging from the name Ro*din*.

for Un-

"He was a poet and hated the approximate [*das Ungefähre*]," notes the narrator in Rilke's novel *The Notebooks of Malte Laurids Brigge*, first published in 1910, in reference to an author who puts off dying just long enough to explain to "a rather uneducated nun" at his deathbed how the word "corridor" should be pronounced correctly.[1] "[O]r perhaps he was concerned only with the truth; or it annoyed him to be taking along as his last impression the thought that the world would continue to go on so carelessly."[2] The narrator, who unlike the nun is in no way "uneducated," seems uncertain: Is it that he hates what is "approximate," does he care about the truth, or is this just a stalling tactic that so unsettles the poet at the moment of his death? At the end of the passage he pushes "the approximate" out of his mind and decides that the dying man must have been concerned with the truth.

But the poet in the *Malte* novel (behind whom Rilke is hiding), who describes himself as "the *bee of the invisible* [*Biene des Unsichtbaren*]," who stores the "honey of the visible [. . .], in the great, golden beehive of the invisible," is just copying it all down.[3] Neither the disapproval of "the approximate" nor the possible temptation to prefer something other than the truth accounts for what the "secretary of the invisible" takes down and what remains unwritten.[4] In his work Rilke prefers to follow the "insight, that so often unexpectedly overpowered [him], ever more impartially and independently," and forces him not to regard anything in life as the opposite to life.[5] The contrast between life and death must be mercilessly deconstructed, for this opposition leads, according to Rilke, to a renunciation of life. An affirmative stance toward death "should be understood *not* in that sentimental-romantic sense of rejecting life, of opposition to life, but rather [as] our friend, precisely at *that* moment when we most passionately and most devastatingly affirm being-here, striving, nature, love. Life is always saying, at one and the same time: Yes and No. Death, in fact (I implore you to believe it!), is the actual yes-sayer. It says *nothing but*: Yes. In the face of eternity."[6]

In his poems Rilke often and emphatically uses the prefix "un-" (or its equivalents, "in-," "im-," and "ir-"). Many of these "un-" words are not supposed to conjure anything "approximate" ("*ungefähr*"), but rather open up a space of *in*stability and openness that conveys a persistent sense of unease in the context of the concrete and poignant images around them.

> I want to stand up front as in a boat,
> huge and unfurled like a flag.
> Dark, but with a golden helmet that
> gleams restlessly [*unruhig*]. And lined up behind me
> ten men [. . .]
> with helmets that flash the way mine does [*unstät sind*].[7]

Rilke's "un-"words work so effectively in his poetry because of their contrast with the extremely concrete words that surround them. "And you wait, you wait for that one thing/that will infinitely [*unendlich*] enlarge your life;/the gigantic, the stupendous [*Ungemeine*],/the awakening of stones,/depths turned round toward you."[8] The vague indeterminacy of the "infinitely" becomes the precise description of a heightened expectation, when Rilke loads the next stanza's metaphors with details: "The volumes bound in rust and gold/flicker dimly on the shelves." In light of the adjectives "rust" and "gold," the "infinitely" and the "stupendous" ("*Ungemeine*") in the first lines cannot be taken as filler words that the poet turns to in the absence of more precise adjectives, but rather as precise descriptions with the same function as "rust and gold." The "un-" words do not render the poem less precise, they are not a cop-out on the part of the poet; rather, they succeed at marking precisely the uncertainty in the experience being described, at delineating precisely what is imprecise. To paraphrase Walter Benjamin: In Rilke the description of the approximate is no approximate description. When the poet in the *Malte* novel says that he hates what is "approximate," he means descriptions that present themselves approximately, not the inherent imprecision and vagueness in the world. As a poet Rilke often aims at nothing other than capturing precisely the imprecision found in life and in the world.

In "The Island," from *New Poems*, the inhabitants of the island "seldom talk,/and each sentence is like an epitaph/for something washed ashore, unrecognized,/that comes without an explanation and stays."[9] "Unrecognized" and "without an explanation" ("*unerklärt*") are not cop-outs here, but rather precise descriptions, since the islanders come in contact only with things sent from outside the island or that wash up on shore—that is, things largely foreign to them. In the 1904 poem "Orpheus. Eurydice. Hermes," Eurydice is described as "untouchable" in the underworld. But this inaccessibility and untouchability is not the opposite of a former state of Eurydice's availability, but rather an ontologically different, and even positive, characteristic. Rilke describes her "untouchability" not as a loss or refusal, but rather as the organic condition of a "young flower": "She was in a new virginity/and untouchable; her sex had closed/as a young flower at approach of evening."[10] At the poem's end Rilke repeats the two lines containing the decisive description of the dead Eurydice in the underworld; this turns the word "uncertain" into a positive quality, to which the dead Eurydice acquiesces and of which her new essence is now comprised: "its steps, constrained by long winding-sheets,/uncertain, gentle, and without impatience [*Ungeduld*]."[11]

Rilke's "un-" words are supposed to strip the negative connotations from states of nonbeing. They are not the opposite of something that exists but rather stand on their own as the inexperienceable element of his work, independent, immovable, irrevocable. "Most events are unspeakable," writes Rilke in an early letter, but these are the events his poetry is about.[12] They should not be read as negation any more than the creative silence in the first of the sonnets to Orpheus: "Yet even in that silence/a new beginning, beckoning, change appeared."[13]

As "bee of the invisible," Rilke notes down—in spite of the poet's inclination for the truth, as noted in the *Malte* novel, and his hatred for anything "approximate"—a huge number of "un-," "in-," "im-," and "ir-" words in his poems and prose texts. This common usage lies at the heart of Rilke's belief that the reality of the world and our experience is in no way limited to straightforward, recognizable, knowable categories. With this insight that the unconscious is not the *opposite of consciousness* and the untimely is not the *opposite of the timely*, Rilke's work offers a new understanding of reality, which no longer originates with truth but with the unconcealment of what exists. This irrepressible conviction places Rilke's poetics in the context of attempts by Nietzsche, Freud, and Heidegger not to think of "un-" as a negation. The "unconscious" is a crucial dimension of our existence, as Freud explains in his work; the "untimely," as Nietzsche understands it, reveals the truth of an epoch; and the unconcealed, according to Heidegger's thesis, is something "which does not show itself, but announces itself through something which does show itself."[14] For Rilke, these are especially the occurrences of childhood, which (also according to Freud) remain unexpressed, un-understood, and unconscious until the child commands enough experiences to frame and contain the extremity of these occurrences. Before that has happened, they can, according to Rilke, only "be registered [. . .] as some kind of *un-un-un*":

> You have to consider the existence of children from the perspective of such experiences, and consider their disappointments and often incommensurate hardship for which they cannot yet fully account while they suffer them. Everything which we now understand retrospectively could register at the time when it was suffered only as un-happiness, un-pleasantness, as some kind of *un-un-un*.[15]

But Rilke is neither a philosopher nor an analyst: Every one of his "actually affirmative" "un-" words appears ultimately in a specific and not at all imprecise context in his writings with the express purpose of delineating more precisely the imprecise dimension of our existence.

As a poet, Rilke surrounds all the "paths into unknown regions, [. . .] unexpected encounters, [. . .] days of childhood, that have not yet been made clear," with the things, creations, and angels of his poetry.[16] He turns the "un-" words into the origin and center of his creation. For they are supposed to express "what is un-experienceable to us" and make "unforgotten" the dimension of life to which the "light excerpts" of our experience can correspond only "un-equally."[17] With his poetry, which he calls the "dictation of existence," Rilke hoped to transform everything as yet "un-grasped" through an "inconspicuous word" into something sensible.[18]

But this "magnificent sense" that Rilke hopes for is not a positive counterpoint to his "un-" words. Neither of them should be thought of as negative. There is no basis for something that exists, or for existence in general, that is not also the lack of such a basis; all that is positive emerges from the same source as all that is negative. This source, according to Rilke in another letter, is the "not-knowing-ourselves." "It's hopeless," he writes, when considering the human urge to repress and dispose of everything that cannot be understood, "the *kinds* of things toward which people turn in their helpless, disoriented curiosity about themselves. While in fact all of our sources originate from this not-knowing-ourselves."[19] In a poem that remained unpublished during his lifetime, Rilke describes this source as "exposed on the heart's mountains."[20] We encounter our existence exposed, without root or home—deep in our heart, which Rilke limns in this poem as an inner mountain towering above all "words," all "feeling," and all "knowledge"; only afterward do we engage, in one way or another, with being in the form of all that exists. And only *then*, after and because of this condition of "ungroundedness," the world divides itself into being and nonbeing, exact and inexact, truth and falsehood, known and unknown, familiar and unfamiliar, happiness and unhappiness.

Just as Freud tried to take the negativity out of the unknown and the unconscious (in the unconscious, according to Freud's thesis, there is no word for "no"), Rilke wants to understand "ungroundedness" as the precarious basis for our existence. Parallel to Freud, for whom dreams, as is well-known, were the royal road into the unconscious, Rilke finds evidence for the productive dimension of our "not-knowing-ourselves" during the night, when each of us has unshared experiences in his sleep, which "terrify him with his un-conquered interiority [. . .] [and] let his un-accepted suffering draw closer."[21] Heidegger's attempt to understand the experience of the world from its "un-concealedness," instead of fixing the world to a concept like existence, presence, revelation, or truth, may in fact be grounded in Rilke's reflections. This would be why Heidegger praised Rilke's *Notebooks of Malte Laurids Brigge* in 1925, because there he found "the elementary coming-to-the-word, i.e. an uncovering of existence as being-in-the-world," to which he devoted his own work.[22]

Because Rilke faces his life "unknowingly," as he put it in an ultimately discarded fragment for *Duino Elegies*, he wants to "undo" all wishes, since every wish can offer an occasion for disappointment. Rilke wants to practice this renunciation by "accustoming" his heart "to what is most remote from us." We could consider this practice of training your heart for what is farthest, most remote, and unattainable as the motto for Rilke's poetry, for which there exists nothing negative. Even "when something becomes an unbearable burden," we find, exposed as we are in the world, not nothing, but rather an "onslaught of being," and "there we stand at the verge of its transformation."[23] But don't think, "What a rosy-eyed fool," for Rilke emphatically distances himself from the idea that he wants to gloss over unhealthiness, unhappiness, uneasiness. As diligent secretary of our existence, he indulges a "passion for the whole," which will not let anything go unsaid. "The artist belongs to the company of those who, with single, irrevocable affirmation, have renounced all gains and losses [. . .] This finally free affirmation of the world raises the heart to another level of experience. The dice cast by him are no longer happiness and unhappiness, his poles are no longer marked as life and death. His range is not the distance between two opposites."[24]

"Fool," you think, still unpersuaded, "happiness is happiness and unhappiness is unhappiness, life is life and death is death," even when the poet's heart doesn't "irrevocably" agree. But Rilke does not say anything except that we ought to realize that happiness and unhappiness, life and death, originate in the same source to which we are exposed in equal measure. That we can think about existence and nonexistence at all, even though our existence is finite, is possible because the source of such thinking is our heart, where "intransience/rests without settling down"[25]—so whispers Rilke even before Heidegger tries to think of being and time—even though we can never experience either of them fully. We know about "intransience" in a world in which everything passes irretrievably, since we experience the fullness of being in the moments of fulfillment to which our heart exposes us, unconcealed as we are in this world, in great pain or bliss.

When Rilke evokes this paradoxical experience of the "majestic space of the heart," from which humans muster the courage to put themselves on the line again and again, contrary to all the wisdom and experience available to them, and thus to render themselves capable of extreme happiness and deep wounds, he wants to overcome the difference between being and nonbeing.[26] All that happens in the name of affirmation, for Rilke does not want to end up like the young girls from good homes in the *Malte* novel who stand in front of the tapestries of the *Lady à la Licorne* and do not "notice how in everything they draw they are merely suppressing inside themselves the unalterable life that in these woven pictures has radiantly opened in front of them, infinite and unsayable."[27] The "unalterable life," in all its infinite unsayability, is not meant to be repressed in Rilke's work, or to remain unspoken. As a poet Rilke is "unexpectedly seized" by this unresolved task to speak this truth "ever more impartially and independently." It is the poet's task to let life itself speak, by being impartial with regard to both pain and bliss.

"And what else?" Rilke asks on the first page of the *Malte* novel, "*und sonst?*"[28] "Un-" in Rilke's work characterizes nothing negative, but is rather the center and the heart of all that which is ungrasped, unspoken, repressed, exposed or marked as an opposite, and around which Rilke's work moves like a breeze around a blossom.

V

for Vagabond, or Being Outside

Where is the outside of a poem? In a love letter to his fiancée, Clara Westhoff, written on October 23, 1900, Rilke paints a picture of a country idyll on the moor of Worpswede (an artist's colony in northwestern Germany) that presents the young woman with her husband at her side.

"In a little house a soft light would burn, a gentle, shrouded lamp, and I would stand at the stove preparing your dinner: some nice vegetables or grits,—and on a small glass plate thick honey would glisten, and cold butter as pure as ivory would stand out against the bright colors of a Russian tablecloth. There would have to be bread, strong, whole-grain dark bread and zwieback, and on a long, narrow platter some pale Westphalian ham laced with stripes of white fat like the evening sky with its long and narrow clouds [. . .] Large lemons, cut into slices, would sink like the sun into the golden twilight of the tea, illuminating it softly with their radiant flesh, and the clear, flat surface of the tea would shiver with the rising threads of sour juices."[1]

The idyll doesn't last long. Rilke himself shivers and moves on and away, to Paris, into the possibility of a vagabond's life of free creation, of poetry, of life without connections. Starting in 1902, Rilke and Clara Rilke lived separate lives. Their daughter, Ruth, remained with Clara's parents in the north of Germany, and Clara Rilke herself went like her husband to Paris, where she studied sculpture—near him, but not with him. Breaks such as this abrupt departure from the idyll in the north of Germany will structure Rilke's life. He never hangs his hat in the same place for long; he never becomes more than a spectator but remains committed to the identity of the poet as vagabond. While he cultivates an attitude of openness toward life, he steps only occasionally out of the role of the spectator and really enters into a particular scene. And when that happens—when Rilke allows himself to become close to something (rarely) or someone (more frequently)—then he usually gets out of it fairly quickly. Life seizes him. He meets women. Loves them. Attaches himself. They take an apartment together. He prepares dinner for them, on a little makeshift stove, or an omelet in the morning. Departs the scene. Reattaches himself. Breaks away again. Until, finally, ultimately, after a bout with leukemia, the vagabond steps outside for one last time.

Rilke's lifelong search for an outside leaves its trace in his life not only in the form of broken-hearted women. It can also be seen in his urge to travel and his seemingly spontaneous decisions to set off, to break away, to start again. The wish to be "outside" feeds Rilke's skepticism toward and growing distance from literature as a profession, that self-sustaining brand of the author and the fame machine, which the poet nonetheless feeds with every word. Being "outside" means to live his life in new, different, and possibly greater ways than before, without ever being enclosed by an order, an understanding of reality, a philosophical system, an identity, or another person. Rilke wants to keep his life open to alternatives, for he sees it as "already lived and over/and like some legend lost in farthest distance," and from this perspective he would like to keep alive the hope of "learn[ing . . .] that space is granted [him]/for yet a second, ampler life, in time uncharted"[2] ("*daß ich Raum/zu einem zweiten, zeitlos breiten Leben habe*").[3] But these lines offer no guarantee of a "space" far outside. The metaphorical land grab is a poetical fiat; the poet wants space, the poet expects to be granted this space, but the true expansion of his life is in no way certain. If being "outside" promises a "second life" inside the first one, is this second life the opposite, or else the complete questioning of the first, "already lived" life? And if the "second life" stands in opposition to our actual life, how is it possible to talk about being "outside" in this way from within the first life, if this is really supposed to be a completely unoccupied space, where (literally or metaphorically) we leave behind all previous life the moment we set foot in it? From what position does Rilke's poetry promise the possibility of a new conception of one's life?

Rilke's urge to be "outside" seems to explain the poet's repeated and often painful escape from connections and relationships. And nevertheless the possibility of being "outside" first arises in the context of love affairs, from which he so often breaks away. The possibility of overcoming oneself—that is, the possibility of making the self into something new—is for him possible only through the burning desire to be near a beloved person. In the second Duino elegy, Rilke describes lovers as those who, in their love for another person, expand their personality, depth, and will to live, and ultimately exceed themselves:

> You, though, who in the other's passion
> grow until, overwhelmed, he begs you:
> "no *more* . . ."[4]

> Ihr aber, die ihr im Entzücken des anderen
> zunehmt, bis er euch überwältigt
> anfleht: *nicht* mehr—[. . .]

Rilke's recognition that being "outside" is only ever possible through the experience of love, which he repeatedly flees in his urge to be outside, is suspended between the second and third lines of the passage just quoted: The beloved "overwhelms" the lover through pure "passion," although he is in fact loved—these lines show Rilke's typical reconciliation of the difference between active and passive, loving and being loved. Rilke uses the word "overwhelmed" here as a verb as well as an adjective, for the lover, "overwhelmed [. . .] begs you." The lover is both overwhelmed and overwhelming: He overwhelms us but also begs us, while overwhelmed himself, to stop. The "*more*," to which only the lovers have access, is suspended between these two lines and thus also, implicitly, between the lovers and belongs to neither of them; no one grants it to the other, but rather both of them are exposed to its excess in the same way, in loving and being loved.

Being "outside" is on the one hand an empirical separation—moving on, setting off to travel, the search for distance (Rilke's notorious pursuit of solitude; the flight from Westphalian ham in the homey idyll). But there is the possibility of experiencing the "outside" not only as the end

of human closeness but also as an ecstatic overcoming of the self;
according to the atheist Rilke, we know of this possibility only through
the experience of love. "For our own heart always/exceeds us."[5] Since this
"exceeding" is a transcendence without a higher being and belongs neither
to the lover nor to the beloved, but rather overwhelms both of them
together, it becomes a teaching about "emptiness" (*Leere*) in *Duino
Elegies*: "Don't you know *yet*? Fling the emptiness out of your arms/into
the spaces we breathe; perhaps the birds/will feel the expanded air with
more passionate flying."[6] Rilke is playing with alternate meanings of the
word here. The German word for emptiness, "*Leere*," is a homophone of
"*Lehre*," "lesson." In this case, the lesson is that even in a godless world
there is something more, something "outside." We reach our arms out
into an empty space (*Leere*), but we find nothing there. The birds, whose
flight man would imitate in his longing to be outside, feel and fill, as an
image of the imagination, the empty space to which we—without
possessing anything ourselves—nevertheless contribute. The wish to be
"outside" is the wish for the fulfillment of all wishes. Yet we have nothing
to give but "emptiness" (*Leere*), since our arms are filled with longing. If
our emptiness is added to the emptiness of space, something more is born,
which surpasses us.

In Rilke's seven phallic poems from 1915, the concept of being "outside"
in outer space disappears at the unification of the lovers, like time and
matter into a black hole. "That innerness here/in which the being-outside
of stars chases" ("*in das das Draußensein der Sterne jagt*") means the simul-
taneity of absolute self-relinquishing—"so as to fling into your soft night/
with the soaring of womb-dazzling rockets/more feeling than I am quite"
("*mit dem Schwung schooßblendender Raketen/ mehr Gefühl zu schleudern,
als ich bin*")—and absolute self-being in orgasm.[7]

So the path to being "outside" is sex? It certainly is for Rilke, time and
again, at least until the night or the poem comes to an end. But being
"outside" is always more than this path, since it lays out the possibility of
an ecstatic experience, a self-produced intensification and heightening of
our being. It is the experience that is deepened in and through sex and
then, paradoxically, is also left behind there: the ecstatic loss of self,
which, according to Rilke, reminds us that I can no longer be "as I am."
Yet in one such case, and here Rilke is being consistent, being "outside"
is not just the orgasmic, indescribable "being outside of the stars," which
drives in and out of him in bed like a rocket, but also the banal or dramatic

exit from a relationship, fleeing from closeness, the separations and breakups, the morning after.

With the metaphors of marbled ham and nighttime rockets, Rilke outlines an understanding of what it means to be "outside," to which human existence has access in two different ways. Being "outside" can mean the highest happiness: a life beyond the tedium of stability and security, life outside the tedium of ham in Worpswede, life as ecstasy, as precarious balance between being overwhelmed by and overwhelming one's lover. Being "outside" can also mean a difficult existence: life without a foothold and without security, life without a guarantee of the "second, ampler life, in time uncharted," within this one that Rilke hoped for, life as "emptiness," life as the loneliness of the vagabond.

Being "outside" is therefore not a philosophical concept that powers poetry, like a mental motor driven by internal distinctions or psychological bifurcations—between desire and satisfaction, presence and unquenchable desire, referential speech and the loss of language. Rilke did not know the certainty found in a coherent and logical system of thought. Nor did he know the stability of a mutually secured relationship with another person, or a socially sanctioned identity with a steady income and other assurances. He left his marriage just as he would ultimately break with most of the poetic forms that he had used in his work. He especially distrusted philosophical systems that elevated a word such as "outside" to the level of a concept.

But even this distrust is not of a philosophical nature. Rilke was not a philosophical thinker and knew that he was "completely incapable of examining a whole system."[8] He distrusted the notion that an individual could develop a coherent explanation of his or her world: "whenever a system emerges from an individual's philosophical development, I have an almost dejected feeling of constriction, of intentionality, and every time I try to locate the person in whom the fullness of his experience still remains alive, still disordered and unarranged, not unified through the delimitation and accommodations which every systematic ordering demands."[9]

"Outside" is where something "still disordered and unarranged" "remains alive" inside a person, whether through him or perhaps even against him. Being "outside" is neither maxim nor concept. Being "outside" has its roots neither in philosophical thought nor in Rilke's life, but rather remains "outside" any systematic ordering, regardless of whether this ordering takes the form of a philosophical system or of the pattern or model of an existing life (such as, in Rilke's case, his roles as lover, father, husband, dandy, poet, prophet, priest). Nevertheless being "outside" is not the *opposite* of a philosophical system or normative pattern. It denotes for us the open space where "the fullness of [. . .] experience still remains alive, still disordered and unarranged."[10] With this formulation Rilke emphasizes that something lives in, through, and *out of* man. The urge toward being "outside" is more than a reaction to the demands of the system or parting ways from it. How then to understand an "outside" that is neither an opposite nor a reaction, nor refutation, antithesis, or appeal? A first step is to free being outside from the double prong of the quotation marks, which elevate it out of language and life to the level of a concept.

In Rilke's work, being outside is that which allows life to be lived to the fullest for each of us. Some do this better than others. And while this is going on, partly in contradiction to it, life, as if without us as the person who is living, keeps living to the fullest. In the elegies this possibility of living a full and direct life, unruly and wild like a vagabond, headed into the emptiness of yet uncharted (unnamed) space, remains both a promise and a danger. In an earlier poem from 1901, from "The Book of Pilgrimage" in *The Book of Hours*, this was still pure potential for Rilke, or a promise and a warning:

And yet, though every man struggles
as though out of a prison cell that holds him, hates him,—
there is a great wonder in the world:
I feel it: all life must be lived.[11]

Und doch, obwohl ein jeder von sich strebt
wie aus dem Kerker, der ihn haßt und halt,—
es ist ein großes Wunder in der Welt:
ich fühle: *alles Leben wird gelebt.*[12]

That "all life" is lived in spite of our occasional efforts to stop it means that it is just as impossible to run away from one's own life as to opt out of it. Being outside is neither a flight nor an alternative to life, but rather that which lives out to the fullest in our life: It is life itself.

To overvalue and fetishize being outside as a private or political alternative to a life governed by norms—or as a genuine life in the midst of the phony ones—as Rilke's famous and often-quoted final line in "Archaic Torso of Apollo" from *New Poems* in 1908 ("you must change your life"[13]) has misled many readers to do, is a misunderstanding. To change your life means to expose yourself to the possibility that the familiar life no longer exists: that you may lose more, through a change, than what bothers you right now. The fetishization of being outside misunderstands the basis of our existence to be something in which we are trapped by the difficulties of life that we would like to escape. To be outside means to let oneself fall into the heaviness of life, not to withdraw from this weight and thereby from life itself:

> He must re-learn, through constant trying,
> to fall and rest in heaviness,
> he who had visions of out-flying
> the birds in his presumptuousness.[14]

> Eins muß er wieder können: *fallen*,
> geduldig in der Schwere ruhn,
> der sich vermaß, den Vögeln allen
> im Fliegen es zuvorzutun.[15]

The point is to notice *what* it is in life that lives (if it is not *us* who do the living) to the fullest. One could guess that Rilke's poetry, which he cited as a pretext every time he left a lover, is a blueprint for how to be outside. Ultimately he emboldens us to throw "the emptiness out of [our] arms/ into the spaces we breathe," which can be understood to mean that literature opens a deeper dimension to life, or at least promises one. Then poetry would not be a flight from the world, but rather a way out from the identities and roles and ideologies in which we are constantly trapped. Rilke's poetry would promise contact with a genuine model of life and an authentic experience.

At least this is how literary scholars have understood what Rilke means by being outside. They claim that in opposition to a false, regulated, and normalized life Rilke proposed in his poetry no less than the conscious, authentic, aware, correct, fulfilled life. And thus being outside becomes an alternative. But in its actual incoherent radicalness, being outside can

also mean the absence of an alternative to a correct life. From a comple-
mentary, if less ambitious, perspective on this reception of Rilke by
various philosophers, Rilke's work had also been read as the political
expression of his attachment to being outside. This is how Rilke, who was
born in Prague, viewed the attacks on him from the German-nationalist
press in 1925, after he apparently said in an interview that he had no
homeland. He published a correction and put an end to the "Rilke affair,"
but with the remark that he did not care about the question of his nationality and that ultimately his work (at this time he was working on poems
in French) was his home, saying, "I am my accomplishments."[16]

More recent interpreters shy away from the pathos of the conflation of
language and life. To grasp the radicalness of Rilke's being outside, some
interpreters define the term as a concept outside of all contexts: as a word
absolutely without reference, which marks the path from "our interpreted
world," in which "we are not really at home," to a language where literal
and figurative sense cannot be distinguished.[17] Rilke's "outside," then,
marks the necessary departure from intellectual contexts and the deconstructive end of the kind of poetry that harmoniously aligned language
and life and granted meaning to individual experience.

There is a certain irony in such interpretations, since these interpreters
turn being outside into something Rilke did not consider himself capable
of: an abstract concept of openness and a philosophical term, which marks
a "half-baked philosophy."[18] In their adamant consistency and the
sharpness of their thought, which we cannot ignore, these interpreters
only skirt the radicalness and contingency of Rilke's outside. Rilke's
outside moves beyond philosophical coherence, which seems to block a
return to descriptive language, which would constitute a relapse into the
language of being, the possibility of meaning. Yet, with this term his work
opens itself once again onto a concrete, determined, referential, and
expressive language, and not onto a disenfranchisement of language. His
work opens onto life.

Rilke's outside is not the opposite of a normalized life, not a flight from
meaning or referential language into an absolute language, not an
abolition of poetry in favor of abstract thinking, and not a philosophically
coherent step into a pure or absolute language. This space, delineated by,
among others, Michel Foucault, is not the end of language, but rather
language succumbing to its own noise, to "its silence, that is hiding not
the intimacy of a secret, but rather a pure outside, where words dissolve

irrevocably."[19] For Rilke the notion of an outside dissolves in just the sense that Foucault insistently and, one could say, incessantly linked to the being of corporeal existence. It is not a turn against the referential dimension of language. Being outside is that which cannot be stopped, the directionless and unforeseeable transformation of abstraction into meaning, from referent into figure, from biographical contingency into linguistic expression. And back again.

This can be seen from one line in Rilke's last poem, "Come, then, you last one, whom I acknowledge." Rilke penciled this poem in late fall of 1926 in a notebook, as he lay dying of leukemia in a hospital bed in Valmont in Switzerland. The poem is a desperate and at the same time euphoric invocation of the experience of pain, which was ravaging his body. In his despair, Rilke wants to understand this pain as a part of his world and not as its negation. But in the end he believes that one can understand pain as little as one can understand being outside: "it is our task not to dissolve pain in our consciousness; it does not tolerate being interpreted. You have to, so to speak, let it burn itself out in its particular spot, without examining in the light of its flickering blaze any object of our spirit or of the unaffected parts of life. Pain is reasonable only on the side where it faces nature, on the other side it is absurd, raw material, unhewn, without form and surface, ungraspable . . ."[20] For Rilke, pain means not leaving the world, but rather being too much in the world. And this being-too-much-in-the-world is then a way into a free space. Rilke explains this to Lou Andreas-Salomé a few weeks before his death in December 1926:

"And now, Lou, I do not know how many hells, you know how I have accommodated such pain, such great physical pain, albeit as an exception and then again as a retreat into the open [*Rückweg ins Freie*]. And now. It is covering me. It is dismembering me. Day and night!

"Where shall I find the strength?"[21]

Rilke's last poem piles up images and figures from his letters and many of his poems into a horrific pyre:

Komm du, du letzter, den ich anerkenne,
heilloser Schmerz im leiblichen Geweb:
wie ich im Geiste brannte, sieh, ich brenne
in dir; das Holz hat lange widerstrebt,

der Flamme, die du loderst, zuzustimmen,
nun aber nähr' ich dich und brenn in dir.[22]

Come, then, you last one whom I recognize,
boundless pain lodged in the body's weave:
how I burned in spirit, look, I burn
in you; the wood resisted long
to join the flames with which you blaze,
but now I nourish you and burn in you.

The metaphor of poetic creation melts together with the pain that is
no longer figurative, only physical. But this poem is more than the
apotheosis of the work in an auto-da-fé, in which the poet makes his
work glow one last time and then burns up with his own images. Rilke
cannot protect all the images of this world from the pain that they were
supposed to keep outside. The pain breaks in. This is followed by two
lines in this stirring farewell poem, which interrupt Rilke's grandiose and
constantly failing intention to recognize life and death, pleasure and pain,
as equally valid components of being:

O life, life: to be outside.
And I in flames. No one who knows me.[23]

O Leben, Leben: Draußensein.
Und ich in Lohe. Niemand, der mich kennt.

To rise up from this sickbed in the Valmont clinic one more time, to draw
a deep breath once more, to open your eyes, to live, to once more be
recognized, be touched, to see yourself one more time (for love, as shown
above, was the possibility Rilke saw for becoming free of oneself): Is that
what Rilke is promising in these imploring lines? What is it, then, to be
outside, this *Draußensein*, if not the life of the healthy, for whom the
"fullness of his experience lives on, still uncompiled and unarranged," as
opposed to the sick man, who burns out in pain and anguish? But what
else, after the strange repetition and colon of "life, life:," is outside if not
the pain in which someone burns beyond his own recognition? The point
where life lives itself out?

Life, Life, wonderful time
reaching from contradiction to contradiction
[. . .]
O most impenetrable, o course of life.

Of all the many bold existences
can any be more radiant and daring?
We stand and push against our limits
And pull in some object beyond recognition.[24]

O Leben Leben, wunderliche Zeit
von Widerspruch zu Widerspruche reichend
[. . .]
O unerklärlichste, o Lebenszeit.

Von allen großgewagten Existenzen
kann eine glühender und kühner sein?
Wir stehn und stemmen uns an unsre Grenzen
und reißen ein Unkenntliches herein.[25]

This is a draft from winter 1913–14, in which Rilke is already gathering metaphors, like kindling, for his final poem, of which he could not yet have known anything: It was still outside. There he names the burdensome "limits" beyond which stands the inexplicable and yet so banal *outside* of his last poem.

In this final poem, being outside is the opposite and end of life, but at the same time its intensification as something hidden within life: the intrusion of the unknowable, which remains unsaid in this draft. Being outside is no rhetorical trick with which Rilke ignores or disenfranchises the "language of being," in which life and expression can still be conflated in the metaphors of interiority. Being outside rather marks the reality that our life is already doubled and fractured. Thus it brings us to recognize the possibility of a second life that is still a part of this life.

The emphatic invitation to pain in Rilke's last poem is his refusal to recognize death: At the last moment, he wants to welcome pain, nothing but pain, as though nothing else is coming after it. Being outside is therefore the "second, ampler life, in time uncharted," which is aimed against life itself, and at the same time also the pain, which is no longer the figure of life but which Rilke also does not wish to regard as the end.

Being outside is for Rilke both escape from the contingencies of life and contingency itself. Being outside means being finally free, to stand free in life, but in doing so to be so out on a limb that it causes only pain. "O life, life": Life is doubled by our possibility of living differently, of finding a second life in the first, of elevating our lives again and again of our own accord, to deepen it, to interrupt it. This doubling is not the attainable path away from the language of expression and communication to a language completely free of reference; rather it is life, which for Rilke can only be lived doubled, since it is always both inside and outside of language at the same time. We live our lives, and all of life is lived. Pain is a symptom of this condition.

The outside can be described as the flight from the contingencies of the world into the imaginary realm. But the respective meanings of these words turn into their opposites, as Rilke also uses "outside" for those contingencies out there in the world, which can be overcome only by our indescribable and overwhelming internal being:

> Outside worlds, the world,—how much, how much,
> but who will describe
>   the happiness and excess of counterplay,
>   that drives our face and essence on.
> Outside airs, greetings, wishes, flights
> victory, deceit—
>   but inside, blooming satisfactions
>   and an indescribable connection.[26]

> Draußen Welten, Welt—, wieviel, wie vieles—;
> aber wer beschreibt
>   Glück und Übermaß des Gegenspieles,
>   das in uns Gesicht und Wesen treibt.
> Draußen Lüfte, Grüße, Wünsche, Flüge,
> Übertroffenheit, Betrug—,
>   aber innen blühende Genüge
>   und der unbeschreibliche Bezug.[27]

Being outside marks, in Rilke's work, the ever-growing distance from a tenable, coherent philosophical position, which with being outside is turned into a concept.

On the philological level it can easily be shown that Rilke's being outside is not a departure from just any form of language. Long before his final, grasping note on his deathbed, Rilke was already "outside." The word "*Draußensein*" appears countless times in his correspondence. And there, outside of poetry, being outside denotes two things: first, the empirical circumstances, which refuse Rilke access to his own inner world (or which, as in the poem quoted above, are balanced out by the internal "blooming satisfactions"). "Outside worlds, the world [. . .] victory, deceit" describes the long, uncanny period of Rilke's difficulties in writing during the First World War in Munich and Vienna, before he managed to flee to Switzerland in 1919 and return to his work. "What a change, the turn back to work. How long was I 'outside' [*wie lange war ich 'draußen'*]—and the way inwards leads: par tous mes ténèbres [through all my shadows]. And is still the only correct way."[28] But then, in the same letter, being outside means just the opposite of such an "outside" of work, where Rilke had spent such a long time. Being outside constitutes, to put it simply, the place where Rilke could flee back into his work— Switzerland. Refuge and deathbed, exile and grave, resting place and clinic, life and poetry: being outside of being "outside"—that is neutral Switzerland. Switzerland is for Rilke outside of Germany and therefore a great refuge, true salvation, a new beginning, recuperation. But Switzerland is also a place of exile that grows more and more limiting—suffering, the sanatorium, the incurable illness, then such a painful death, the churchyard, the simple grave. Three months after arriving in Switzerland Rilke writes, on September 12, 1919, to Gertrud Knoop:

"Imagine, being 'outside' [*das 'Draußen'-Sein*] was almost difficult at first. You couldn't do it quite right, you could only spend half a day at it (or was that just me?), to read the names of the elegant drugstores, Houbigant, Roger and Gallet and Pinaud; yes, for one moment this was the name of freedom,—who would have thought it possible. For a long time the pastry shops made such an impression on me, I still have not bought any chocolate, but soap did it to me, I was truly defenseless against such a cleanly abundant display window in the Bahnhofstrasse in Zurich."[29]

These two literal and contradictory meanings of the term "outside" in Rilke's letters refute the claim that Rilke is calling for a language without similes and without concrete reference.[30] Being outside can be located: It can be Switzerland, just as "freedom" can have an actual reference, for an instant, such as "Houbigant" or "Roger and Gallet." For such banal, Swiss references keep erupting in Rilke's language, which in fact becomes a language without interiority.

Neither the philosophically awkward poet nor his language provides the philosophical coherence of which Rilke was so skeptical. Being outside keeps turning into the reference for a circumscribed location. Rilke is serious about being outside, and for this reason he continually opens his poems on linguistic levels that philosophers easily overlook from a distance, since they are not stopping to browse through his letters, where Rilke unfolds his language more openly than in most of the poems. Being outside is certainly among other things the departure from referential language, but being outside is transformed just as quickly into Rilke's distance from his work in Germany during the war, then far away from Germany, into "cheesy Switzerland." And it does not end there. Living precariously, with a temporary residence permit in Switzerland, Rilke was not spared another, political-legal dimension of being outside there, where he was at last "outside" again.

If poetry is the equivalent of an outside, then it must do more than speak of this being outside or extricate itself from *one* function of language (the referential or communicative). It must surrender to this being outside and thereby distance itself from itself, and must allow several functions of language to erupt into any line; possibly, it must surrender being poetry. Be life. Be no longer. Be Swiss, from time to time.

for Worm

In a letter written on May 3, 1944, the German poet Gottfried Benn
describes his irresolute attitude toward his predecessor Rilke: "My feelings
about him will always be ambivalent. I can never imagine him otherwise
than creeping along, as a worm, who has a unique way of moving along
and can segment himself without any breaks, but doesn't quite belong to
the proper animals. This feeling is foremost in my mind . . ."[1]

 With his toxic remark, Benn wants to distance himself from his predecessor. This ambivalence extends even to Benn's most intimate and
personal moments, when the poet wants, perhaps more than in his public
statements, to break from any association with Rilke. In 1954 Benn's
longtime lover, Astrid Claes, complains to him that he never addresses
her by name in his love letters out of his fear that they may be published
and reveal Benn's identity. Benn responds: "for at least twenty or thirty
years [I have] not written a single letter to a woman in which even a trace
of tenderness, affection, dedication could be found. No Rilke-letters will
ever appear from me. Just to be clear."[2] But Benn's worm analogy, to
dismiss Rilke, can be linked without any breaks to an episode in Rilke's
1910 novel, *The Notebooks of Malte Laurids Brigge*. In his biting remark,
Benn may not be so far off, after all: Near the end of Rilke's only novel,
there is a worm. A literal worm, like a worm in an apple.

The Notebooks of Malte Laurids Brigge begins with death: "So this is where people come to live; I would have thought it is a city to die in."[3] But the novel ends with love, for Rilke the only possibility for us humans to transcend ourselves. In love, a person does more than yield to emotions and passion. The beloved enters the world of the lover differently from everything else that exists: He alone *transforms* the lover into a lover, into someone for whom another can be everything. "You make me who I am," sings a mysteriously bewitching young Danish woman at an elegant and shallow party in Venice at the end of *The Notebooks of Malte Laurids Brigge*. The young woman's song is the only proper poem in the novel. "You, only, are always reborn; and the moment when/I let go of you, I hold on to you everywhere."[4] You turn me into what I want to be, since only through you do I become a lover, and I can remain a lover even if I lose you.

Love makes us greater if we do not hold on to the beloved as someone known and familiar, but as someone ever new who ignites our love anew, someone "reborn" each time in our consciousness and our perception.

In the first of the *Duino Elegies* (completed in 1922), Rilke uses for the lover the image of the arrow, which "endures the bowstring's tension" for one moment of highest excitement, "so that/gathered in the snap of release it can be more than/itself."[5] Then in "The Second Elegy": "for our own hearing always exceeds us."[6] And finally in "The Ninth Elegy," where the "urgent command" becomes overly intense: "Superabundant being/wells up in my heart."[7] Rilke insists throughout his work that man contains something superabundant in himself that can be revealed and set free only through love. The lover stands trembling like the arrow on the bowstring just before release—and he is *less* once he has hit the target. For Rilke, love is greatest when it has no goal, no *telos*, object, or intention, when it becomes pure motion. The metaphors change; the program stays the same: "Isn't it time, that we lovingly/freed ourselves from the beloved?"[8]

Rilke may have been enthralled by such absolute love because he suspected that he was not truly capable of it. In her memoir Marie von Thurn und Taxis reflects: "Love, the great love that [Rilke] so admired in others—he considered himself incapable of ever truly experiencing it."[9] Later critics have sought to protect Rilke from this apparent shortcoming by saying that there are "no pure negatives in the reckonings of the soul

[. . .] and so Rilke may have extracted from this weakness [his inability to love] an openness for being."[10] But whether or not Rilke was capable of loving completely, there is, in the openness that he extracts from his ideal image of life or from his own inability, a worm.

In the last part of the *Malte* novel Rilke develops the idea of true love by rewriting the legend of the prodigal son. At this point in the book, Rilke has lined up a veritable guard of deeply unhappy, bitterly disappointed women and tragic mystics—with the status of patron saint granted to Gaspara Stampa—who according to Rilke successfully sublimated the sorrows of their unrequited loves into high art. Rilke idealizes these female writers, who in their writings and letters redirected their heightened feelings away from the worthless beloved back to themselves as now self-less lovers who are transformed by this love and thus nearly lifted out of the worldly realm. This experience of love without an object, which only in its initial stages is tied to pain and sorrow, Rilke sees as an opportunity for expanding existence itself. In his novel, Rilke also takes the biblical figure of the prodigal son to create another symbol of such objectless love. Love for other people seems to him overly concrete: The lover is "very close" to the unboundedness of being, except that "the beloved" is "there/blocking the view."[11] Only when there is no more expectation, satisfaction, or obligation, love is no longer work or exertion but a "direction of the heart," as Rilke calls what he considers the "*one* power of the human, with which one may accomplish everything."[12]

The prodigal son is Rilke's version of the mythic hero in his quest for an authentic sense of self, represented ubiquitously in literature and during Rilke's lifetime particularly prominently by Hermann Hesse, in his 1922 retelling of the life of Siddhartha: a young man, given much and loved by all, from a well-to-do background, with devoted family and friends, and well-meaning parents—who then "departs forever."[13] Why? Because all of them, in Rilke's version of this myth, all of the friends and family and loyal dogs, with their gentle hands and their wet snouts, forced this free man to become "what they thought he was." Love does this, in Rilke's view: It compresses the other into an image and buries him under caresses and embraces. In Rilke's telling, the prodigal son creates distance from his lovers by paying them. Gold necklaces and brooches, a fine dinner, and an elegant scarf are the sort of gifts the young man in Rilke's novel bestows on beautiful young women, on the mornings after, to keep these objects of affection at bay. In Hesse's version of the Siddhartha story, the seeker, who "started to feel that the love of his father and the love of his mother, and also the love of his friend [. . .] would not bring him joy forever and ever, would not nurse him, feed him, satisfy him [. . .] Unstoppable like the arrow shot from the bow," he left his homeland.[14] In Hesse's novel the eponymous Siddhartha finally becomes a ferryman and recognizes that everything in life is constantly in flux, and ebbs and flows and then connects again. Rilke's nameless globetrotter, by contrast, becomes a shepherd, and this "thin, cloaked figure [. . .] [does] not love, although he [does] love simply being."[15] Rilke continues in the tone of legend or myth: "The base love of his sheep [. . .] spread out around him and shimmered softly over the meadows."[16] And a gentle, bearded, and white-locked God glanced beatifically down from his place in the clouds. At least that is how it seems here, where Rilke describes a life, "which then began the long love for God, that quiet work with no end."[17] Rejection of the worldly, painful renunciation, bodily visitation, abstinence, wandering, errancy, life in the simplest of conditions, transcendence: a *via dolorosa* into nirvana.

"And this time he hoped for exaltation. His whole being, having become prescient and unerring in its long solitude, promised him that the one whom he intended to love understood with a piercing, radiant love."[18] Most scholars have interpreted these words one-sidedly, and thus overlooked their sense: "The sense of this feeling [of love] completes itself not in relation to a concrete person, but rather far beyond him in transcendence. And the sense of love, for Rilke, consists in becoming an endless feeling that raises the person up above oneself."[19]

This would mean that Rilke's prodigal son wants to free himself from the world and its "concrete people." And it seems that Rilke here is not far at all from the poet who judged him so harshly, the cold Gottfried Benn, who wrote at age sixty-five: "Love is the Elysium for the unproductive ones, for those who cannot think and express their thoughts. When pushed toward his utmost potential the extreme man no longer shares his love, but rather keeps it for himself."[20]

Other scholars, fearful of endorsing Rilke's coldhearted rejection of real people in favor of abstract love, refer to his letters. There they find ample evidence for Rilke's inability to love concrete people and sufficient grounds for mocking the poet who loved expensive soap and fresh roses, but who in his novel raved about the "ulcers [. . .] like emergency eyes against the blackness of tribulation" of the shepherd's life. Who dumped his girlfriends with eloquent explanations as soon as he wanted to get back to his desk, in order to let ripen the "fruits of his prolonged solitude."[21]

Ah, the jury trial conducted by scholars and biographers.

Charges: the glorification of suffering and a false promise of transcendence, in order to justify and exonerate his own selfish behavior.

Exhibit A: "Oh mon Amie" (December 16, 1920; a letter written in questionable French, with passages in German, to Baladine Klossowska, known as Merline, Rilke's lover):

> Imagine a Malte, who in this dreaded city of Paris would have a lover or even a friend! Would he ever have penetrated so deeply into the confidence of things? For the things (he often shared this with me in our intimate conversations) through which you wish to comprehend real life, first direct the following question to you: Are you available? Are you prepared to sacrifice all of your love to me, to lay yourself down with me?[22]

Rilke invokes the Malte character from his novel to forbid his lover, the real flesh-and-blood Merline, from visiting him and to justify his neglect of her. He distances himself from her in the name of his art. And finally even the page-long letters—which Rilke considered a "breathing through the quill"—are not intended for Klossowska, who had worked tirelessly to render inhabitable the nearly abandoned house called Muzot, and who managed his household for a time.[23] He is not fending off Merline Klossowska's requests to be allowed to visit him. Rilke doesn't have her in mind at all; he is writing against his own desire to see her:

> Dearest, make no mistake, everything I have written to you is not intended to defend myself against your appeal. [. . .] It is the appeal that I continually feel inside myself and which draws me towards you, against which I defend myself—let me make this clear: I am speaking with myself in your presence, please understand that, my friend.[24]

Understand this, my dear, Rilke writes to the woman he loves (this is the intention of many of his letters): I am not speaking to you as a human and I am not listening to, or choose to ignore, your overly concrete and therefore somewhat predictable requests to spend time with you. Above all, I am concerned with expelling my own love and longing for you in order to overcome and to prepare myself for something greater.

Nonpossessive love? The letters to Baladine Klossowska are pages of proof that this concept has nothing to do with reality. On the contrary: The idea of nonpossessive love allows Rilke to remove himself, apparently, from reality and its demands. Kurt Pinthus described with great amazement how "Rilke [drilled] with such enthusiastic fervor into the images of reality that he pushed through it and entered into the kingdom of the divine."[25] Whether Rilke's critics follow Pinthus and defend Rilke's conception of man as a "drilling" but ultimately transcending being or dismiss Rilke's conception of nonpossessive love as "creeping along," self-serving, and ultimately not quite proper—they all overlook the worm in Rilke's text. In a crucial passage in Rilke's novel, the "quiet work with no end" of loving God, through which the prodigal son in the *Malte* novel gets rid of the object of his love to finally love freely, hits on a figure that wrests itself free from both transcendence and biographical explanation. While the shepherd learns that God will offer no reciprocal love, Rilke writes: "He had found the philosopher's stone, and now he was being forced to ceaselessly transform the quickly produced gold of his happiness into the gross lead of patience. He, who had adapted himself to infinite space, had now become like a worm crawling through crooked passageways, without exit or direction."[26]

The worm has neither eyes nor ears: He has no organ for perceiving the God for whom he searches. God is forgotten amid the hard work of loving him. The lover "adapted himself to infinite space" when he began to grasp the great distance between himself and God. Empty space itself became his world, without any further thoughts of God, for whom alone he had once meant to cross this space. Imperceptibly the journey became the goal, just as imperceptibly as the noble and biblical metaphors gave way to the worm. And in this space the prodigal son goes missing amid all of his conceptions. Instead of continuing to "fling himself into space" toward God, he becomes a worm who creeps this way and that, without any hope of arriving. The way has transformed itself into the goal, but the worm remains a worm. He twists out of the allegory that concludes Rilke's novel and creeps along as a segment of reality that cannot be transcended or sublimated, as the excrement of reality, through the text, just as Rilke writes at the beginning of the novel, in this poignant passage:

"Near these bedroom walls [of a partially demolished house] there remained, along the entire length of outer wall, a dirty-white space through which crawled, in unspeakably nauseating, worm-soft, digestive movements, the open, rust-spotted channel of the sewage pipe."[27]

In an early poem dedicated to Lou Andreas-Salomé, Rilke wrote: "Put my eyes out: I can hear you/seal my ears shut: I can hear you."[28] Marianne Schuller has interpreted this love poem as showing, in poetry, the "intangibility of what is alive."[29] But in claiming universal validity, the otherwise astute critic has missed something. For Rilke, what is alive is not intangible. The blind and deaf "worm" in *The Notebooks of Malta Laurids Brigge* is not something "intangible." It is and remains a "worm," and it cannot be translated into anything less or interpreted as a metaphor for something else; it cannot—even as an instance of negativity—be transcended. If you carefully peel open and dissect the *Malte* novel, this little piece of text creeps out, naked, helpless, without signifying.

The "worm" is Rilke's anticharacter, a word worm that replicates itself even when critically dissected. This worm anchors *in the world* Rilke's promise of man's ability to elevate himself above himself through precise poetic vision, which he proffers at the beginning of his novel and in much of his poetry. But Rilke chooses a figure with no allegorical meaning. That "endless feeling that raises the person up above oneself," that is, love, is pulled back from the heaven of abstraction and out of the promise of allegory (that is, a meaning that transcends everything) and into the earthly realm, and becomes ultimately a concrete, *earthly*, immanent, invertebrate creature. That, at least, seems "irrevocable," as Rilke describes the fact that we have once been of this earth, in the ninth of the Duino elegies.

Rilke's "worm" resists those attempts at exegesis that uncover a greater meaning behind every word and in every verse. The worm defies Rilke's academic critics: It is that earthy element in his text that renders Rilke's poetry uncannily relevant for so many readers. What is supposed to be hiding behind the boneless worm, which no longer knows its way and digs and tunnels blindly?

In his disdainful dismissal of Rilke as gushing and sentimental, Gottfried Benn picked out the worm in Rilke's work. In doing so Benn unintentionally weakened his critique of Rilke, whom he viewed as striving, "creeping along" with all his might upward, toward heaven, unable to reach true transcendence. Since Rilke, in Benn's medically trained view (he was a doctor by profession), "doesn't quite belong to the proper animals," he cannot stand up fully by himself and ever reach those heights. But this is precisely what makes the worm, in Rilke's text, the concrete, earthly, and immanent counterweight to those passages where Rilke's poetry risks losing itself in religion, without which the soaring poetry would turn into empty ritual, and without which the notion of nonpossessive love would become an unattainable promise.

After the worm analogy, Benn continues without any breaks, his own sentence twisting wormlike: "nevertheless, as I said, [Rilke] has my admiration, and he is the last poet of the twentieth century with whom I could dispense."[30] Even for the *Herr Doktor*, there has to be a worm.

X

for Xaver

In 1929, the Rilke Archive published, at the initiative of Rilke's widow, Clara Rilke; his daughter, Ruth; and his son-in-law, Carl Sieber, the small volume of ten letters that have made Rilke famous with art students everywhere: *Letters to a Young Poet*. Only a few letters but no full collection had been published before that date. With the first comprehensive edition of letters, beginning in the year 1930, Rilke's editor Anton Kippenberg, in collaboration with Clara and Ruth Rilke and Carl Sieber, sought to cultivate a particular image of the poet. For the first few decades after Rilke's death, his editor Kippenberg and Rilke's family mainly published letters about art, especially Cézanne, and descriptions of travel as well as commentary on his own work, all with the intention of creating an image of Rilke as a learned and important writer on subjects ranging from aesthetics to literature and philosophy.

The publication of *Letters to a Young Poet*, however, served a different purpose. The slim volume was supposed to provide direction to a generation of young readers that, in 1929, Ruth Sieber-Rilke and Carl Sieber saw as in desperate need of orientation. The letters to Franz Xaver Kappus, a young student at the same military academy where Rilke had gone to school, were supposed to give hope to the interwar generation (which was not yet aware they were headed into a second world war) before that generation went in the wrong direction. These ten poignant and urgent letters, without a doubt the most widely read letters by any poet in the world, were intended in the first instance to save Germany and Europe from the looming catastrophe.

The name of Rilke's correspondent, Franz Xaver Kappus, was removed and replaced by the anonymity of "young poet," as if this name were from the outset nothing but an empty placeholder and, quite literally, an arbitrary X in Rilke's work. This made the letters world-famous: Every reader can recognize himself in the X of the "young poet."

But what Ruth Sieber-Rilke and her husband, Carl, hoped for from these letters did not come to pass. Rilke's calls, articulated with great passion and a visionary sense of what would take over a century to be recognized as a fundamental human right to love, including a desperately needed recalibration of the relation between the sexes, fell on deaf ears. A sizable portion of the German youth for whom these letters were first published went on to become the backbone of the Third Reich, instead of stylizing themselves, after the disillusioning 1920s, into the first Generation X—that is, a generation of people skeptical of master narratives who prefer to live their lives outside of grand ideologies, as slackers and poets. Gottfried Benn gives an impression of the attitude of this generation:

> Maintaining order, fighting for form against the collapse of Europe! European nihilism: an animalistic theory of evolution without an anthropological idea of domination to complete it, the final stadium of the movement of history that began with the end of feeling and seeing the world in classes, species and orders, and with the farewell to the seven days of creation, once more: "Each one according to its own kind." Now the dissolution of species, ranks, distinctions under the popular babble of mothers, a listless retreat into swampy symbols, pressing all the seeds and juices into an old keg, in short: the obliteration of the noble principle of form, subordination of the will to cultivation and style, the supremacy of lowly, practical projects and developments—, after the imperial military transcendence of antiquity, the religious realism of the Middle Ages, now the plausible, the flat, science as the theoretical interpretation of the world—Nietzsche's situation.
>
> This is the situation my generation was born into. It witnessed how Rilke grew soft and allowed himself to be driven by every instance of gloom toward any possible rhyme and to God Himself [. . .][1]

Benn is not a good reader of Rilke here, for Rilke's "dear God," to name just one example, is certainly close to the "religious realism of the Middle Ages." *Letters to a Young Poet* was surely a horror for Benn, since Rilke accuses men in general, all men, categorically, of offering only "a world of lust and restless, intoxicating highs burdened with the old prejudices and arrogance with which man has distorted and brought down love" and diagnoses "something narrow, somehow wild, spiteful, temporary, transient" in a man's capacity for love, which must be overcome.[2] If anything, Rilke faults man for his inflexible attitude in love, his unimaginative rigidity, which Benn wants to activate as the salvation of the West in decline.

The letters to Franz Xaver Kappus begin with Rilke's dry remark that the young poet's poems "are not distinctive in any way" and are "not yet anything in and of themselves, nothing independent."[3] Rilke's critique, which would crush any young poet, made the letters a bestseller. Countless readers feel personally addressed by this opening salvo of a devastating critique, just as if they could shed their own hopes and fears in their identification with the sharply criticized young poet and so be able to listen more attentively. Benn considered the wish to dispense with one's own hopes and fears feminizing and preferred the rigor of military order to Rilke's cult of femininity.

Today the X in the middle of the name of Franz Xaver Kappus, the addressee of the letters with which Rilke's daughter hoped to save the Germans from the impending barbarism, marks a different spot on the map of world literature. Today these letters are read by young people on all continents who want to reenter life, to get out of the traps and snares (of success, of others' approval, of acclaim) that so easily lead us away from an artist's life, or even just a meaningful life, in the sense of a life that corresponds with and takes full advantage of one's personal strengths and predilections. The fact that these letters were once published in the hopes of saving a particular generation of young Germans in 1930 from their own worst impulses, who then undid this noble wish so terribly through their participation in the catastrophe inflicted by Germany on Europe's Jews, the other European nations, and the world—this gives the current popularity of *Letters to a Young Poet* a melancholy note.

for Y

Everything was supposed to be an impetus and a mission for Rilke—even a Y. When writing, to carry out this mission would be

> as if one were flipping through an encyclopedia and, immediately following something completely different, suddenly starting reading under Th or Y.
>
> Indeed, if one were as confident in one's work as one ought to be, even with a head cold, one wouldn't be unnerved by this: one would simply encounter and create new things out of this state of affairs.[1]

Were, ought to, wouldn't be unnerved, *would* encounter, *would* create. But since one is rarely as confident in one's work "as one ought to be," even when not bothered by a cold, the Y unnerves me. From the state of complete confidence in one's creative powers, we can "encounter and create" anything, even out of a random Y. So get to work.

Z

for Zero

Rilke from A to Z: Z promises a summary, a completed picture, closure. Z is the end. Everything has been spelled out: zero left. But Rilke did not want to believe in the end any more strongly than in the beginning. Death was supposed to become a part of life; we are supposed to lose our fear of it. To come to Z and not yet be at the end, to always stay in motion, those were Rilke's goals. "The Ninth Elegy" ends with the great and enigmatic discovery that there is always more:

> Look, I am living. On what? Neither childhood nor future
> grows any smaller . . . Superabundant being
> wells up in my heart.[1]

> Siehe, ich lebe. Woraus? Weder Kindheit noch Zukunft
> werden weniger. . . . Überzähliges Dasein
> entspringt mir im Herzen.[2]

Nothing is over, neither the past "nor future grows any smaller," but rather there is "superabundant being." This idea of being counts more than what? If being is superabundant, what is the zero point from which Rilke started counting?

This zero point is neither the end nor the origin for Rilke, neither misery nor fulfillment. One should not turn either joy into the beginning or misery into the ending, because "to get used to misery as such, to slip it a bit of sugar from your coffee every day, so that eventually it settles beneath your table and does not want to leave again, means to train this phantom in a manner contrary to its nature. The poet should not take distress as his lover, but rather incorporate every affliction and blessing into his work."[3]

Not to take any experience too seriously, not to bind oneself firmly to anyone, not to feed any experience, however wonderful or terrible it may be, with the metaphorical sugar of one's attention. Neither misery nor happiness should be preferred. Nothing that befalls us is sufficient to open to us the full context of our life. Even death should not be understood as an end; finiteness should not be made into an absolute horizon, but rather seen as the entrance into another point of reference: "how enormous are life and death, if you don't always see both in one glimpse, and almost make no distinctions between them. But that is a matter for angels, not for us, or else for us only on an exceptional basis, for moments earned through long-lasting pain."[4] Rilke's explanations that death is not to be understood as the end are practically endless; in his correspondence they fill many pages. The frequency and length of these explanations attest to Rilke's desire to write on beyond the "end" (or to resolve the contradiction in his experience). Rilke writes:

"Throughout time there have always been those who thought that they had sufficient proof that this so-called death signifies an end, a condition of decay and the harsh disintegration of all living matter, but the very opposite opinion has also always found its supporters and defenders, and they have gone so far as to define death as a more intensive degree of life. Its immobility is then cited as proof of the greater intensity of vibration to which death is subject, and hence more alive than we are. Our everyday perception would not contradict this: for instance, we still feel the movements of a high-speed train with our entire body while based on our experience we should have to interpret the vastly greater speed of the earth as a standstill.

"To me (since you ask), it has seemed probable from my youth that death is nothing less than the opposite and refutation of life; my inclination always tended toward making death into the center of life as if we would be housed and sheltered in it quite well as if in the greatest and most profound intimacy. I cannot say that any experience has ever contradicted this assumption; yet I have also always refrained from imagining this being-in-death in any way, and all existing descriptions of a 'beyond' have always left me quite indifferent."[5]

This "center of life" in which we "would be housed and sheltered" corresponds to that combination of insignificant words, "the dictation of existence," as Rilke describes his work in a letter from December 21, 1913, in which he tries to take down all the world's meanings.[6] This dictation reveals to us our position for individual moments, only to immediately fall apart again into individual words. What ultimately counts for Rilke are—always together, always both—the individual letters and words as well as our knowledge about the entire dictation. That means that we must pay attention both to every individual word and to the overarching themes, that we must read carefully and become familiar with the full body of work. It means that Z does not weigh any more heavily than any other letter in the dictation.

Compared to life, numbers are too abstract for Rilke. In *The Notebooks of Malte Laurids Brigge,* in the episode about the petty official Nikolai Kusmich, who gets time and money all mixed up, Rilke writes almost in the style of a Gogolian fable: "it's obvious that [numbers] shouldn't be granted too much importance; they are, after all, just a kind of arrangement created by the government for the sake of public order. No one had ever seen them anywhere but on paper. It was impossible, for instance, to meet a Seven or a Twenty-five at a party. There simply weren't any there."[7]

And nevertheless we, like the petty official Kusmich, cannot avoid having to count in our lives.

Z is a Zorro-like stroke of the tongue: You cringe a little when you read a German Z.[8] Rilke did not close himself off to this sound. It courses like a comet's fiery tail through "Elegy," written in Rilke's final summer in the year 1926 and dedicated to Marina Tsvetaeva (but not included in *Duino Elegies*), just as if the first letter of Tsvetaeva (transliterated into German as Zwetajewa) were determining the keynote:

As angels draw marks as a signal on the doors of those to be saved
we, though we seem to be tender, stop and touch this or that.
Ah, how remote already, how inattentive, Marina,
Even in our innermost pretense. Signalers: nothing more.[9]

Wie die Engel gehen und die Türen bezeichnen jener zu Rettenden,
also rühren wir dieses und dies, scheinbar *Zärtliche*, an.
Ach wie weit schon Entrückte, ach, wie *Zerstreute*, Marina,
auch noch beim innigsten Vorwand. *Zeichengeber*, sonst nichts.[10]

"Elegy" hisses along with the German words "*Zärtliche*" (tender), "*Zer-streute*" (inattentive), and *Zeichengeber*" (signalers), and the following lines repeat the strong German Z sound, with words like "*Zugriff*" (grip), "*Zartheit*" (delicacy), "*zahllosen*" (numberless), and (Rilke's creation) "*Zugvogelziel*" (destination for migrating birds). But in the end what is central to our thoughts is the word "*Zahl*" at the beginning of the poem. When Rilke insists on leaving nothing out, on embracing everything, on spreading the poetic grace of his metaphors fairly over sorrow and happiness, is there any all-encompassing cipher that brings it all together? Don't the *Duino Elegies* of 1922 promise such a wrapping-up, since they saved Rilke from a creative and personal crisis that had lasted from 1913 to 1922? The tension for Rilke is between our longing to be finished, "to be united with all that [the spacious openness]," and at the same time to exceed ourselves, not to miss any opportunities that comprise our being, not to resign. Rilke describes the "spacious openness" in different ways. In the passage from the *Malte* novel quoted here, it is the "approach of spring," which we would gladly accept, in Rilke's view. Yet, our approach brings "an astonishment in the air" and in our "presentiment," which we would like to keep open to every experience of the world, the "weight of [our] limbs" displaces itself, and "something like the possibility of becoming ill" emerges.[11] Rilke wants equilibrium in ecstasy. He knows that precisely this desire prevents it: "But we, who have undertaken to achieve God, we can never become perfected. We keep postponing our nature; we need more time. What is a year to us? What are all the years? Before we have even begun God, we are already praying to him: let us survive this night. And then illness. And then love."[12] If we add up our being, we also count something else too: We want to add up the account of being, but more than that we are afraid to reach a final figure. Out of the "we need more time" speaks our fear of seeing the present as everything.

This is Rilke's two-part claim: The dictation of existence is complete in every moment, and not a single word is missing; the present is everything that there is. But at the same time another word can always be added to it. Such a word would be, for example, the word *"Zahl"* (number, sum).

Rilke is looking for a number to which everything accrues and yet that has no limit or final amount. The Z sound continues through the lines of the elegy to Tsvetaeva:

> Oh the losses into the All, Marina, the stars that are falling!
> We can't make it larger, wherever we fling ourselves, to whatever
> star we may go! In the Whole, all things are already numbered.
> So when anyone falls, the perfect sum is not lessened.[13]

> O die Verluste ins All, Marina, die stürzenden Sterne!
> Wir vermehren es nicht, wohin wir uns werfen, zu welchem
> Sterne hinzu! Im Ganzen ist immer schon alles gezählt.
> So auch, wer fällt, vermindert die heilige Zahl nicht.[14]

"The perfect number" (*die heilige Zahl*) includes everything that can or cannot be, what no longer is, and what can and will be. This number is the starting balance of "the God of completeness," which Rilke cites in a letter of October 21, 1924, as an appropriate instance of "the miserable diversity" of life, from which the poet may not subtract a thing.[15] We have landed at Z: I no longer need to emphasize that Rilke does not believe in God. In Rilke's great attempt to gather everything together, and to understand losses not as a negation of what is but rather as independent experiences *within* life and not *outside* of it, the final balance of this grand reckoning is the perfect sum, but without a God. Neither a deliberate sacrifice nor any form of self-abandonment can add to this perfect sum ("wherever we fling ourselves, to whatever/star we may go!"), nor does an undesired death subtract anything from it ("when anyone falls, the perfect sum is not lessened"). Because it is constant, the perfect sum can, to follow Martin Heidegger's interpretations of other Rilke poems, be understood as "the center of the totality of what exists" and as "being."[16]

But the concept of "being" is abstract. And since even what could never "be" is included in Rilke's perfect sum, Heidegger's terminology is possibly misleading here. Rilke himself does not speak of "the totality of what exists." To give this concept more depth, I quote Rilke's simile of life as a great dice cup, inside of which we all count for the same amount (before being cast out):

There you rest like a die in a cup. Surely, an unknown gambler's hand shakes the cup, casts you out, and out there you count upon landing either for a lot or very little. But after the die has been cast, you are put back into the cup and there, inside, in the cup, no matter *how* you come to lie, you signify all of its numbers, all of its sides. And there, inside the cup, luck or misfortune are of no concern, but only bare existence, being a die, having six sides, six chances, always again all of them—along with the peculiar certainty of not being able to cast oneself out on one's own and the pride in knowing that it takes a divine wager for anyone to be rolled from deep within this cup onto the table of the world and into the game of fate. [. . .] It is an honest game, unpredictable, and always begun anew, beyond one and yet played in a way that no one is ever worthless for an instant, or bad, or shameful: for who can be responsible for falling this way or that out of the cup?[17]

In the cup is "being"; with every throw we are once again "bare existence" with all our "surfaces," our "chances." As metaphorical dice in the cup we are *every* number. How we then fall or get thrown into life is unforeseeable and changes nothing about the total sum of all our sides and possibilities.

That means that we cannot grasp the total sum of what it means to be a die, although we constitute a part of this sum. Only outside do we come to lie, to fall in accordance with good or bad fortune, but we never know what the total number inside the dice cup is. Rilke calls "the totality of what exists" in the elegy to Tsvetaeva "the perfect sum," since we will never know this number, but it is nevertheless the composite of our "mere beings." "Perfect" does not mean transcendent, but rather something like: indispensable, of great meaning to us, decisive. And yet, the perfect sum that would hold the whole cosmos together, that could bring the Rilke alphabet to a close and whose sum lies in a dice cup, is unknowable.

Why? Because our happiness and our sorrow are based not on what we *know* but on what we *experience*, how we are thrown out of the cup. Because we always have all the "chances, always again all of them," good as well as bad, "luck" as well as "misfortune," but never *know* all of these chances. "The peculiar certainty of not being able to cast oneself out on one's own" means that being and nonbeing can never be fully known but must be experienced.

Rilke chooses the metaphor of a game of chance, because luck in a game, as studies show, can awaken the feeling even in nonbelievers that a player can reach alignment for a moment (the moment of luck) with the motion of the cosmos, even though everything is dependent on chance.[18] The game breaks down into familiarity (with the rules) and knowledge (skill) on the one side and, on the other side, into this great feeling of belonging, into the experience, movement, event: into the game. You experience the falling dice in a game, but not as knowledge. In the same way, you experience your place in the world as good or bad fortune, but not necessarily as knowledge.

Moreover, the metaphor of the dice cup draws upon the experience of weight, which for Rilke is suspended between knowledge and experience, between law and freedom. For Rilke, weight simultaneously denotes something hard to overcome, the actual experience of weight, and the law of gravity. In the elegy for Tsvetaeva he laments: "Oh the losses into the All, Marina, the stars that are falling!" Oh our past loves, all the people lost forever. He chooses for this the image of the "stars that are falling" because for the stars in space there is no up and down; they fall but cannot fall *down*. Our "losses" (they are ours, for otherwise Rilke would not have written "Oh") correspond to the "stars that are falling," and therefore the weight of human existence is placed parallel to the directionless falling—and therefore potential ascendance—of the stars. The final lines of "The Tenth Elegy," in which Rilke tries to think of our existence from the perspective of the dead, express this thought:

> And we, who have always thought
> of happiness as *rising*, would feel
> the emotion that almost overwhelms us
> whenever a happy thing *falls*.[19]

> Und wir, die an *steigendes* Glück
> denken, empfänden die Rührung,
> die uns beinah bestürzt,
> wenn ein Glückliches *fällt*.[20]

Here Rilke writes "almost overwhelms us," since his whole body of work seeks to reevaluate the negative meaning of falling. That which "over-whelms us," according to Rilke, could be the reevaluation of rising and falling, which illuminates for us, as soon as we no longer see our falling as an end, or no longer see death as "the opposite and refutation of life" and no longer see ourselves only in relief against the absolute horizon of the transience of life. Perhaps this seemingly abstract thought of the reevaluation of falling can be clarified with examples of how "to fall" is sometimes neither negative nor positive, but rather denotes the revelation of the world: "to fall in love," or in French, *"tomber amoureux."* Rilke does not just use the word "fall" differently, i.e., poetically, and define it differently, but simply puts it in a broader context—here one that includes what happens in outer space. As soon as we see our losses in this greater context, it is less clear what is falling and what is rising.

To express this once again using the metaphor of the dice: To fall is to fall into life, not out of it. Being cast into the world. And weight is one of the surfaces of the die like all the others and at the same time the force that causes us to fall. The reevaluation of the meaning of "falling" belongs to Rilke's attempt to rehabilitate the word for "weight" and "heaviness" (which also signifies "difficulty" in German):

> What do you have against heaviness? That it can kill you. It is indeed strong and powerful. You know that about heaviness, but what do you know about lightness? Nothing. We have no memory of lightness at all. Even if you could choose, wouldn't you have to choose weight? Don't you feel that it is close to you? [. . .] And are you not in harmony with nature when you make that choice? Do you think it wouldn't be easier for the seedling to remain buried in the ground?—Light and heavy do not exist. Weight is life itself. And you do want to live?[21]

But we do not need to remember weight. "In the Whole, all things have always already been counted." Only we don't know the "perfect" total sum. And weight, which Rilke calls life itself, also denotes for him the force of gravity, which supports us. According to Heidegger, Rilke's "gravity" is "in contrast to physical gravity, which one is accustomed to hearing about, the middle of the totality of existence."[22] Anyone who has—perhaps while reading Heidegger—shaken a dice cup will remember the interaction of emptiness, weightlessness, and weight in the cup, in which the dice are always weightless for a moment. That is the image that Rilke chooses for the experience of "mere being." For Rilke, weight, that is, life, is not an object of knowledge, but rather the truth of an experience. It is everything that we are, and yet we do not know it.

There are two poems in which Rilke writes that we should forget about the total sum. One of them is "Be Ahead of All Parting," from *The Sonnets to Orpheus*:

> Be—and yet know the great void where all things begin,
> the infinite source of your own most intense vibration,
> so that, this once, you may give it your perfect assent.
>
> To all that is used-up, and to all the muffled and dumb
> creatures in the world's full reserve, the unsayable sums,
> joyfully add yourself, and cancel the count.[23]

> Sei—und wisse zugleich des Nicht-Seins Bedingung,
> den unendlichen Grund deiner innigen Schwingung,
> daß du sie völlig vollziehst dieses einzige Mal.
>
> Zu dem gebrauchten sowohl, wie zum dumpfen und stummen
> Vorrat der vollen Natur, den unsäglichen Summen,
> zähle dich jubelnd hinzu und vernichte die Zahl.[24]

The thought in the first stanza quoted here could be expressed as follows: The possibility of being happy in life is most accessible in moments of change, when one's own movements resonate by chance with the movements of life and of time—the shaking of the cup, existence itself. For our inner vibrations might come into harmony with the most drastic change, or for a moment with our own weight, with the falling of the planets through space, with nonbeing, which Rilke conceives of as the weightlessness of the dice. Then we can be aligned for a few moments to time, the ungraspable basis of the present. But this is not about a "thought," but rather an experience, which cannot be transmitted as knowledge. Nothing can support or account for Rilke's statement about the "infinite source" of our being in nonbeing except for the rhyme itself. So our being floats over nonbeing, as the poem floats on account of this rhyme.

The second of the two poems that deal with the "total sum" is "The Fifth Elegy," which Rilke wrote in 1922 in memory of Pablo Picasso's painting *Family of Saltimbanques*, which he had occasion to contemplate in detail while staying in a friend and patron's Munich apartment during the summer of 1915:

> And suddenly in this laborious nowhere, suddenly
> the unsayable spot where the pure Too-little is transformed
> incomprehensibly—, leaps around and changes
> into that empty Too-much;
> where the difficult calculation
> becomes numberless and resolved.[25]

> Und plötzlich in diesem mühsamen Nirgends, plötzlich
> die unsägliche Stelle, wo sich das reine Zuwenig
> unbegreiflich verwandelt—, umspringt
> in jenes leere Zuviel.
> Wo die vielstellige Rechnung
> zahlenlos aufgeht.[26]

The "difficult calculation becomes numberless" and is "resolved," and the "unsayable sums" (in "Ahead of All Parting") of nature are annihilated, because nonbeing is as unknowable as being: One does not know that one is; rather, one *is*. For Picasso's tumbling acrobats, this is the moment in which rising transforms into falling (for example at the peak of a trampoline jump). The momentary experience of weightlessness, which any child can reach at the highest point on a swing, is the experience of non-experience. It is the "empty Too-much" that overcomes us, without establishing any connection to transcendence. The line break after "empty Too-much" enacts the "unsayable spot" where "the pure Too-little" "leaps around." But this is not expressed explicitly: With every line break, Rilke's poem and these thoughts transform themselves—until the difficult calculation of the great elegy is resolved metrically. This understanding of the "empty Too-much" fits Heidegger's description of poets as those "who are more daring than life itself."[27] For Rilke it is the moment between two breaths, the moment between jumping up and falling down, the syncope between two heartbeats. the missing moment between up and down, forward and back, in and out. It is the experience of being in time: "We must accustom ourselves to living in a pause in the breathing of God, between two of his breaths: for that is what it means: to be in time."[28] Life is the heaviness between being and nonbeing, which is not heavy but is our "inner oscillation." The moment of emptiness that is fulfillment.

NOTES

PREFACE: "THE WHOLE DICTATION OF EXISTENCE"

1. *ALT* 1:454.
2. *ALT* 1:454.
3. Musil, "Rede zur Rilke-Feier," 75. Cited in Baer, "The Perfection of Poetry," 171–89.
4. De Man, *Allegories of Reading*, 56.
5. Musil, "Rede zur Rilke-Feier," 70.
6. See Rainer Maria Rilke, *Letters on Life*, ed. and trans. Ulrich Baer (New York: Random House, 2008).
7. Rainer Maria Rilke, *The Notebook of Malte Laurids Brigge*, 53.

A FOR ASHANTI

1. "The Modern Lyric" (speech given in Prague on March 5, 1898), in *SW* 5:388.
2. Peter Altenberg, *The Ashantee*, trans. Katherina von Hammerstein (Riverside: Ariadne Press, 2007).
3. Ralph Freedman, "*Das Stunden-Buch* and *Das Buch der Bilder*: Harbingers of Rilke's Maturity," in Erika A. Metzger and Michael M. Metzger (eds.), *A Companion to the Works of Rainer Maria Rilke* (Rochester, NY: Camden House, 2004), 125.
4. Letter to Clara Rilke, October 19, 1907, in *GB* 2:433.
5. *BOI*, 69.
6. "Die Aschanti," in *SW* 1:394–95.
7. Heidegger, *Elucidations of Hölderlin's Poetry*, 118.
8. "The Ashanti," in *BOI*, 69.
9. Letter to Clara Rilke, October, 19, 1907, in *GB* 2:433.
10. "The Ashanti," in *BOI*, 69.
11. "Die Aschanti," in *SW* 1:395.
12. Ibid.

13. Altenberg, *Ashantee*, 24.

14. *BOI*, 69.

15. De Man, *Allegories of Reading*, 45.

16. Ibid., 47.

17. *VOC*, 63.

18. De Man, *Allegories of Reading*, 56.

19. Letter to Clara Rilke, March 8, 1907, in *GB* 2:279–90 (trans. Baer).

20. "Turning-Point," in *AAP*, 127.

B FOR BUDDHA

1. *SW* 6:1467.

2. Bahr, *Die Bücher zum wirklichen Leben*, 2.

3. Ibid., responses by Camill Hoffmann and Richard Schaukall (6, 14).

4. *SW* 6:1020–21.

5. *MLB*, 39.

6. Ibid., 43

7. Ibid.

8. Ibid., 42.

9. *SW* 6:1021–22.

10. Letter to Richard Schaukal, August 2, 1904, quoted in *KA* 4:983.

11. *MLB*, 198.

12. "Requiem for Wolf Graf von Kalckreuth," in *JBL*, 210; Benn, *Sämtliche Werke* 1, 654.

13. Letter to Baladine Klossowska, December 16, 1920, *NAL* 2:100–101.

14. Celan, *Der Meridian*, 156.

15. "Archaic Torso of Apollo," in *AAP*, 61.

16. *SW* 1:317.

17. Wallis, *Dhammapada*, xiii.

18. *ALT* 1:25.

19. *Das Testament*, 23.

20. Neumann, *Die Reden Gotamo Buddhos*.

21. The citations from Mann, Hesse, Shaw, and Hofmannsthal are found in Neumann, *Die Reden Gotamo Buddhos*.

22. Cited in Neumann, *Die Reden Gotamo Buddhos*.

23. Letter to Clara Rilke, September 8, 1908, in *ALT* 1:252.

24. Ibid., 248 et seq.

25. Later, after the First World War, Rilke's rejection of Buddhist teaching takes a decidedly anti-Buddhist turn: "But let us resist the introduction of oriental traditions, Hindu, Buddhist and the others . . . What they will impose on us one day is not their strange wisdom, made for them and not for us, but rather Bolshevism" (*WUN* 2:1139). It is important to keep in mind that "Bolshevism" was a fairly common pejorative in educated circles in those days. This is why Lord Chatterley, in D. H. Lawrence's *Lady Chatterley's Lover*, calls his wife a "Bolshevik" at the first sign of her unfaithfulness, when she suddenly grows cool toward him. Rilke's thinking here has less to do with the content than with the form of a principle that understands itself as a mobilization of the masses.

26. *SW* 6:891

27. Letter to Clara Rilke, September 20, 1905, in *ALT* 1:112.

28. "Corpse-Washing," in *NP*, 219.

29. "Buddha," in *NP*, 47.

30. "Buddha (Als ob er horchte)," in *SW* 1:496.

31. Letter to Clara Rilke, September 4, 1908, in *ALT* 1:250.

32. *NP*, 47.

33. "Buddha (Als ob er horchte)," in *SW* 1:496.

34. Ibid.

35. Ibid.

36. *NP*, 117.

37. "Buddha (Schon von ferne fühlt)," *SW* 1:528.

38. Letter to Baladine Klossowska, undated (July 1921), in *ALT* 2:244.

39. *NP*, 117.

40. "Buddha (Schon von ferne fühlt)," *SW* 1:528–29.

41. "Buddha in Glory," in *AAP*, 75.

42. "Buddha in der Glorie," *SW* 1:642.

43. *WUN* 2:728–29.

44. *AAP*, 75.

45. "Buddha in der Glorie," *SW* 1:642.

46. Ibid.

47. Ibid.

48. *NP*, 117.

49. Ibid.

C FOR CIRCLE

1. Letter to Nanny Wunderly-Volkart, October 29, 1924, in *WUN* 2:1192.

2. Letter to Victor von Gebsattel, January 14, 1912; *NAL* 1:392.

3. Letter to Magda von Hattingberg, February 21, 1914, in *HAT*, 158.

4. Engel, *Rilke-Handbuch*, 250.

5. *LOU*, 476–77.

6. Between January and July of 1925, Rilke saw André Gide regularly while the latter worked on *The Counterfeiters*, which was first published in 1925 in the *Nouvelle Revue Française*, where Rilke's French poems also appeared shortly afterward.

7. Letter to Lou Andreas-Salomé, December 12, 1925, in *LOU*, 479.

8. Ibid., 480.

9. Cited in Schank, *Rainer Maria Rilke*, 148.

10. *LOU*, 483.

11. Ibid.

12. "I live in expanding rings," in *JBL*, 28.

13. The term "*dépense*" comes from Georges Bataille's critique of a bourgeois morality that condemns waste.

14. Letter to Witold Hulewicz, November 13, 1925, in *NAL* 2:375.

15. "The Third Elegy," in *AAP*, 345.

16. Ibid.

17. Ibid., 349.

18. Ibid., 345.

19. Buddeberg, *Rainer Maria Rilke*, 483.

20. Rilke, *On Love and Other Difficulties*, 45.

21. "The Second Elegy," in *AAP*, 343.

22. Freud, Sigmund, ed. *Wiener psychoanalytische Diskussionen* (Vienna: Psychoanalytische Vereinigung, 1915), 138. Other psychoanalysts questioned whether "onanists" who have given up their compulsive masturbation necessarily succumb to neurosis (as Freud suggests) and are thus faced with "the anxious choice between neurasthenia or neurosis" (Wilhelm Stekel, in *Wiener psychoanalytische Diskussionen*, 33).

23. Andreas-Salomé, *Rainer Maria Rilke*, 104.

24. Ibid.

25. Ernst Pfeiffer, "Nachwort," in *LOU*, 635.

26. Ibid., 626.

27. Ibid., 628.

28. Prater, *A Ringing Glass*, 384.

29. Freedman, *Life of a Poet*, 532.

30. Laqueur, *Solitary Sex*.

31. *SW* 1:277.

D FOR DESTINY DISRUPTED

1. "You who never arrived," in *AAP*, 131.

2. Ibid.

3. "Apprehension," in *POR*, 77.

4. "Bangnis," in *SW* 1:396.

5. De Man, *Allegories of Reading*, 45.

6. "Die fünf Briefe der Nonne Marianna Alcoforado," in *SW* 6:1000.

7. "Die Bücher einer Liebenden (Comtesse Anna de Noailles)," *SW* 6:1019.

8. "Die fünf Briefe," in *SW* 6:999.

9. *MLB*, 207.

10. *NP*, 241.

11. "Die Parke VII," in *SW* 1:607.

12. *POR*, 471.

13. "Judiths Rückkehr," in *SW* 2:38.

14. "Erlebnis," in *SW* 6:1040.

15. Rilke, *Unknown Rilke*, 87.

16. Schnack, *Rainer Maria Rilke*, 718.

17. *LOU*, 275.

18. Ibid.

19. *The Notebooks of Malte Laurids Brigge*, 152.

20. Cavell, *Contesting Tears*, vii.

21. Barthes, A *Lover's Discourse*, 2.

NOTES TO PAGES 45–57

E FOR ENTRAILS

1. Letter to Nora Purtscher-Wydenbruck, August 11, 1924, quoted in Werner Günther, *Weltin-nenraum: Die Dichtung Rainer Maria Rilkes* (Berlin: Erich Schmidt, 1952), 36.

2. "Es winkt zu Fühlung," in Rilke, *Die Gedichte 1910 bis 1922,* ed. Manfred Engel (Frankfurt: Insel 1996).

3. Maurice Blanchot, *L'espace littéraire* (Paris: Gallimard, 1988), 141.

4. Egon Schwarz, *Das verschluckte Schluchzen. Politik und Poesie bei Rainer Maria Rilke* (Frankfurt: Athenäum, 1972), 3.

5. Letter to Alexandrine Schwerin, May 16, 1922, in *ALT* 2:363.

6. Letter to Margot Sizzo, January 1923, in *Briefe an Gräfin Sizzo* (Frankfurt: Insel, 1977), 49.

7. Ibid., 52–53 (trans. Baer in *LOL*, 110–11).

8. Trans. Baer.

9. Manuscript in "In und nach Worpswede. Verse für meinen Lieben Heinrich Vogeler, 1899–1900" (Harvard University Houghton Library/Richard von Mises Collection).

10. "Requiem für eine Freundin," in *SW* 1:647.

11. Ibid.

12. Ibid., 648.

13. Ibid.

14. Ibid., 647.

15. Ibid., 648.

16. Ibid., 647.

17. Ibid.

18. Ibid.

19. Ibid.

20. William Rauscher, "Bodies in Motion: Four Inquiries into Flesh and Voice in Rilke" (unpublished manuscript, New York, December 2003).

21. Letter to Sidonie Nádherný von Borutin, August 1, 1913, in *LOL*, 113–14.

22. Trans. Baer.

23. Samuel Beckett, *Disjecta: Miscellaneous Writings and a Dramatic Fragment* (New York: Grove Press, 1984), 67.

F FOR FROGS

1. Quoted in Arnold, *Rilke*, 40, 47.

2. Ibid., 44.

3. Letter to Clara Rilke, September 13, 1907, in *ALT* 1:176.

4. Letter to Carl Sieber, November 10, 1921, in *ALT* 1:256.

5. Letter to Maximilian Harden, February 1, 1901, in *NAL* 1:80 (emphasis added).

6. Letter to Ludwig Fischer, November 12, 1919, in *BZP*, 292.

7. From October 12, 1917, to May 7, 1918, Rilke lived in the Hôtel Continental in Berlin, which Karl von der Heydt, who was supporting Rilke financially, called "one of the most expensive hotels in Berlin." "The question, L.R. [*lieber* Rilke], 'don't you need something?' has, to be honest, not entered my mind," writes von der Heydt, visibly put off by the high-class address and Rilke's repeated requests for more money. Rilke, *Briefe an Karl und Elisabeth von der Heydt*, 410.

8. Letter to Nanny Wunderly-Volkart, October 7, 1921, in *WUN* 1:566.

9. Letter to Nanny Wunderly-Volkart, April 18, 1921, in *WUN* 1:408.

10. Letter to Ludwig von Ficker, November 12, 1919, in *BZP*, 293.

G FOR GOD

1. Brecht, *Gesammelte Werke*, 18:60. Reinhold Grimm emphasizes that Brecht considered Rilke "otherwise a really good man," which means, in the "language of sports and especially of boxing," which Brecht was prone to use, "a sound and solid, a proper man, experienced in his job, and worthy of respect." See Grimm, *Von der Armut*, 44.

2. Karl Kraus, letter to Sidonie Nádherný, June 8, 1915, quoted in Arnold, *Text und Kritik: Rilke?*, 30.

3. Rudolf Kassner, quoted in Arnold, *Text und Kritik: Rilke?*, 50.

4. Franz Blei, quoted in Arnold, *Text und Kritik: Rilke?*, 43.

5. "Wendung," in *AAP*, 129.

6. Thomas Mann, quoted in Arnold, *Text und Kritik: Rilke?*, 44.

7. Grimm, *Von der Armut und vom Regen*, 8.

8. Hans Carossa, quoted in Arnold, *Text und Kritik: Rilke?*, 40.

9. "Autumn Day," in *AAP*, 15.

10. *POR*, 21–23.

11. Ibid., 27.

12. *TAX* 1:38.

13. *JBL*, 28.

14. Ibid.

15. *SW* 1:255.

16. Letter to Clara Rilke, September 3, 1908, in *ALT* 1:245.

17. *SW* 1:312.

18. Ibid., 312–13.

19. Rilke, *Briefe an einen jungen Dichter*, May 14, 1904, 39 (author's translation).

20. Kidder, *The Book of Hours*, 15.

21. *SW* 1:259.

22. Bertolt Brecht, "Rudern, Gespräche," *Buckower Elegien, Gesammelte Werke* 7:20.

23. Rudolf Kassner, quoted in Arnold, *Text und Kritik: Rilke?*, xxxvii.

24. *SW* 1:259.

25. Kidder, *The Book of Hours*, 17.

26. *SW* 1:260.

27. "Ach wehe, meine Mutter reißt mich ein," *SW* 1:101–2.

28. *SW* 1:264.

29. Kidder, *Book of Hours*, 31.

30. Ludwig Goldschneider, ed., *Klabunds Literaturgeschichte* (Vienna: Phaidon, 1930), 322.

31. Rudolf Kassner, quoted in Arnold, *Text und Kritik: Rilke?*, 50.

32. "How well I now understand those strange pictures in which things meant for limited and ordinary uses stretch out and stroke one another, lewd and curious, quivering in the random lechery of distraction. Those kettles that walk around steaming, those pistons that start to think, and the

indolent funnel that squeezes into a hole for its pleasure. And already, tossed up by the jealous void, and among them, there are arms and legs, and faces that warmly vomit onto them, and windy buttocks that offer them satisfaction. And the saint writhes and pulls back into himself; yet in his eyes there was still a look which thought this was possible: he had glimpsed it." (*MLB*, 184–85.)

33. Letter to Nanny Wunderly-Volkart, September 23, 1923, in *WUN*, 918.

34. *ANI*, 17.

35. Ibid., 23.

36. *LOL*, 192.

37. Ibid., 193.

38. Ibid., 194.

39. Ibid.

40. *ANI*, 42–43.

41. Letter of March 15, 1920, in *WUN* 1:184.

H FOR HAIR

1. "The Rose Window," in *NP*, 53.

2. "O Lacrimosa," in *AAP*, 187.

3. "The Hand," in *POR*, 555.

4. "Gong," in *AAP*, 199.

5. Ibid.

6. 2 Samuel 1:26, New International Version.

7. "Lament for Jonathan," in *JBL*, 151.

8. Ibid.

9. *KA* 1:964.

10. "The Tenth Elegy," in *AAP*, 389.

11. *UP*, 124.

I FOR INCA

1. "Progress," in *BOI*, 91.

2. "Fortschritt," *Buch der Bilder*, in *SW*, 1:197.

3. *JBL*, 46–47.

4. Letter from Anton Kippenberg, April 7, 1914, in *KLP* 1:507 (trans. Baer).

5. Ibid., 505–6 (trans. Baer).

6. The letters in question are eleven letters and one card written in 1896 to Richard Zoozmann, to whom Rilke dedicated the volume *Dream-Crowned*.

7. Andreas-Salomé, *Rainer Maria Rilke*, 9.

8. Ibid., 10.

9. "Progress," *BOI*, 91.

10. Letter of December 17, 1922, quoted in Schnack, *Rainer Maria Rilke*, 7 (trans. Baer).

11. Rainer Maria Rilke Papers, Harvard University, Houghton Library, Ger 58.2.

12. *TAX* 1:39 (trans. Baer).

13. Ibid., 1:151.

14. Ibid., 1:175.
15. *TSV*, 46.
16. *TAX* 1:52.
17. *SID*, 326; *LOU*, 300.
18. *TAX* 1:52.
19. *SW* 2:132.
20. Pahl, *R.M. Rilke*, 5.
21. *TAX* 1:341 (trans. Baer).
22. "Narcissus," in *UP*, 59.
23. "Narziß (Narziß verging)," *SW* 2:56.
24. *BSF*, 209.
25. Jacques Derrida, *Sauf le nom* (Paris: Gallimard, 1993), 58.
26. *TAX* 1:102.
27. From Rilke, *Lettres françaises à Merline 1919–1921*, 81.
28. Ibid., 81 [colored page inserted into book].
29. *BSF*, 721 (trans. Baer).

J FOR JEW BOY

1. *ALT*, 2:284–85. The wording differs slightly from the copies of the letter given by Ilse Blumenthal-Weiß to the Houghton Library, Harvard University, in the 1950s. The Altheim version is quoted here.
2. Ibid., 600.
3. Ibid., 285.
4. Letter to Marie von Thurn und Taxis, December 17, 1912, in *TAX* 1:246.
5. "The First Elegy," in *AAP*, 333.
6. Ibid.
7. *ALT* 2:286 (trans. Baer).
8. Ibid., 438.
9. "Nature Is Happy," in *Poems 1906–1926*, 235.
10. "Natur ist glücklich," *SW* 2:449.
11. "The Second Elegy," in *AAP*, 339–41.
12. Letter to Lou Andreas-Salomé, February 19, 1922, in *SW* 1:690.
13. *NAL* 2:248.
14. Ibid. Emphasis follows Ilse Blumenthal-Weiß's typescript copy of the letter, Houghton Library, Harvard University.
15. Ibid., 249.
16. Ibid.
17. Ibid.
18. Vivian Liska, "'Roots Against Heaven,' an Aporetic Inversion in Paul Celan," in *New German Critique* 91 (2004), 41–56.
19. Heine, *Sämtliche Werke*, 282.
20. Letter to Ilse Blumenthal-Weiß, April 25, 1922, in *NAL* 2:249.
21. Ibid.

22. Moses, ed., *Lösung der Judenfrage*, 7.

23. Ibid., 282.

24. Ibid., 215.

25. *SW*, 6:1004.

26. Ibid., 1005.

27. Ibid.

28. Schwarz, *Ich bin kein Freund*, 193–94.

29. Letter to Eva Cassirer, August 20, 1908, in *GB* 3:37.

30. Ibid.

31. Ilse Blumenthal-Weiß did not find Rilke's letter to be anti-Semitic. Critics such as Egon Schwarz have a point in not considering such personal opinions alone "to be the deciding factor." Schwarz, *Ich bin kein Freund*, 182, note 7.

32. Rilke, *Florenzer Tagebuch*, 103.

33. Schwarz, *Ich bin kein Freund*, 193.

34. "The First Elegy," in *AAP*, 331.

35. *WUN* 2:848–49.

36. *NAL* 1:282.

37. *TAX* 1:309.

38. Although Rilke admired Werfel's poetry, he criticized his *Not the Murderer* as "tasteless." See *WUN* 1:273.

39. *TAX* 1:323.

40. Ibid., 323–24.

41. "The First Elegy," in *AAP*, 331.

42. *TAX* 1:312.

43. Ibid., 328 (trans. Baer).

44. Ibid., 309.

45. *SW* 6:1046.

46. Ibid., 1048.

47. Ibid., 1055.

48. Ibid., 1053.

49. *SW* 6:1053.

50. *WUN* 2:1025.

51. *Florenzer Tagebuch*, 103.

52. *TAX* 2:966.

K FOR KAFKA AND KING LEAR

1. Letter to Princess Marie von Thurn und Taxis, January 6, 1912, in *TAX* 1:92.

2. "The First Elegy," in *AAP*, 331.

3. Letter to Princess Marie von Thurn und Taxis, February 11, 1922, in *TAX* 2:698.

4. Letter to Anton Kippenberg, February 9, 1922, in *ALT* 2:308.

5. Letter to Lou Andreas-Salomé, February 11, 1922, in *ALT* 2:311.

6. Letter to Countess Sizzo, March 17, 1922, in *SIZ*, 24.

7. Nossack, *Insel-Almanach auf das Jahr 1967*, 92.

8. Schnack, *Rainer Maria Rilke*, 662.

9. *SW* 6:1086.

10. Ibid., 1087.

11. Ibid.

12. Ibid.

13. Ibid.

14. Ibid., 1090.

15. Rilke hoped that Adolf Koelsch would carry out this experiment in the Swiss town of Rüschlikon. See Rilke and Forrer, *Briefwechsel*, 21–22, and Schnack, *Rilke*, 663.

16. *SW* 6:1091.

17. Quoted in Angela von der Lippe, "Translating a Life," afterword to Andreas-Salomé, *You Alone Are Real to Me*, 136.

18. Rilke most likely read Kafka's book immediately upon its publication. Rilke was familiar with Kafka since at least 1914. (See Schnack, *Rilke*, 484.)

19. Letter to Kurt Wolff, February 17, 1922, quoted in Schnack, *Rilke*, 787.

20. *MLB*, 19–20.

21. Ibid., 52–53.

22. *TAX* 1:322.

23. Marie von Thurn und Taxis, *Erinnerungen*, 48.

24. *SW* 6:1089.

25. *TAX* 1:86.

26. Ibid.

27. Shakespeare, *King Lear*, act 2, scene 4, line 72.

28. Friedrich Kittler, *Gramophone, Film, Typewriter*, trans. Geoffrey Winthrop-Young and Michael Wutz (Stanford: Stanford University Press, 1999), 80.

29. Ernst Kantorowicz, *The King's Two Bodies: Studies in Mediaeval Political Theology* (Princeton: Princeton University Press, 1997).

30. "Aus der Trübe müde Überdrüsse," in *SW* 2:223.

L FOR LAREAN

1. Letter to Witold Hulewicz, November 13, 1925, in *ALT* 2:483.

2. Freud, "For a Scientific Psychology," in *The Complete Letters of Sigmund Freud to Wilhelm Fliess*; Benjamin, "The Work of Art in the Age of Mechanical Reproduction," in *Illuminations*; Heidegger, "The Origin of the Work of Art" and "The Thing," in *Poetry, Language, Thought*; Breton, "Du surréalisme dans ses oeuvres vives," in *Manifestes du surréalisme*; Lacan, *La chose freudienne* and *Le séminaire X*; Wittgenstein, *Notebooks 1914–1916*.

3. *Brockhaus Konversations-Lexikon*, 14th ed. (Leipzig: Brockhaus, 1893). The *Oxford English Dictionary* cites the most recent attestation in English of the root word "*lar*" in 1889.

4. Letter to Witold Hulewicz, November 13, 1925, in *ALT* 2:483.

5. "Nicht um-stoßen, was steht," in *SW* 2:176.

6. *ALT* 2:483.

7. Letter to Ellen Key, April 3, 1903, in Rilke, *Briefwechsel mit Ellen Key*, 26–27.

M FOR MUSSOLINI

1. *BZP*, 642.
2. Ibid, 671–72.
3. Schwarz, *Das verschluckte Schluchzen*, 3.
4. Ibid., 22.
5. Ibid., 23.
6. Ibid., 72.
7. *BZP*, 715.
8. Ibid., 701–2.
9. Nalewski, foreword to *NAL* 1:31; Storck, "Politisches Bewußtsein bei Rilke," in *BZP*, 701–2.
10. Letter to Baladine Klossowska, in Rilke, *Briefwechsel mit Rolf von Ungern-Sternberg*, 44.
11. Although he praises rhyme here, Rilke writes in another letter that one is "unnoticeably abused and alienated [. . .] when one must take what one most wants to express, and put it in a form that is deforming, coddling, and even a bit debasing." A changing understanding of freedom accounts for these contradicting statements. *ANI*, 46.
12. Quoted in *BZP*, 677, 679.
13. Croce, *Scritti e discorsi politici (1943–47)*.
14. Derrida, *Otobiographies*, 29.
15. Gallarati-Scotti's reply is here translated from the German translation by Frauke Schwanke in "Rilkes *Lettres Milanaises* in deutscher Übertragung mit einem Kommentar" (dissertation at Washington University in St. Louis, 1977), in *BZP*, 681.
16. Ibid., 682.
17. Ibid., 683.

N FOR NATURE

1. "The Eighth Elegy," in *AAP*, 377.
2. Agamben, *The Open*, 57.
3. Hart, *Nowhere Without No*, 8.
4. Wolfram Malte Fues, in Groddeck, *Gedichte von Rainer Maria Rilke*, 162. Of course this claim is only a feint. The critic then plays the poetry against philosophy. In such games, there is usually no winner.
5. "The Second Elegy," in *AAP*, 341.
6. "The Eighth Elegy," in *AAP*, 377.
7. *SW* 5:11.
8. Ibid., 12.
9. "The Tenth Elegy," in *AAP*, 389.
10. Ibid., 391.
11. Ibid.
12. Barbara Indlekofer, in Groddeck, *Gedichte von Rainer Maria Rilke*, 196.
13. Rilke made this remark to his French translator Maurice Betz in *KA* 1:1004.
14. "The Dog," in *NP*, 313.
15. Rilke to Magda von Hattingberg, *Rilke and Benvenuta*, 77.

16. For example Beda Allemann, who persuasively explicates Rilke's "conception of the hollow center" from which "a great movement continually [. . .] seeks new places to go." Allemann, *Zeit und Figur*, 102, 105.

17. For instance, Barbara Indlekofer, in Groddeck, *Gedichte von Rainer Maria Rilke*, 199. This is in contrast to Paul de Man's reading of Rilke: "The notion of a language entirely freed of referential constraints is properly inconceivable" (De Man, *Allegories of Reading*, 49).

P FOR PROLETARIAN

1. "The Painter," in *Visions of Christ*, 89.
2. *SW* 3:140.
3. Rilke praised the novel *Jörn Uhl* by Gustav Frenssen, because it "tried to make the Sermon on the Mount unsentimental." *SW* 6:1418.
4. Letter to Ilse Erdmann, December 21, 1913, in *ALT*, 417.
5. Ibid.
6. This break in style uses Christian thought to free Rilke's use of "proletarian" from the limitations of Marxist revolutionary thinking, as for example Alexander Blok does in his poem "The Twelve," which is about the Russian revolution and ends with an image of Christ.
7. *GB* 2:392.
8. Hamburger, *Rilke in neuer Sicht*, 64.
9. *SW* 1:356.
10. Quoted in Pongs, *Dichtung und Volkstum*, 111 et seq.
11. Rilke, *Briefwechsel mit Anton Kippenberg* 1:154.
12. Marcuse, *Triebstruktur und Gesellschaft*, 141, 143. Marshall Berman criticized Rilke's reckoning from a Marxist angle. (See Berman, *Adventures in Marxism*, 145–46.)
13. Rilke, *Briefwechsel mit Ellen Key*, 25.
14. Grimm, *Von der Armut*, 10, 13.
15. Ibid., 17.
16. Ibid., 19.
17. Ibid., 64.
18. "The Painter," in Rilke, *Visions of Christ*, 89.
19. *SW* 3:140.
20. Grimm, *Von der Armut*, 77.
21. Letter to Margot Sizzo, March 17, 1922, in *NAL* 2:235–36.

Q FOR *QUATSCH*

1. "Wladimir, der Wolkenmaler," in *SW* 4:588. Translation by Baer.
2. Ibid.
3. Balzac, *The Girl with the Golden Eyes*.
4. Ibid.
5. Agamben, *Man Without Content*, 9.
6. *SW* 4:591.
7. Agamben, *Man Without Content*, 10.

8. *GB* 1:162.

9. *SW* 4:591.

10. Ibid., 587.

11. Ibid., 589.

12. Ibid., 588.

R FOR ROSE

1. "Rose O reiner Widerspruch," in *SW* 2:185.

2. *WUN* 2:1192.

3. While writing this, I learned that Rolf Selbmann subsequently made the same discovery. See: "Rainers Widersprüche" in *Blätter der Rilke-Gesellschaft*, 24.

4. Wolfgang Leppmann, "Zauberwürfel," in Reich-Ranicki, *1000 Gedichte*, 372.

5. "Sonnets to Orpheus, First Part," in *AAP*, 419.

6. Walter Benjamin, "On Language as Such and on the Language of Man," in Benjamin, *Selected Writings* 1:65.

S FOR STAMPA

1. "The First Elegy," in *AAP*, 333.

2. "Die Erste Elegie," *Duineser Elegien*, SW 1:686.

3. *ALT* 2:361.

4. *SW* 6:937; *WUN* 1:643–44.

5. Letter to Nanny Wunderly-Volkart, April 12, 1922, *WUN* 2:730.

6. Schnack, *Rainer Maria Rilke*, 315.

7. Ibid., 316.

8. Barthes, *A Lover's Discourse*, 189.

9. "The First Elegy," in *AAP*, 331.

10. *MLB*, 213.

11. Ibid., 212.

12. Rilke and Pozzi, *Correspondance*, 67–68.

13. "Die Liebenden," in *SW* 2:293–94.

14. Joyce, *Ulysses*, 644.

15. *SW* 6:903–4.

16. Ibid., 936. Also in Rilke, *Letters on Life*, 197.

17. Ibid., 897.

18. Schnack, *Rainer Maria Rilke*, 315.

19. Harold Bloom in a letter to the author, November 6, 2004.

20. Letter to Annette Kolb, January 23, 1912, in Rilke, *Mitten im Lesen schreibe ich Dir*, 141.

21. Waters, *Poetry's Touch*, 38.

22. Guardini, *Zu Rainer Maria Rilkes*, 50.

23. *MLB*, 236.

24. Ibid., 236–37.

25. *LOU*, 19.

26. Letter to Theodor Fontane, quoted in Schnack, *Rainer Maria Rilke*, 42.
27. "The First Elegy," in *AAP*, 333.
28. "The Problem of Sublimation" in Lacan, *Seminar of Jacques Lacan*.
29. "The Third Elegy," in *AAP*, 345.
30. Untitled poem ("To Lou Andreas-Salomé") in *AAP*, 97–99.
31. *KA* 2:18.
32. Letter to Margot Sizzo, April 12, 1923, in *ALT* 2:598.
33. *SW* 6:1016.

T FOR TOWER

1. "The Ninth Elegy," in *AAP*, 387.
2. Ibid., 385.
3. Wittgenstein, *Notebooks*, 83.
4. "Archaic Torso of Apollo," in *AAP*, 97.
5. Rilke, *Auguste Rodin*, in *SW* 5:150.
6. Ibid., 163–64.
7. *MLB*, 52–53.
8. *Auguste Rodin*, in *SW* 5:146.
9. Ibid., 200.
10. *MLB*, 53.
11. Ibid.
12. Ibid.
13. Rilke, *Briefe 1902–1906*, 89.
14. *MLB*, 53.
15. *ALT* 1:454.
16. "The Seventh Elegy," in *AAP*, 373–75.
17. *JBL*, 28.

U FOR UN-

1. *MLB*, 167.
2. Ibid.
3. Letter to Witold Hulewicz, November 13, 1925, in *NAL* 2:375–76.
4. The term "secretary of the invisible" comes from Czesław Miłosz's poem "Secretaries," in *Hymn of the Pearl*.
5. *SIZ*, 49–55.
6. Ibid.
7. "The Boy," in *POR*, 63.
8. "Memory," in *POR*, 85.
9. "The Island," in *NP*, 133.
10. "Orpheus. Eurydice. Hermes," in *NP*, 141.
11. Ibid., 147.
12. Letter to Franz Xaver Kappus, February 17, 1903, in *LYP*, 4.

13. "The Sonnets to Orpheus," in *AAP*, 411.

14. Heidegger, *Being and Time*, 52.

15. Letter to Countess M. December 2, 1921, in *ALT* 1:710.

16. *SW* 6:724; *WUN* 1:618.

17. *SW* 6:1087, 1091.

18. Letter to Ilse Erdmann, December 21, 1913, in *ALT* 1:454.

19. Letter to Nanny Wunderly-Volkart, June 2, 1921, in *WUN* 1:473.

20. "Ausgesetzt auf den Bergen des Herzens," in *SW* 2:95.

21. Letter to Yvonne von Wattenwyl, August 21–22, 1919, in *Mitten im Lesen*, 58–59.

22. Petzet, *Auf einen Stern*, 24, 244.

23. *ANI*, 34.

24. Rilke, *Das Testament*, 23.

25. *SW* 2:123.

26. "Gegen-Strophen," in *SW* 2:136.

27. *MLB*, 133.

28. *MLB*, 4.

V FOR VAGABOND, OR BEING OUTSIDE

1. Letter to Clara Westhoff, October 23, 1900, in *ALT* 1:24.

2. "I love the darker hours of my existence," in *POR*, 29.

3. *SW* 1:254–55.

4. "The Second Elegy," in *AAP*, 341.

5. Ibid., 343.

6. "The First Elegy," in *AAP*, 331.

7. "The Seven Phallic Poems," in Rilke, *On Love and Other Difficulties*, 45, 49.

8. Letter to Alexander Benois, July 28, 1901, in Asadowski, *Rilke und Rußland*, 293.

9. Ibid.

10. Ibid.

11. *SW* 1:557.

12. Ibid., 317.

13. "Archaic Torso of Apollo," in *AAP*, 67.

14. "When from My Window Something Falls," in *JBL*, 73.

15. *SW* 1:321.

16. *BZP*, 656, 666–67.

17. "The First Elegy," in *AAP*, 331.

18. Heidegger, *Poetry, Language, Thought*, 96.

19. Foucault, *Dits et écrits*, 152.

20. *LOL*, 102.

21. Ibid., 484–85.

22. *Gedichte 1910 bis 1926* 2:412 (trans. Ulrich Baer).

23. Ibid.

24. "O Leben, Leben, wunderliche Zeit," in *SW* 2:411.

25. Ibid.

26. "Draußen Welten," in *SW* 2:230.

27. Ibid.

28. *WUN* 1:340.

29. Letter to Gertrud Ouckama Knoop, September 12, 1919, in *NAL* 2:27.

30. For the notion of "pure language," see "The Task of the Translator" in Benjamin, *Illuminations.*

W FOR WORM

1. Letter from Benn to F. W. Oelze, in Hauschild, ed., *Insel-Almanach auf das Jahr 1997,* 142.

2. Benn, *Briefe an Astrid Claes,* 25.

3. *MLB,* 3.

4. Ibid., 249.

5. "The First Elegy," in *AAP,* 331.

6. "The Second Elegy," in *AAP,* 343.

7. "The Ninth Elegy," in *AAP,* 387.

8. "The First Elegy," in *AAP,* 333.

9. Marie von Thurn und Taxis, *Erinnerungen,* 71.

10. Guardini, *Zu Rainer Maria Rilkes,* 52.

11. "The Eighth Elegy," in *AAP,* 377.

12. Letter to Sophie Liebknecht, June 22, 1917, in Rilke, *Briefe zur Politik, 170.*

13. *SW* 6:199.

14. Hesse, *Siddhartha,* 6, 9.

15. *SW* 6, 199.

16. Ibid.

17. Ibid.

18. Ibid.

19. Otto Bolnow, *Rilke,* 208.

20. Letter from Benn to Edgar Lohner, February 19, 1952, in Benn, *Briefe an Astrid Claes,* 139.

21. Rilke, *Lettres françaises à Merline,* 57.

22. Ibid., 58.

23. Ibid.

24. Ibid., 62.

25. Pinthus, *Zur jüngsten Dichtung,* quoted in Arnold, *Text und Kritik,* 30.

26. *MLB,* 257–58.

27. *MLB,* 46.

28. *POR,* 35.

29. Groddeck, *Gedichte,* 25.

30. Letter to F. W. Oelze, *Insel-Almanach auf das Jahr 1997,* 142.

X FOR XAVER

1. Benn, "Lebensweg eines Intellektualisten," in *Gesammelte Werke,* 8:121.

2. *LJD,* 18. Translated by Ulrich Baer.

3. Ibid., 7. Translated by Ulrich Baer.

Y FOR Y

1. Letter to Clara Rilke, October 4, 1907, in *ALT* 1:180.

Z FOR ZERO

1. "The Ninth Elegy," in *AAP*, 387.

2. "Die Neunte Elegie," *Duineser Elegien*, in *SW* 1:720.

3. Letter to Thankmar Freiherr von Münchhausen, December 27, 1913, in *ALT* 1:461.

4. Letter to Marie von Thurn und Taxis, December 29, 1913, in *TAX* 1:346.

5. Letter to Anita Forrer, February 22–24, 1920, in *LOL*, 50.

6. Letter to Ilse Erdmann, December 21, 1913, in *ALT* 1:454.

7. *MLB*, 173.

8. The German Z is invariably pronounced as a "ts" sound—as in "pizza" or "Mozart." The name of the letter on its own is pronounced "tset." —Trans.

9. "Elegy," in *AAP*, 207.

10. "Elegie an Marina Zwetajewa-Efron," in *SW* 2:272.

11. *MLB*, 237.

12. Ibid., 238.

13. "Elegy," in *AAP*, 207.

14. "Elegie an Marina Zwetajewa-Efron," in *SW* 2:271.

15. Letter to Hermann Pongs, October 21, 1924, in *BZP*, 437.

16. Heidegger, "What Are Poets For?" in *Poetry, Language, Thought*.

17. Letter to Nanny Wunderly-Volkart, April 1, 1924, in *LOL*, 24.

18. See Lears, *Something for Nothing*.

19. "The Tenth Elegy," in *AAP*, 395.

20. "Die Zehnte Elegie," *Duineser Elegien*, in *SW* 1:726.

21. Rilke, "Eine Morgenandacht," *SW* 5:681.

22. Heidegger, *Poetry, Language, Thought*, 93.

23. "Be Ahead of All Parting," in *AAP*, 487.

24. "Sei allem Abschied voran," in *SW* 1:759–60.

25. "The Fifth Elegy," in *AAP*, 361.

26. "Die Fünfte Elegie," *Duineser Elegien*, in *SW* 1:704.

27. Heidegger, *Poetry, Language, Thought*, 102.

28. *WUN* 1:467–68.

WORKS CITED

TRANSLATIONS OF RILKE

Rilke, Rainer Maria. *Ahead of All Parting. The Selected Poetry and Prose of Rainer Maria Rilke*. Translated by Stephen Mitchell. New York: Modern Library, 1980. (AAP)

———. *The Book of Hours: Prayers to a Lowly God*. Translated by Annemarie S. Kidder. Evanston: Northwestern University Press, 2001.

———. *The Book of Images*. Translated by Edward Snow. New York: Farrar Straus Giroux, 1991. (BOI)

———. *Letters on Life*. Edited and translated by Ulrich Baer. New York: Modern Library, 2006. (LOL)

———. *Letters to a Young Poet*. Translated by Stephen Mitchell. New York: Vintage, 1986. (LYP)

———. *New Poems*. Translated by Edward Snow. New York: Farrar Straus Giroux, 2001. (NP)

———. *The Notebooks of Malte Laurids Brigge*. Translated by Stephen Mitchell. New York: Vintage International, 1982. (MLB)

———. *The Notebooks of Malte Laurids Brigge*. Translated by Burton Pike. Champaign: Dalkey Archive Editions, 2008.

———. *On Love and Other Difficulties: Translations and Considerations of Rainer Maria Rilke*. Translated by John J. L. Mood. New York: Norton, 1975.

———. *Poems 1906–1926*. Translated by J. B. Leishman. New York: New Directions, 1957.

———. *The Poetry of Rilke*. Translated by Edward Snow. New York: Farrar Straus Giroux, 2009. (POR)

———. *Selected Works, Volume 2: Poetry*. Translated by J. B. Leishman. New York: New Directions, 1960. (JBL)

———. *Uncollected Poems*. Translated by Edward Snow. New York: Farrar Straus Giroux, 1997. (UP)

———. *The Unknown Rilke*. Translated by Franz Wright. Oberlin: Oberlin College Press, 1990.

———. *Visions of Christ: A Posthumous Cycle of Poems*. Translated by Aaron Kramer. Boulder: University of Colorado Press, 1967.

Rilke, Rainer Maria, and Magda von Hattingberg. *Rilke and Benvenuta: An Intimate Correspondence*. New York: Fromm International, 1987.

Rilke, Rainer Maria, and Catherine Pozzi. *Correspondance* (French edition). Paris: Editions de la Différence, 1990.

RILKE'S WORKS IN GERMAN

Rilke, Rainer Maria. *Briefe*. 2 vols. Wiesbaden: Rilke Archiv, 1980. (ALT)

———. *Briefe*. 2 vols. Edited by Horst Nalewski. Frankfurt: Insel, 1991. (NAL)

———. *Briefe 1902–1906*. Frankfurt: Insel, 1930.

———. *Briefe an die Schweizer Freunde*. Edited by Rätus Luck. Frankfurt: Suhrkamp, 1994. (BSF)

———. *Briefe an einen jungen Dichter*. Frankfurt: Insel, 1969.

———. *Briefe an Gräfin Sizzo*. Frankfurt: Insel, 1977. (SIZ)

———. *Briefe an Karl und Elisabeth von der Heydt*. Frankfurt: Insel, 1986.

———. *Briefe an Nanny Wunderly-Volkart*. 2 vols. Edited by Rätus Luck. Frankfurt: Insel, 1977. (WUN)

———. *Briefe an Sidonie Nádherný von Borutin*. Frankfurt: Insel, 1973. (SID)

———. *Briefe zur Politik*. Edited by Joachim Storck. Frankfurt: Insel, 1992. (BZP)

———. *Briefwechsel mit Ellen Key*. Frankfurt: Insel, 1993.

———. *Briefwechsel mit Rolf von Ungern-Sternberg*. Frankfurt: Insel, 2002.

———. *Das Testament*. Frankfurt: Suhrkamp, 1976.

———. *Florenzer Tagebuch*. Frankfurt: Insel, 1994.

———. *Gedichte 1910 bis 1926*. Edited by Manfred Engel and Ulrich Fülleborn. Frankfurt: Insel, 1996.

————. *Gesammelte Briefe.* Edited by Ruth Sieber-Rilke and Carl Sieber. Frankfurt: Insel, 1930–37. (GB)

————. *Lektüre für Minuten.* Edited by Volker and Ursula Michels. Frankfurt: Insel, 1988.

————. *Lettres françaises à Merline.* Paris: Seuil, 1950.

————. *Mitten im Lesen schreibe ich Dir.* Edited by Rätus Luck. Frankfurt: Insel, 1996.

————. *Sämtliche Werke.* 6 vols. Frankfurt: Rilke-Archiv, 1987. (SW)

————. *Werke.* Annotated edition in four volumes. Edited by Manfred Engel, Ulrich Fülleborn, Horst Nalewski, and August Stahl. Frankfurt: Insel, 1996. (KA)

Rilke, Rainer Maria, and Lou Andreas-Salomé. *Briefwechsel.* Frankfurt: Insel, 1975. (LOU)

Rilke, Rainer Maria, and Anita Forrer. *Briefwechsel.* Frankfurt: Insel, 1982. (ANI)

Rilke, Rainer Maria, and Magda von Hattingberg. *Briefwechsel mit Magda von Hattingberg.* Frankfurt: Insel, 2000. (HAT)

Rilke, Rainer Maria, and Anton Kippenberg. *Briefwechsel mit Anton Kippenberg.* Frankfurt: Insel, 1995.

Rilke, Rainer Maria, and Marie von Thurn und Taxis. *Briefwechsel.* Edited by Ernst Zinn. Frankfurt: Insel, 1986. (TAX)

Rilke, Rainer Maria, and Marina Zwetajewa. *Ein Gespräch in Briefen.* Edited by Konstantin M. Asadowski. Frankfurt: Suhrkamp, 1973.

SECONDARY SOURCES

Agamben, Giorgio. *The Man Without Content.* Stanford: Stanford University Press, 1999.

————. *The Open: Man and Animal.* Stanford: Stanford University Press, 2004.

Alleman, Beda. *Zeit und Figur beim späten Rilke. Ein Beitrag zur Poetik des modernen Gedichts.* Pfullingen: Neske, 1961.

Altenberg, Peter. *The Ashantee.* Translated by Katherina von Hammerstein. Riverside, CA: Ariadne Press, 2007.

Andreas-Salomé, Lou. *Rainer Maria Rilke.* Frankfurt: Insel, 1928.

Arnold, Heinz Ludwig, ed. *Rilke. Kleine Hommage zum 100. Geburtstag.* Munich: Edition Text und Kritik, 1992.

Arnold, Ludwig, ed. *Text und Kritik. Rilke?* Munich: Edition Text + Kritik, 1975.

Asadowski, Konstantin, ed. *Rilke und Rußland. Briefe, Erinnerungen, Gedichte.* Frankfurt: Insel, 1986.

Bahr, Hermann, ed. *Die Bücher zum wirklichen Leben.* Wien: Hugo Heller, 1908.

Balzac, Honoré de. "The Unknown Masterpiece," in *The Girl with the Golden Eyes and Other Stories*, trans. Peter Collier. New York: Oxford University Press, 2012.

Barthes, Roland. *The Lover's Discourse: Fragments.* Translated by Richard Howard. New York: HarperCollins, 1978.

Beckett, Samuel. *Disjecta. Miscellaneous Writings.* New York: Grove Press, 1984.

Benjamin, Walter. *Angelus Novus.* Frankfurt: Suhrkamp, 1988.

———. *Illuminations.* New York: Schocken, 1969.

Benn, Gottfried. *Briefe an Astrid Claes.* Stuttgart: Klett-Cotta, 2002.

———. *Gesammelte Werke.* Edited by Dieter Wellershof. Munich: DTV, 1979.

Berman, Marshall. *Adventures in Marxism.* New York: Verso, 2001.

Blanchot, Maurice. *L'espace littéraire.* Paris: Gallimard, 1955.

Brecht, Bertold. *Gesammelte Werke.* Frankfurt: Suhrkamp, 1967.

Breton, André. Du surréalisme dans ses œuvres vives (1953), in *Manifestes du surréalisme.* Paris: Gallimard, 1979.

Brockhaus Konversations-Lexikon, 14th ed. Leipzig: Brockhaus, 1893.

Buddeberg, Else. *Rainer Maria Rilke. Eine innere Biographie.* Stuttgart: Metzler, 1954.

Cavell, Stanley. *Contesting Tears: The Hollywood Melodrama of the Unknown Woman.* Chicago: University of Chicago Press, 1996.

Celan, Paul. *Der Meridian. Endfassung, Vorstufen, Materialen.* Frankfurt: Suhrkamp, 1999.

Croce, Benedetto. *Scritti e discorsi politic (1943–47).* Bari: Bibliopolis, 1963.

De Man, Paul. *Allegories of Reading: Figural Language in Rousseau, Nietzsche, Rilke, and Proust.* New Haven: Yale University Press, 1979.

Derrida, Jacques. *The Ear of the Other: Otobiography, Transference, Translation.* Lincoln, NE: University of Nebraska Press, 1988.

———. *On the Name.* Stanford: Palo Alto, 1995.

———. *Otobiographies. L'enseignement de Nietzsche et la politique du nom proper.* Paris: Gallimard, 1984.

Engel, Manfred, ed. *Rilke-Handbuch.* Stuttgart: Metzler, 2004.

Foucault, Michel. *Dits et écrits.* Paris: Gallimard, 2001.

Freedman, Ralph. *Life of a Poet.* Evanston, IL: Northwestern, 1996.

Freud, Sigmund, ed. *For a Scientific Psychology.* In *The Complete Letters of Sigmund Freud to Wilhelm Fliess, 1887–1904.* Jeffrey Masson, ed. and trans. Cambridge, MA: Harvard University Press, 1985.

———. *Wiener psychoanalytische Diskussionen.* Vienna: Psychoanalytische Diskussionen, 1915.

Goldschneider, Ludwig, ed. *Klabunds Literaturgeschichte.* Vienna: Phaidon, 1930.

Grimm, Reinhold. *Von der Armut und vom Regen. Rilkes Antwort auf die soziale Frage.* Königstein: Athenaeum, 1981.

Groddeck, Wolfram, ed. *Gedichte von Rainer Maria Rilke.* Stuttgart: Reclam, 1999.

Guardini, Romano. *Zu Rainer Maria Rilkes Deutung des Daseins. Eine Interpretation der zweiten, achten, und neunten Duineser Elegie.* Grünewald: Schönigh, 1996.

Günther, Werner. *Weltinnenraum. Die Dichtung Rainer Maria Rilkes.* Berlin: Erich Schmidt, 1952.

Hamburger, Käte. *Rilke in neuer Sicht.* Stuttgart: Kohlhammer, 1971.

Hart, Kevin, ed. *Nowhere Without No: In Memory of Maurice Blanchot.* Melbourne: Vagabond, 2003.

Hauschild, Vera, ed. *Insel Almanach auf das Jahr 1997.* Frankfurt: Insel, 1997.

Heidegger, Martin. *Being and Time.* Translated by John MacQuarrie and Edward Robinson. New York: Harper, 2008.

———. *Erläuterungen zu Hölderlins Dichtung.* Frankfurt: Klostermann, 1996.

———. *Poetry, Language, Thought.* Translated by Albert Hofstadter. New York: Perennial, 2001.

Heine, Heinrich. *Sämtliche Werke.* Edited by Fritz Strich. Munich: Georg Müller, 1928.

Joyce, James. *Ulysses.* New York: Random House, 1986.

Kantorowicz, Ernst. *The King's Two Bodies.* Princeton: Princeton University Press, 1997.

Kittler, Friedrich. *Gramophone, Film, Typewriter.* Palo Alto: Stanford University Press, 1999.

Lacan, Jacques. *La chose freudienne.* Paris: Seuil, 1950.

———. *The Seminar of Jacques Lacan: The Ethics of Psychoanalysis.* New York: Norton, 1992.

Laqueur, Thomas W. *Solitary Sex.* Cambridge, MA: Zone Books, 2004.

Lears, Jackson. *Something for Nothing: Luck in America.* New York: Penguin, 2004.

Liska, Vivian. "'Roots Against Heaven,' an Aporetic Inversion in Paul Celan." *New German Critique* 91 (2004): 41–56.

Marcuse, Herbert. *Triebstruktur und Gesellschaft. Ein philosophischer Beitrag zu Sigmund Freud.* Frankfurt: Suhrkamp, 1979.

Metzger, Erika A., and Michael M. Metzger, eds. *A Companion to the Works of Rainer Maria Rilke.* Rochester, NY: Camden House, 2004.

Miłosz, Czesław. "Secretaries," in *Hymn of the Pearl*, trans. Miłosz and Robert Haas. Ann Arbor: Michigan Slavic Publications, 1982.

Moses, Julius, ed. *Die Lösung der Judenfrage.* Berlin and Leipzig: Modernes Verlagsbureau Curt Wigand, 1907.

Musil, Robert. "Rede zur Rilke-Feier." Cited in Ulrich Baer, "The Perfection of Poetry," *New German Critique* 91 (2004): 171–89.

Pahl, Grünte. *R. M. Rilke.* Berlin: Goldstein, 1933.

Pannewick, Friederike, ed. *Martyrdom in Literature.* Wiesbaden: Reichert, 2004.

Perloff, Marjorie. "Reading Gass Reading Rilke," in *Parnassus: Poetry in Review*, January 1, 2001.

Petzet, Heinrich. *Auf einen Stern zugehen, Begegnungen und Gespräche mit Martin Heidegger 1929–1976.* Frankfurt: Societäts Verlag, 1983.

Pongs, Hermann, ed. *Dichtung und Volkstum*, vol. 37. Stuttgart: Metzlersche Verlagsbuchhandlung (1936).

Prater, Donald. *A Ringing Glass: The Life of Rainer Maria Rilke.* Oxford: Clarendon, 1986.

Reich-Ranicki, Marcel, ed. *1000 Gedichte.* Frankfurt: Insel, 1996.

Schank, Stefan. *Rainer Maria Rilke.* Hamburg: DTV, 1998.

Schnack, Ingeborg. *Rainer Maria Rilke. Chronik seines Lebens und seines Werkes.* Frankfurt: Insel, 1996.

Schwarz, Egon. *Das verschluckte Schluchzen. Poesie und Politik bei Rainer Maria Rilke.* Frankfurt: Athenaeum, 1972.

———. *Ich bin kein Freund allgemeiner Urteile über ganze Völker. Essays über österreichische, deutsche und jüdische Literatur.* Berlin: Erich Schmidt, 2000.

Selbmann, Rolf. "Rainers Widersprüche," in *Blätter der Rilke-Gesellschaft* 24, 2002.

Shakespeare, William. *King Lear.* New York: Random House, 2009.

Thurn und Taxis, Marie von. *Erinnerungen.* Frankfurt: Insel, 1994.

Wallis, Glenn. *Dhammapada: Verses on the Way.* New York: Random House, 2004.

Waters, William. *Poetry's Touch: On Lyric Address.* Ithaca: Cornell, 2003.

Wittgenstein, Ludwig. *Notebooks 1914–1916.* Chicago: University of Chicago Press, 1984.

INDEX

abstinence: admission to heaven, 156–57; fan-shaped jewelry box, 157; Stampa, Gaspara, 150, 158; unrequited love, 149, 156
abstract art, 141–42
abstraction of numbers, 206
Adorno, Theodor, 83
Africans in human exhibitions, 1–2
Agamben, Giorgio, "The Eighth Elegy" (Rilke), 126
Alcoforado, Marianna, *Letters of a Portuguese Nun,* 40
"All of life is lived," 14–15
allegory, word as, 167–68
Altenberg, Peter, *Ashantee,* 1
Andreas-Salomé, Lou, 27; birdcall in letter, 42; letter concerning masturbation, 28–29; letters, publication, 33; onanism of Rilke, 28–31; Rilke's name, 79, 81; Rilke's style change, 80
angel of my affirmations, 153; hypothetical negation, 157; poetic imagination, 156
animals: dreaming from their point of view, 5; *versus* humans, 125–26; pure space, 125; sealed inner life and, 5. *See also* nature

"Apprehension" (Rilke), 38–39
the approximate, 171, 173
"Archaic Torso of Apollo" (Rilke), 184
arrow image for lover, 193
art: abstract, 141–42; impersonal, 165; *Letters to a Young Poet* (Rilke), 200–2; modern, 142
artistic creation, 107–8; dictation and, 107–9
artists: internal vision, 8; observation and, 8–9
Ashantee (Altenberg), 1
Ashanti, 1–9; *The Book of Images* and (Rilke), 4; recognition by observer, 5–6; Rilke's lack of description, 6–7; Rilke's seeing, 4–5
The Ashanti (Rilke), 1–2; racist images, 2–3; sexuality, 3–4
authentic life, Jew and, 99
autonomy of words, 164
"Autumn Day" (Rilke), God, 62–63

Babel, 169
Bahr, Hermann, *Books for Real Life (Die Bücher zum wirklichen Leben),* 10
balance, 18–19
Balthus, 54

Balzac, Honoré de, "The Unknown Masterpiece," 141
Barzun, Henri, simultaneanism, 107
beauty, 15
Becker, Paula. *See* Modersohn-Becker, Paula
being, 208–9; falling into life, 208–12
Benn, Gottfried, 13; break from Rilke, 192; *Letters to a Young Poet* (Rilke) and, 201–2
Bibliothèque Nationale, 11
birdcall: destiny and, 37–42; disruption and, 42–43; as everything, 43; "Experience" (Rilke), 41; as idée fixe, 42; "Improvisations from the Capri Winter" (Rilke), 41–42; "Judith's Return" (Rilke), 41; lamentation and, 40; letter to Lou Andreas-Salomé, 42; letter to reader, 44; *New Poems* and, 40–41; rhetorical possibilities, 39–40; rounded, 44; the unique and, 40–42
Blanchot, Maurice, "The Eighth Elegy" (Rilke), 126
blasphemy, 66–67
blessed contemplation, 9
blessedness, identity and, 79
Blumenthal-Weiß, Ilse: Jewish nationality, 90; "Letter on Faith" (Rilke), 87–88
The Book of Hours (Rilke), 14; God, 63–64; Kassner on, 62, 66–67; "On Poverty and Death," 135–36; onanism, 34–35; prayer book comparison, 63, 67; religous relationship, 66
The Book of Images (Rilke): "Apprehension," 38–39; fear of seeing the Ashanti, 4; unconscious, 76–77
books: life and, 11–13; path to life, 12; power of, 11–12
Books for Real Life (Bahr), 10
Books for Real Life survey, 11–12
borborygmus, 51–52

Borutin, Sidonie Nádherný, 100, 102–3
branding, 76–77, 79; Adorno, Theodor W., 83
breath metaphor, 72
Brecht, Bertold: *Buckow Elegies*, 66; Rilke's gayness over God, 61–65, 70
Buckow Elegies (Brecht), 66
Buddha, 14–15; "Buddha in Glory," 24–26; centrality, 24–25; consciousness and, 20; contemplation, 18; materiality, 23–24; metaphors and, 19–20; *New Poems* (Rilke), 19–22; "passion for the whole" and, 19; pilgrims, 22–24; stillness, 20–21; *The Teachings of Gotama Buddha*, 16–17
Buddha at Rest sculpture, 18

cat's eye metaphor, 71
Celan, Paul, 13–14
children, proletarian, 133
Christ, *Visions of Christ* (Rilke), 134–35
circle: masturbation, 28–31; psychoanalysis and, 27–28
closure, 204
column, tower. *See* tower
consciousness, 20; "The Eighth Elegy" (Rilke), 130–31
creation: poetic, dictation, 167; word's significance, 164–65
cult of poverty, 136–37

de Man, Paul, on Rilke's method, 6
death, 205; entrails and, 50–51; grief, 51; human awareness of, 125–26; "Requiem" (Rilke), 47–50; séances, 49; suppression of, 47–48; world's inner space and, 47
deathbed, 27–28; masturbation as cause of suffering, 28
deceit, Stampa and, 155
deconstruction of language, 165
desire, Gaspara Stampa, 152–53
destiny, 36–7; disruption, 38–44

Dhammapada, 14–15
Diaspora, inner space and, 92
dice cup metaphor for life, 208–12
dictation, 206; artistic creation and,
    107–9; of *Duino Elegies*, 104–5;
    poetic creation and, 167; primal
    sound and, 106, 109–10
dictation of existence, 174–75;
    completeness, 207–8; proletarian
    and, 134
dictatorship tolerance, 119–20
diversions of modern world, 128–29
dogs, nature and, 129–30
Draußensein, 187, 190
dreaming, from animal's point of
    view, 5
Duino Elegies (Rilke), 29; dictation,
    104–5; God and, 90; God as tower,
    169–70; intentions, 161; onanism
    and, 30–32; Thurn und Taxis, Marie
    von, 108–9

Eastern thought, 15
"The Eighth Elegy" (Rilke):
    consciousness, 130–31; human/
    animal differences, 126; nature and,
    125–28; religiosity, 127
"Elegy" (Rilke), Z words, 206–7
endings, 204–5
entrails: borborygmus, 51–52; death
    and, 50–51; *Ulysses* (Joyce), 52
epitaph on Rilke's gravestone, 146–48
erotic poems, 32
existence: dictation of, 174–75; turning
    away, 2–3
experience, being and, 209
"Experience" (Rilke), birdcall, 41

falling into life, 208–12
Family of Saltimbanques (Picasso),
    212–13
fan-shaped jewelry box, 157
fascism: appeal of, 120–21; Italian,
    120–21; riddle of, 121–22

fate, 36–37, 43; unrequited love, 151–52
feminine-aesthetic, 62
"The Fifth Elegy" (Rilke), 212–13
final poem, 188
Five Songs (Rilke), 118
foreign, contact with, 3–4
Forrer, Anita, 62, 67–69
Foucault, Michel, 185
Freedman, Ralph, onanism and, 33–34
freedom, 119; outside, 189; political,
    language and, 124
Freud, Sigmund, 27–28
frogs letter, 58–59

Gallarati-Scotti, Aurelia, 116
gayness over God, 63–66
gender equality, love and, 65
gender-specific roles, 62
George, Stefan, 78
ghost story in "Requiem," 48–49
God: "Autumn Day" (Rilke), 62–63;
    blasphemy, 66–67; *The Book of
    Hours* (Rilke), 63–64; *Duino Elegies*
    (Rilke), 90; erotic connection, 64; as
    father, 64; Jews and, 87–88; Jews
    drawing comfort, 96; *Letters to a
    Young Poet* (Rilke), 67–68; naming
    things and, 85; relationship to, 64;
    religious relationship, 66; Rilke's
    gayness over, 63–66; Rilke's use, 61,
    63; standing before, 67; as tower,
    169–70
Goethe's Correspondence with a Child, 17
gramophone construction, 105
gravestone, 146–48
grief, 51; King David, 73–74; *New
    Poems* (Rilke), 72; pubic hair
    metaphor, 73
guide to life in Rilke, 10–11
guilt, over onanism, 29

hair: different meanings, 74; love-
    snakes, 75; pubic hair metaphor,
    72–73

Heidegger, Martin, "The Eighth Elegy" (Rilke), 126
Heller, Hugo, 10
Hesse, Hermann, 194–95
homosexual love defense, 69
house dieties, 112
Hulewicz, Witold, 111
human exhibitions, 1–2
human potential: Judaism, 93
hypothetical negation, angel of my affirmations and, 157

identity: Andreas-Salomé, Lou, 79, 81; George, Stefan, 78; Inca, 82–83; name as unit, 83; names throughout his life, 80–81; naming things, 85; nicknames, 80–81, 83; rechristening, 76; RMR, 78–79; signature, 79–80; style change, 80; wish to be nameless, 82
impersonal art, 165
"Improvisations from the Capri Winter" (Rilke), birdcall, 41–42
"In the Penal Colony" (Kafka), 107
Inca, 82–83, 85–86
individualism, 97; Jew boy term, 102
inner space: human potential and mobility, 94; loss of openness, 127; metaphor and, 72; mission and, 98–99; mobility, 92–93, 97–100; rechristening and, 80. See also world's inner space
internal vision of an artist, 8
Italian fascism, 120–21

Jacobsen, Jens Peter, 12
the Jew, 90–91
Jew boy, 100–2; individuality, 102
jewelry box, fan-shaped, 157
Jews: advantages, 94; authentic life, 99; bad qualities, 91; comfort from God, 96; God and, 87–88; Jewish nationality, 90; Jewish question, 94–96; mission, 97–98; modernity

and, 92; Rilke's behavior toward, 100–1; Rilke's friendship, 98; rootlessness, 92; speaking as Jews, 87–88. See also inner space; Judaism
Joyce, James, Ulysses, 52
Judaism: anti-Semitism, 91, 94–96; as direction of the heart, 89; potential of the human, 93; Rilke's disturbance, 93–94; Zionism, 93
"Judith's Return" (Rilke), birdcall and, 41

Kafka, Franz, "In the Penal Colony," 107
Kappus, Franz Xaver, 200–2
Kassner, Rudolph, on The Book of Hours, 62, 66–67
King David's grief for Jonathan, 73–74
King Lear (Shakespeare), 109–10
Kippenberg, Anton, Rilke's name, 77–78
Klossowska, Baladine, 54; distancing from, 196–97
Klossowski, Pierre, 54

lamentation, birdcall, 40
language: deconstruction, 165; as existing material, 168; Mussolini, 116–17; Mussolini and, 123–24; of poetry, 106–7; poetry and, 123–24; political freedom and, 124; in service of communication, 168; similes, 190–91; transcendence and, 168–69; word use in poetry, 162
larean value of things, 111–15
Lares, 112
"Letter on Faith" (Rilke), 87–88
Letters of a Portuguese Nun (Alcoforado), 40
Letters to a Young Poet (Rilke), 200–2; God, 67–68; Jacobsen, Jens Peter, 12
life: absence of alternative to correct life, 184–85; books and, 11–13; falling into, 208–12; living to the fullest, 184

life changes, 184
linguistic balance, 18–19
literature, creation of meaning, 167
lived love *versus* sublimation, 159–60
love: abstract, 195–96; arrow image for
lover, 193; lover renewed, 193; men's
incompetence, 156; narcissitic, 159;
nonpossessive, 196–97; objectless,
194; outside and, 180–81; Rilke's
capability, 193–97; self-deceit of,
161; true love, 193–94. *See also* unrequited love

Marcuse, Herbert, 136
Marx, Karl, proletarian, 133–34
Marxism, proletarian, 134
masturbation. *See* onanism
materiality, Buddha, 23–24
meaning, as task, 165
meditation, 20
Merline. *See* Klossowska, Baladine
metaphors: breath, 72; Buddha and,
19–20; cat's eye, 72; pubic hair,
72–73; reversal with subject, 74–75;
standing on its own, 71
mission: inner space and, 98–99; Jews,
97–98
modern art, 142; things and, 164
modern diversions, 128–29
Modersohn-Becker, Paula, 48–49;
"Requiem" (Rilke), 47
Monument to Work, 165–66
Moses, Julius, 94–96
mottos from Rilke's work, 13–14
Mussolini: admiration for, 116–17;
enthusiasm for, burial, 118–19;
language of, 116–17, 123–24; political
ignorance of Rilke, 123–24;
tolerance for dictatorship, 119–20
Muzot (tower), 169–70
mythical hero, 194–95

namelessness, 82
Nanny Wunderly-Volkart, 57–58

narcissistic love, 159
National Socialism, 118
nature: as absolute metaphor, 128;
dogs, 129–30; human understanding, 126; interest in humans,
127–28; "never nowhere without the
No," 125–26; reality, 128–31;
Romantic poets and, 126; "The
Tenth Elegy" (Rilke), 128; transcendence and, 128
"Nature is Happy" (Rilke), 90
"never nowhere without the No,"
125–26
New Poems (Rilke), 19, 21–22; birdcall,
40–41; Buddha, 19–22; "Buddha in
Glory," 24–26; dreaming from
animal's point of view, 5; grief,
72–74
nicknames, 80–81, 83
"The Ninth Elegy" (Rilke): column,
tower, 168–69; ending, 204
Noailles, Anna de, 40
nonpossessive love, 196–97
The Notebooks of Malte Laurids Brigge
(Rilke), 11, 193–94; Stampa,
Gaspara, 150–51; worm, 192
numbers: abstraction, 206; perfect
number, 208

objective thing poems, 2
objects. *See* things: coming into existence, 113
observation: artists and, 8–9; blessed
contemplation, 9
old maids. *See* unrequited love
"On Poverty and Death" (Rilke),
135–36
onanism: *The Book of Hours* (Rilke),
34–35; as cause of illness, 28–29;
circles and, 28–31; defenders of the
time, 32–33; *Duino Elegies* (Rilke)
and, 30–32; guilt over, 28–31;
usefulness discussion, 34
Only You (movie), 36–37, 43–44

onomatopoeia, 143–44

opposing principles of Rilke's poetry, 163–64

outside: absence of alternative to correct life, 184–85; as concept, 182, 189–90; connections, 180; corporeal existence and, 185–86; difficulty, 190; freedom, 189; as life, 183; living life, 184; love and, 180–81; phallic poems, 181; philosophical thought and, 182–83; of a poem, 178; relationships, 180; Rilke's attachment to, 185; Rilke's life, 179; sex and, 181–82; as word without reference, 185

pain, 186–87

"passion for the whole," 19

patrons of Rilke, 53–54; daughter and, 55–56; Thurn und Taxis, Marie von, 53–54; toads, 56–57; Wittgenstein, Ludwig, 56–57

perfect number, 208

perpetuity, 154–55

phallic poems, outside and, 181

philosophical thought, outside and, 182–83

phrenology, 107

Picasso, Pablo, 212–13

poems: erotic, 32; final, 188; lasting love and, 155–56; outside, 178; thing poems, 114–15

poetry: artistic creation and, 107–8; bodily analogy for inspiration, 106–7; dictation, 167; freedom, 119; grumbling of the body as, 52; language and, 123–24; modern, 107; opposing principles in Rilke, 163–64; word use, 162–63

poets, *The Notebooks of Malte Laurids Brigge*, 11

political freedom, language and, 124

political ignorance of Rilke, 123–24

poverty: cult of, 136–37; proletarian and, 137–38; spiritual wealth and, 134–36

power of books, 11–12

prayer book comparison, *The Book of Hours* (Rilke), 63, 67

predetermination, disruption, 38–40. *See also* destiny; fate

prefix un-, 171–77

primal sound, 106; dictation of poetry and, 106, 109–10

"Primal Sound" (Rilke), 105; romanticism rejection, 110

prodigal son figure, 194–95

proletarian: dictation of existence, 134; Marx, Karl, 133–34; Marxism, 134; poverty and, 137–38; *Visions of Christ* (Rilke), 133–35

protofascism of Rilke, 118

psychoanalysis, 27–28

pubic hair metaphor, 72–73

Qualm, 144

Quatsch, 143

racism, 6–7; *The Ashanti* (Rilke), 2–3

reality: nature, 128–31; "The Tenth Elegy" (Rilke), 128–29

rechristening, 76; Andreas-Salomé, Lou, 79, 81; George, Stefan, 78; Inca, 82–83; inner life and, 80; name as unit, 83; names throughout his life, 80–81; nicknames, 80–81; RMR, 78–79

religion: circus of the masses, 61; "The Eighth Elegy" (Rilke), 127; faith, renewed, 63; suppression of death and, 47. *See also* Jews; Judaism

religious relationship, 66

"Requiem" (Rilke), 47–50

reversal of spaces, 72

rhetorical inversions, birdcall and, 39–40

Rilke, Clara. *See* Westhoff, Clara

Rilke, Rainer Maria: books, relationship to, 10; name as unit, 83;

names, 80–81; racism, 6–7; renaissance, 14; self-help section, 13;
Shakespeare and, 109; women and,
179
Rilke, Ruth, patronage money and,
55–56
RMR, 78–79
Rodin, Auguste, 17–18; meaning in art,
164–66; *Monument to Work*, 165–66;
as secretary, 78; surface of sculpture,
164–65
Romantic poets, nature and, 126
rootlessness of the Jew, 92–93
rose, 146–48
rounded birdcall, 44

"Santa Claus of loneliness," 13
séances, 49
seeing: fear of being seen, 4, 7–8; Rilke
seeing the Ashanti, 4–5
sentimental poems, 2
sexual relationships: outside and,
181–82; women as unhappy, 158
sexuality: *The Ashanti* (Rilke), 3–4;
female, fan-shaped jewelry box, 157
Shakespeare, *King Lear*, 109–10
Sieber, Carl, 55; *Letters to a Young Poet*
(Rilke) and, 200–2
Sieber-Rilke, Ruth, *Letters to a Young
Poet* (Rilke) and, 200–2
signature, 79–80
smoke in "Vladimir, the Cloud
Painter," 142–44
The Solution to the Jewish Question
(Moses), 94–98
The Sonnets to Orpheus (Rilke), 29–30
spaces, reversal, 72
speechlessness of Rilke, 105
spiritual wealth, poverty and, 134–36
Stampa, Gaspara, 149–50, 157; absti-
nence, 158; angel of my affirmations
and, 153; deceit, 155; desire, 152–53;
fate, 151–52; narcissistic love, 159;
The Notebooks of Malte Laurids

Brigge (Rilke), 150–51; as outlier, 155;
unrequited love and, 150–51
style change after Andreas-Salomé, 80
superabundant existence, 162
supporters of Rilke. *See* patrons of
Rilke

teachings, 15
The Teachings of Gotama Buddha
(Neumann, trans.), 16–17
"The Tenth Elegy" (Rilke): nature in,
128; reality, 128–29
things: artist's task and, 165; larean
value of, 111–12; modern art, 164;
thing poems, 114–15
Thurn und Taxis, Marie von, 53–54;
Duino Elegies (Rilke), 108–9; Jew
boy reference, 101
toads, patronage money, 56–57
total sum, 212–13
tower: God as, 169–70; as labor and
monument, 167; Muzot, 169–70;
"The Ninth Elegy" (Rilke), 168–69;
Rodin's art, 166; word use, 163–64
tower of Babel, 169
transcendence: language and, 168–69;
nature and, 128

Ulysses (Joyce), entrails and, 52
un-, 171–77
un-concealedness, 175
unconscious, 174
ungroundedness, 175–76
"The Unknown Masterpiece" (Balzac),
141
unrequited love, 149–50; abstinence,
149, 156; desire, 152–53; experience as
model, 155; fate, 151–52; men *versus*
women, 158; Stampa, Gaspara,
150–51; surpassing ourselves, 154
untimely, 174

Visions of Christ (Rilke): Christ, 134–35;
proletarian, 133–35

"Vladimir, the Cloud Painter" (Rilke), 139–41

Walter, Reinhold von, 99
Weltinnenraum (world's inner space), 45. *See also* world's inner space
Werfel, Franz, 100–3
Westhoff, Clara, 48; separate life from Rilke, 178–79
Wittgenstein, Ludwig, 56–57
word: as allegory, 167–68; dictation and, 206
word use in poetry, 162–63; autonomy, 164; tower, 163–64
world's inner space, 45; death and, 47; existentialists on, 46

worm, 192; anticharacter, 198; *The Notebooks of Malte Laurids Brigge* (Rilke), 192; perception and, 197–98
writer's block, 58–59

Xaver, 200–2

Y, 203
"You Who Never Arrived" (Rilke), 36–37

Z: "Elegy" (Rilke), 206–7; as the end, 204
zero point, 204–5
Zionism, 93